LICORICIA OF WINCHESTER

Licoricia of Winchester
Marriage, Motherhood and Murder in the Medieval Anglo-Jewish Community

SUZANNE BARTLET
Edited for Publication by Patricia Skinner

VALLENTINE MITCHELL
LONDON • CHICAGO

First published in paperback in 2015 by Vallentine Mitchell

Middlesex House, 814 N Franklin Street
29–45 High Street, Chicago, Illinois
Edgware, Middlesex HA8 7UU 60610
UK USA

www.vmbooks.com

Copyright © 2009 Suzanne Bartlet and Patricia Skinner
First published in hardback in 2009

British Library Cataloguing in Publication Data
Bartlet, Suzanne
  Licoricia of Winchester : marriage, motherhood & murder in
the medieval Anglo-Jewish community. — (Parkes-Wiener
series on Jewish studies)
  1. Licoricia, of Winchester. 2. Licoricia, of Winchester—
Death. 3. Jewish women—England—Winchester—Biography.
4. Jewish businesspeople—England—Winchester—History—To
1500. 5. Murder—England—Winchester—Case studies.
6. Winchester (England)—History.
I. Title II. Series III. Skinner, Patricia.
942.2'735034'092-dc22

ISBN 978 0 85303 822 1 (cloth)
ISBN 978 0 85303 832 0 (paper)

Library of Congress Cataloging in Publication Data
Catalogue record has been applied for

*All rights reserved. No part of this publication may be reproduced in any form or
by any means, electronic, mechanical, photocopying, reading or otherwise, without the prior permission of Vallentine Mitchell & Co. Ltd.*

Printed by Independent Publishers Group, Chicago, IL

Contents

List of Figures	vii
Editor's Preface	ix
List of Abbreviations	xi
Glossary	xiii
Introduction: The Jews in England and Europe	1
1. Licoricia of Winchester	21
2. Winchester: 'The Jerusalem of the Jews'	32
3. David of Oxford and Marriage in the Jewish Community	48
4. Licoricia the Widow	63
5. Licoricia's Family	78
6. The Barons' War	85
7. Benedict the Guildsman	93
8. After the Wars	105
9. The Coin-Clipping Pogrom	119
10. The Final Decade and Expulsion of the Jews	135
Epilogue: Looking for Licoricia	144
Bibliography	145
Index	159

Figures

1. Five Anglo-Jewish Tally Sticks. Photo courtesy of the National Archives — 7
2. The Family of Chera of Winchester — 28
3. The Medieval Winchester Jewry. After Keene, *Survey of Medieval Winchester*, Fig. 46, by kind permission of the Winchester Excavations Committee — 33
4. The Family of Belia — 45
5. Henry III's Effigy. Photo © Dean and Chapter of Westminster Abbey, used by kind permission — 64
6. The Shrine of Edward the Confessor. Photo © Dean and Chapter of Westminster Abbey, used by kind permission — 66
7. The Family of Licoricia — 79
8. The Family of Benedict — 111

Editor's Preface

Sue Bartlet came late in life to medieval history, stimulated by the excavation, being done just outside her back gate, of what turned out to be the medieval Jewish cemetery of Winchester. In an article published in 1999, she attributes to her husband Leslie her discovery of the widow Licoricia, and the temptation to research the life of someone who might just be interred under her house proved too great to resist. Seeking assistance from the medieval history department at Southampton University, Sue met a then quite young historian – me – with a passion for women's history and a developing interest in the history of medieval Jewry. We instantly hit it off, and thus began a decade in which she developed her research work further, gaining her MA in the process, publishing three articles[1] and being invited to participate in conferences and present her findings. It was an exciting journey, but one in which she constantly defended the right to present her research accessibly, unencumbered by academic language and technical terms, and with an occasionally cavalier attitude towards referencing, which was a source of lively debate.

All this was done in the shadow of cancer, which Sue had been fighting since 1987, although she did not tell me this until it returned, and her MA work and subsequent research became punctuated by increasingly destructive courses of chemotherapy. Throughout this time, she tried to read, write, email me with her progress, demand feedback, and hold on to some semblance of normality during the hospital stays that took so much out of her.

She was also in frequent correspondence with those in the academic world whom she thought might be able to help, and received assistance from (among others) Derek Keene, Colin Platt and Cheryl Tallan. In May 2007 Sue sent me the manuscript of this book, asking me to look at it. I spent rather longer than I meant to going through it, and sent her back an annotated copy in the autumn. This coincided with another hospital stay, and Sue's daughter, Emma, emailed me to say how much it had cheered her up to have me say it was publishable, provided she did something about the footnotes! In December 2007 Sue rang me and invited me to lunch. I went up to Winchester, enjoyed a typically good meal (among Sue's many interests was cookery, and she had written an unpublished book about that as well), and then settled into her study with her to discuss Licoricia. But what we discussed was rather more than this – Sue asked me to complete the work on the book, as she was not well enough to do so and wanted to be sure that it would get completed and published. I worked on the manuscript, reconstructing references, for another five months. In May 2008 I sent her a triumphant email and a large padded envelope, looking forward to the discussion we might have about me filling her manuscript with footnotes! But she did not see it – she had passed away the week before I sent it. With the agreement and valued support of Leslie and Sue's family, I pressed on to produce the final version, which is presented here. It is fully Sue's work – I had access to her notes after her death and found that she had gone far further into the archives than her 'clutter-free' (her description) presentation suggested. I have simply restored the clutter, so that academic readers will know where she found information, whilst retaining Sue's text, which was always admirably clear and has moments of Sue's own mischievous sense of humour. If any indication is needed of how the research took over Sue's life, her own words sum it up:

> When I started this project, I thought that I had discovered Licoricia. It seems to me now that Licoricia has discovered me and pervaded my life. Sometimes I fantasize that she might be lying under my house, nagging me to get on with it. I tell her I'm trying.[2]

This then is the story of Licoricia, an astute businesswoman with a strong sense of family. No wonder Sue loved her.

NOTES

1. Suzanne Bartlet, 'Three Jewish Businesswomen in Thirteenth-Century Winchester', *Jewish Culture and History*, 3 (2000), pp.31–54; 'Women in the Medieval Anglo-Jewish Community', in *The Jews in Medieval Britain*, Patricia Skinner (ed.) (Woodbridge: Boydell, 2003), pp.113–27; 'Discovering Licoricia', *The New Light*, 46, 2 (Winter, 2003), pp.35–6.
2. Bartlet, 'Discovering Licoricia', p.36.

Abbreviations

BIHR	Bulletin of the Institute of Historical Research
BIJS	Bulletin of the Institute of Jewish Studies
Ch.R.	Charter Rolls
Cl. R.	Close Rolls
F.R.	Fine Rolls
HUCA	*Hebrew Union College Annual*
JCH	*Jewish Culture and History*
JHS	*Jewish Historical Studies* (continuation of TJHSE)
JMH	*Journal of Medieval History*
JQR	*Jewish Quarterly Review*
Lib.R.	Liberate Rolls
MJHSE	*Jewish Historical Society of England Miscellanea*
Mundill, *Solution*	Robin R. Mundill, *England's Jewish Solution: Experiment and Expulsion, 1262–1290* (Cambridge: Cambridge University Press, 1998)
Pat.R.	Patent Rolls
PREJ	Calendar of the Plea Rolls of the Exchequer of the Jews
PRO	Public Records Office
REJ	*Revue des Études Juives*
Rokeah	*Medieval English Jews and Royal Officials: Entries of Jewish Interest in the English Memoranda Rolls, 1266–1293*, Zefira Entin Rokeah (ed. and trans.) (Jerusalem: The Hebrew University Magnes Press, 2000)

Select Pleas	*Select Pleas, Starrs and Other Records from the Rolls of the Exchequer of the Jews, AD 1220–1284*, J.M. Rigg (ed.) (London: Selden Society Publications 15, Bernard Quaritch, 1902)
Shetaroth	*Shetaroth: Hebrew Deeds of English Jews before 1290*, M.D. Davis (ed.) (London: Jewish Chronicle, 1888)
Starrs	*Starrs and Jewish Charters Preserved in the British Museum*, Israel Abraham and H.P. Stokes (eds) with additions by Herbert Loewe, 3 vols (I, Cambridge: Cambridge University Press for the JHSE, 1930; II and III, London: Spottiswood for the JHSE, 1930–32)
TJHSE	*Jewish Historical Society of England Transactions*

Glossary

Archa	Chest, used to hold documents recording debts owed to Jews and regularly searched by royal officials. The target for any attacks on Jewry as hard evidence of debt vanished with its destruction, and then the loan was a matter of one man's word against another's.
Beth Din	A gathering of Jewish elders to decide on matters of law.
Bezant	Unit of currency.
Bond	Record of a debt.
Chirograph	A document recording the debt, initially containing two and later three copies of the transaction – ripping it and matching the ripped edges was originally a guarantee of authenticity. The third copy came to be kept in the archa.
Chirographer	One of four men, two Christian, two Jewish who serviced each archa. At least two had to be present to witness any changes to the bonds. There were frequent accusations of dishonesty against the chirographers.
Distraint	Seizure of goods or even person to force them to pay a debt.
Emor	A reading of a portion of Leviticus from the Torah.
Escheator	Receiver and evaluator of goods falling to the king through intestate deaths, forfeiture for crimes, or specific taxation such as tallage.
Ketubah	The settlement given to a Jewish bride on her marriage, to support her in her widowhood.
Landgable	Local tax.
Mainpern	To be held as guarantor for an action, usually bringing someone else to court.
Mark	Unit of currency.

Mikveh	A Jewish ritual bathing pool.
Obl'de Musce	Obols of Muscat.
Seisin	The right to hold land (often disputed) unless a better claim is proven.
Starr	A document recording a Jewish transaction.
Tallage	Periodic taxation levied on the Jewish community and others by the king. From the French *taillage*, literally, 'taking a cut'.
Tally	A stick used to record a debt (see Figure 1).
Tocsin	Alarm bell rung to alert citizens to the defence of their city.
Usury	Derogative term used to describe interest levied on a debt.
Virgate	Typically 30 acres.

Introduction:
The Jews in England and Europe

The Anglo-Jewish community of the twelfth and thirteenth centuries has long attracted attention from historians, both amateur and professional. Since the publication of much source material in the late nineteenth- and early twentieth centuries, numerous studies have emerged of the organization and social life of the Jews in England between 1066 and 1290;[1] many regional and local studies have also been completed, providing detailed pictures of individual communities.[2] The fiscal history of the Jews has also been the focus of more interest in recent years.[3] My approach has been from a different angle to that of the usual historical perspective. My starting point has been the city of Winchester, whose Jewish community in the Middle Ages has been strangely ignored, and my focus is on the story of one prominent Jewish businesswoman, Licoricia, and her associates.

Although Licoricia has been the subject of some attention from medieval historians,[4] no attempt has been made to track her remarkable career and relate it to the city in which she finally settled. We trace her emergence in Winchester in the early thirteenth century, follow her through her two marriages and her survival from the attacks of Simon de Montfort as he led the barons into civil war, to her eventual murder, before exploring the continuing career of her successful son, Benedict, who became the only Jewish guildsman in medieval Britain. After his execution in 1279, the survivors of the family and their declining fortunes are examined, until the final eviction of all England's Jewry in 1290. By selecting one individual, Licoricia, and the city in which she was based, Winchester, and tracing her distinctive name through those records that have been documented and transcribed, it has proved possible to elicit not only the outline of her story, but to create an impression of what it was like to be a woman in a small embattled minority group, living at the time of worsening community relations which led in 1290 to the Expulsion of all Jews from England. I have tried to place the Jews in their environment, that is, to compare their position to that of their neighbours, and to try and produce a balanced view of their relationships.

Jews came to England only after the Norman Conquest, and there is no reliable trace of them here any earlier, although individuals may have ventured in from the continent to explore England's possibilities.[5] The earliest ones appear to have been invited by some of the more studious church leaders, such as Bishop Gerard, who wanted translators for Hebrew documents. It is not clear whether they settled here permanently or returned to their original communities in France. The first permanent settlers appear in records as living in London in the late eleventh century, travelling from Normandy and elsewhere in France. They are reputed to have been encouraged by the Conqueror himself who must have known of their potential commercial expertise from Normandy. There is also evidence of their being invited on an individual basis by barons and crusaders meeting them abroad. The returning crusaders had experienced the tastes and riches of a more exotic culture, and some of them were keen to continue the stimulation and enjoyment with others familiar with the culture of the Middle East. They recognized in the Jews that they met abroad, sometimes on the homeward road, like minds who also offered the possibility of making more wealth available to them, and they invited them to come and live in or near their castles. For other Jews, their reason for coming to England was to flee the waves of persecution and expulsion that occurred in their countries of origin. Throughout the Middle Ages, the Jews of Europe were repeatedly hounded from one place to another. There could have been no sense of security, wherever they settled. In the cities of France and Normandy the treatment of Jews fluctuated between tolerance and oppression.[6] Many came to Britain to escape conditions at home and join their co-religionists. Others were attracted by the opportunities for trade and advancement that they heard were on offer. They came mostly from western Europe, but many also from Italy, and one from as far away as Russia.

The German emperor, Frederick Barbarossa, complained at the loss of Jews from his country to England, and some were forced to return to him in 1162. Elsewhere on the continent rulers would expel and then recall Jews, sometimes within a very short space of time. Philip II of France made them leave the royal domain in 1182, benefiting by acquiring the wealth they were forced to leave behind, but he then invited them to return just seven years later after they paid for the privilege of so doing.[7] It must be remembered that the country provided a very worthwhile source of income for them, and there were few alternative places that could offer so much. Nowhere could guarantee any permanence of settlement or safety, and the Jews had long become used to picking up and moving on elsewhere at short notice.

Conversely, English Jews fled to the continent to escape waves of violence and oppression when they broke out here. Many who had continued their business connections in France and maintained their community links were able to move there or send their children and their nurses to safety, as in 1264. Some returned to England again when the situation improved. At other times individual Jews fled England to avoid court cases or excessive tallage demands.[8] The poorest, who were deemed of no use in producing wealth for the king, were ordered to leave, and those who remained suffered increasingly heavy demands on their wealth, as when their traditional exemption from certain royal tolls, such as pontage (income from bridge crossings, destined to maintain the fabric of the structure), was removed.[9] Finally in 1290 all the English Jews were expelled, mostly resettling in France, Holland and the more tolerant German states. Attitudes to these waves of incomers ranged from appreciation of the material advantages that their financial knowledge and experience could bring, to resentment and hatred on religious or xenophobic grounds.

In England, they initially settled in places that promised the greatest potential advantage, so that London had the earliest recorded Jewry, but by 1130 Jews had started to appear outside the capital in Canterbury, Cambridge, York, Oxford, Norwich and Bristol. By the reign of the Conqueror's son, William Rufus, Jews were often in attendance at his court, and many churchmen criticized what they considered to be his over-tolerant attitude towards them, taking it as a sign of his weakness. He is reputed to have arranged for a religious debate between two of the leaders of the opposing religions, cynically promising that if the Jews won the argument he would become a Jew himself. It is more than likely that this story was fabricated to demonstrate his basic indifference to the church, rather than being the account of an actual event, but such debates were a feature of medieval life.[10]

The Jewish immigrants rapidly spread to all parts of the country. By 1159 they had formed nine communities that were self-governing in Jewish matters, one of which was in Winchester. Their financial value to the king was soon in evidence: a consortium of London Jews lent the Crown 5,750 marks in 1177.[11] They could be found in some two hundred different locations by the end of the twelfth century. One is reported in Scotland and some others went to Ireland, although they did not find in either country a rich source of anything except violence, and did not settle.[12] With the beginnings of the Jewish Exchequer to manage royal income from the Jews in 1194, and the regulation that decreed that Jewish moneylenders live only in towns that possessed the *archae* or chests in which their records of debts had to be entered, they became increasingly restricted to twenty-seven towns.[13] Nevertheless, the records frequently mention individuals living in small towns and settlements across the country. While some of these may have been agents working for moneylenders, many others may have been making a living in other occupations. However, by the second half of the thirteenth century, sheriffs were being told to bring all Jews into the approved *archa*-holding centres, and they began to be expelled from the other towns across England and Wales. When they began to be expelled from some of the individual towns where they had established themselves, they crowded into more tolerant towns or into those where they had relatives. Some of these evictions were at the request of the towns themselves where they had enjoyed their own liberty, which had given them a measure of independence. More frequently it was the local lords who demanded their removal for reasons of political expediency or religious bigotry. Leading barons like Simon de Montfort had the Jews expelled from Leicester in 1234; the Queen Mother, Eleanor of Provence, moved them on in 1274 from her dowry towns of Marlborough, Gloucester, Worcester and Cambridge.[14] Slowly the number of Jewries shrank. In 1234 they were also driven from Newcastle-on-Tyne, Warwickshire, Wycombe and East Anglia, in 1237 from Northampton, from Berkhamsted in 1242, and the following year from seven Welsh centres, Newbury, Speenhamland (Speen, Berks.), and a total of twenty-six other places. When the last two named towns expelled the Jews, they were told to return them to Winchester, which implies that they had originated from there in the first place. By 1253 they were forbidden to move to anywhere new, and by 1290 they were restricted to only twenty towns where *archae* were located. Winchester must have been particularly affected in 1236 when Jews were banished from Southampton, and again in 1264 when Romsey was closed to them, although Romsey could not have had a large community. Nevertheless, most of those evicted must have come to Winchester. Although expelled, this did not necessarily mean that they never returned to their former home towns, particularly as they still had debtors in those towns and so needed to attend to their business interests.

In order to service these debts they could pay a fine to gain permission to revisit on a temporary basis, and some were able to maintain living quarters in a few of the larger towns for periodic visits. Indeed the citizens of Bridgnorth complained that the Jews seemed to be more in evidence after expulsion from the town than before.[15]

In common with all estimates of medieval population, it is difficult to assess the size of the medieval Anglo-Jewish community with any accuracy. It was in any case a fluctuating one, with minor exoduses at times of violence provoked by either the king or his rebellious subjects, followed by some groups returning when things seemed to have settled down or the economy became more encouraging. Most historians however estimate that the Jewish population peaked at around 5,000 in 1200 before dipping during the civil wars that followed, and recovered to almost the same number by the 1240s. Others consider that it grew back to that number by the 1240s, but by the time of the 1290 Expulsion it had fallen to some 2000.[16]

THE SOURCES

Part of the problem when estimating numbers of Jews in medieval England stems from the type of records we have of their presence. Almost all that we know derives from sources produced by non-Jews, and much of what we know comes specifically from the judicial and fiscal records generated by England's precociously bureaucratized government. From a relatively early date we can see the day-to-day administration of a raft of fines, royal taxes and tolls exacted from the entire population, including reports from local sheriffs and orders issued from the royal Treasury or Exchequer, all recorded on Rolls which survive in increasing numbers as the twelfth century gives way to the thirteenth. The relative importance of the Jews to this royal revenue machine is indicated by the appointment of specific justices to handle the Jewish business of the Exchequer in 1198.[17]

The financial records only refer to those who were wealthy enough to engage in loans and dealing, while criminal records mention those on trial or convicted. The rolls listing the fines, that is the payments that had to be made for permission to live in or move around the country, to inherit, to marry, and to generally carry on with everyday life, do mention many people besides business men and women, but these are by no means an extensive record.[18] One of the most thorough documents from the Warden of the Tower of London lists those paying for various liberties, and for misdemeanours committed while imprisoned there in 1278/79, awaiting trial for coin-clipping.[19] Yet this cannot list all who were imprisoned at that time, and of course there is no account of those in the community who were freely living outside prison. Other records were the Patents issued by the king, directives to various officials to carry out his instructions, as well as Close Rolls giving decisions to individuals, and Memoranda Rolls covering policy decisions on various subjects.

The Plea Rolls of the Jewish Exchequer were initiated to keep records of those transactions that were of use to the Crown. At the end of the twelfth century, with the massacre of Jews that followed the coronation of King Richard I in 1189,[20] not only were the Jewries plundered of their possessions, but the bonds kept by the individual Jewish creditors were destroyed, and with them a potential source of royal income. In 1194 the king directed Hubert Walter, then Archbishop of Canterbury and later Chancellor of England, to set up a system of recording and storing the records of Jewish money-lending. Walter adapted the *Archa Aaronensis*, which had been established in 1186 to receive all of Aaron of Lincoln's considerable estate. Under the new proposals, an *archa* or chest would be established in twenty-seven designated centres, serviced by two Christians and two Jews called chirographers, with a clerk in attendance. The bonds, or chirographs were written out twice on parchment divided unevenly into two parts, one of which was placed into the chest as an official record.[21]

Earlier accounts of tallage or tax payments as well as the details of some of the moneylending bonds were recorded on strips of wood called *tallies* (see fig. 1).[22] While the earliest legal documents were in Norman French or even Middle English, the official language increasingly became Latin. The signatures of the Jewish moneylenders could be in Hebrew as well as being recorded in Latin, and these can still be read on the surviving tallies, but it was more likely to be in the handwriting of the Jewish chirographer rather than the actual creditors. Nevertheless, there is an account of Jews being asked to identify the signature on a legal document as being the handwriting of a co-religionist, and they were able to do so. All debts had to be recorded along with the subsequent repayments, a copy to be kept in the chest, available for scrutiny in advance of assessing tax or heritage fines.[23] This was then recorded on the rolls of the Jewish Exchequer, which along with the other recordings of legal and administrative activities of the court, has inadvertently provided posterity with a rich source of information about the Jews and

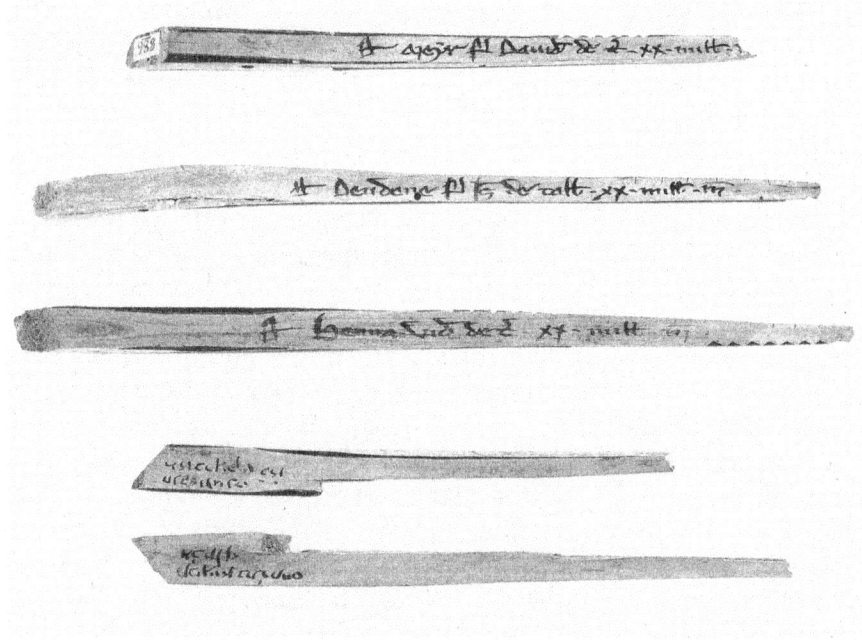

Figure 1. Five Anglo-Jewish Tally Sticks. Photo courtesy of the National Archives.

their clients, albeit from an exclusively Christian and administrative point of view.

Bonds, sometimes also termed *starrs*,[24] were supposed to be returned when the loan was repaid, but this could take a long time, when the debts could be sold on or given to someone else, or the king might confiscate them for various reasons and subsequently give them to his courtiers or soldiers in lieu of wages or as gifts. Simon de Montfort, for example, acquired a considerable debt on behalf of some of his followers in order to have them 'pardoned' by the king, but after his rebellion and subsequent death at Evesham, the pardoned debt was reactivated and assigned to his sons who, because of their subsequent careers abroad, probably did not repay them. In this case the loser was inevitably the unlucky Jewish moneylender, who had originally owned the bond, or the person to whom the king had passed it on as gift or payment. During the civil wars and upheavals of the thirteenth century, the chests were a focus for attack and destruction by the debtors and the documents destroyed or stolen.

There can be little doubt that some of the most prominent Jews of the day were involved in the king's personal business, and Henry III certainly could be benign in his dealings with his favoured Jews.[25] Where individual Jewish moneylenders were allotted to members of the royal family for their own private management they could be very well protected, even to the point of being excused from appearing in the law courts, let alone answering the accusations made against them. Any attempt to disentangle the possible motives for such protection is impossible at this distance. What we would judge to be corruption was rife in the thirteenth century; some of it was institutionalized as payments, fines or fees for any involvement with the authorities, no matter how minor these functionaries were. To obtain a hearing in any official matter required payment to various people. The poor would not have been able to afford recourse to the law in most cases, and if they did, the outcome seemed to depend on who you knew, or were able to buy. Attempting to follow any court case is likely to end in confusion and frustration for the modern researcher. Records of cases are frequently incomplete, either because they have disappeared over time, or perhaps never concluded in a verdict or a sentence. Years go by as the accused or the accuser, the jury members – or sometimes the judges themselves – fail to appear. When the judges call on those who guaranteed the appearance of key plaintiffs or witnesses, they are as likely as not to be absent. In the absence of a verdict, it becomes impossible to know what happened to the person being traced. They sometimes subsequently reappea, having inexplicably survived the seemingly inevitable sentence of death or banishment. There could be intercession by powerful and wealthy citizens, leaving us to guess the reason for such beneficence. Was it money, anticipated advantage, the repayment of a favour or the persuasions of someone even more powerful? We cannot ever know, but those same inadequate and unfinished legal records provide a rich seam of information on the workings of the law for the medieval individual.

We are, however, heavily reliant on the clerks who recorded the court and Exchequer proceedings. The records were never as extensive or as reliable as one might assume, despite being generated by government. The clerks who wrote up the details were of varying ability and efficiency, and cannot be relied on to be accurate. The best of them were able to appreciate the need to record the facts of the cases before them, but many of the others knew nothing of arithmetic, the law or the need for some sort of objectivity, and indeed the latter was not a requirement in the culture of the times. The Rolls are full of repeated facts so that there can be no certainty as to whether we are dealing with the duplicate of a previous case or an entirely new one. Occasionally the entries themselves are unfinished, as if the clerk meant to complete them later but never got round to it. Sometimes the clerk confuses names or even the sex of a witness or defendant. This may have been due to the fact that they were represented in the court by attorneys, or perhaps the accents of newly immigrant Jews were unfamiliar and difficult to understand. The clerks were, with few exceptions, trained and employed by the church and some were clearly hostile to Jews. This antagonism was conveyed in some of the grotesque caricatures of the Jews before them in the courtroom that they drew in the margins of the records.[26] Chroniclers, too, were clerics; it has been said of them that 'They strove to be veracious: their accuracy is on the whole remarkable' but that 'they have little sympathy or charity to spare for the Jewish people'.[27]

When researching the Rolls to try and build up a picture of Jewish life, other complications arise. The medieval calendar was ordered and compiled in a completely different way from the present arrangements.[28] The year was marked by the celebrations of Christian festivals and saints' days, some of which are unfamiliar to us today, such as Hoke Day, or Quinquagesima Sunday. Days that were not a Christian festival were described as being so many days before or after such a day, or as 'eve of'. Nor did the year run from 1 January to 31 December, but commenced with the beginning of the current reign and changed with each succeeding monarch. Thus Henry III's reign began on 28 October, so that was the date that every year began with, being written as '1 Henry III', through to the fifty-seventh year, when he died, written as '57 Henry III'. His son's rule as Edward I, however, starts on 20 November. A chart is essential to navigate the dates on documents, but it has to be said that even the actual dates used are suspect and vary according to when the record was written rather than when the event actually occurred. It is also worth noting that there were no clocks at this period, so time had to be reckoned by the church bells sounding the hours for prayers and the curfew.

More troubling to the researcher than the inefficiency of the clerks and the difficulties in dealing with unfamiliar dating is the disappearance of the records over the centuries. Many were destroyed during the

Barons' Wars and the upheavals of the mid-thirteenth century, when some of the participants who took part went out of their way to destroy not only the records of their debts but in some cases the Jewish creditors themselves. One adherent of Simon de Montfort strangled his Jewish creditor with his bare hands. Over the centuries, repeated fires destroyed numbers of records. In 1298, the first of these occurred in the chapel of St Katherine in Westminster Abbey where many of them had been stored.[29] Another wave of destruction removed more of the records during the Peasants' Revolt of the following century when the building in which they were kept was burnt. In 1834 a fire destroyed the House of Commons where many tallies and chirographs were stored. It is believed that the tallies themselves were being used by the caretakers as fuel for the boilers, and that they sparked the blaze. After 800 years it should not be too surprising that the records are incomplete; in fact it is astonishing that so much has survived at all.

Before moving on, however, it is important to point out a further barrier to research for the uninitiated, caused by the manner in which the fiscal records were published. Look for Licoricia in the list of personal names in an index and you will not find her – she and her co-religionists appear only in the sub-entry of *Jewish* personal names, under the index entry 'Jews, named'. Academic practice in the late nineteenth- and early twentieth century created a Jewish ghetto which certainly did not exist in the medieval period that the documents record.

Alongside the administrative records, we have the evidence of narrative sources, mainly chronicles, only one of which was written by a Jewish author, Ephraim of Bonn, and he was observing Anglo-Jewish events from a European perspective.[30] Ultimately, the voices we hear of Jews in medieval England are filtered through non-Jewish, and sometimes overtly hostile, sources. With patient reconstruction, however, something of the personal lives of individual Jews can be revealed. Licoricia's story is one which can be told in some detail, as we shall see.

JEWISH ACTIVITY IN ENGLAND: AN OVERVIEW

The real value to the Crown of the Jewish presence was not only their financial competence, although one historian believed that they had no specific expertise and 'learnt on the job'.[31] Before the arrival of the Jews, there had been many Christian usurers, sometimes lending large amounts, such as the sheriff of London who was owed £1,040 by the monks of Bury St Edmunds. During their time here the Jewish business men and women developed new practices such as the use of mortgages, although after their expulsion this seems to have been discontinued for several centuries. They also developed dealing in 'futures' when they were not allowed to lend money for a while following the strictures of the Statute for the Jews in 1275 (see p.120). They could access large amounts of wealth through their family or community connections, sometimes across the country, which was particularly useful when the only alternative was to physically transport large, heavy amounts of coinage. More importantly, they made accessible new funding for building castles, cathedrals and abbeys on an unprecedented scale, and through the use of land as security for debts made it available for the accruing of land and enlargement of estates when the debtors failed in their repayments. Moneylending, or rather the interest or usury it earned, was regarded as a sin by the church, and it was forbidden to Christians by the pope. Nevertheless, there were always English Christians who ignored such prohibitions, choosing to risk their souls in the pursuit of wealth.

The first recorded Jewish loan dates from 1130, when the London Jews were creditors to the earl of Chester and the Clare family.[32] Henry II began to use them exclusively for his own private financial needs, while another notable debtor was Thomas Becket, who borrowed 500 marks in 1159 when he was chancellor in order to pay his soldiers. Jews always had competition, and not only from Englishmen but on a much greater scale from French and Italian or Lombard usurers. The latter were also referred to as the 'papal bankers', who were recommended to the church as an approved source of funding. Their business practices and excessive interest charges were cause for complaint from the barons at the Council of Oxford in 1258. Even Bishop Grosseteste, never a friend of the Jews, complained in 1253 about the pope's bankers, saying that they charged the full interest even if the debt was settled early, whereas the Jews only charged interest for the period of the debt. Furthermore, the charge was laid that the Lombards would lend 100 marks but insist that the borrower sign for £100 pounds, a profit of £33 7s 8d, and they would expect the full £100, no matter how soon the loan was paid off.[33] The barons at Oxford complained about Jewish moneylenders only in reference to the selling on, to magnates and monasteries, of the forfeit pledged land. The Templars operated under a special licence from the pope to lend money to pilgrims and crusaders at what was euphemistically called a 'rent'. Without this source of funding, travelling would have been even more hazardous than it was. After a ban on

Jewish money-dealing in 1275 (of which more below), the number of Christian moneylenders rose steeply, some of them initially working in partnerships with Jews. They were able to acquire the land that was forfeit for non-payment of debts from the Jewish creditors, who could not continue to own it for more than one year and a day. As the Jews became more impoverished prior to the 1290 Expulsion, the numbers of English Christians becoming moneylenders increased, much to the disapproval of the church.

The upper limit on usury that the Jews could charge varied between two or three pence per pound per week. The Cahorsins (a term used to denote 'French') and Lombards could charge as much as 50 per cent. Jewish religious tenets also forbade Jews from lending at interest to fellow Jews, although there is evidence that arrangements were made to circumvent this religious stipulation. It is evident that not all Jews and Christians followed the exact rules as laid down by their religious leaders.

How many of the Jewish community were actually involved directly in moneylending? One estimate puts the proportion of the Jewish population working at the highest levels of financial dealing at around 1 per cent, but it seems highly probable that many others lent smaller amounts to their poorer Christian neighbours. Other Jews were either involved in occupations allied to moneylending, such as the manufacture of jewellery and pawnbroking, or working as scribes and agents for their more prosperous co-religionists.[34] The financial records of course only mentioned the wealthiest money-dealers and their family members, at one stage totalling eighty-two individuals in just eighteen families.[35] However, it is frequently noticed that the wealthiest also dealt in very small amounts and some of these loans are recorded in the Exchequer records. When not hounded for the immediate payment of high tax demands, the Jews could be more flexible with their debtors and would sometimes arrange easier payments, or the combination of several debts into one. They tended to be more mobile and they or their agents were more available to what was largely a static population.

The Jews provided an important financial service for the king and his subjects, and in return were granted his protection. This, however, came at a price. King John demanded 4,000 marks from the whole community for licence to deal. They were authorized to use his castles or those of his officials, prisons and other sanctuaries under royal ownership when they were threatened. At a local level, the king appointed teams of local dignitaries as their protectors in times of trouble within the towns and cities in which they lived. These were usually the leading citizens, who were closely involved with the Jews either in their everyday business activities, or on becoming their fellow chirographers, maintaining the Exchequer chest. Those who sided with the king during the many upheavals of the thirteenth century were fully aware that by protecting his Jews they were avoiding his displeasure. For the Jewish community, the king's protection was dangerous, comparable to sheltering in a lion's den, where safety relied on feeding the money-ravenous monarch with plenty of cash-on-demand or with unsolicited gifts. There were many times during the thirteenth century when this strategy failed. Ultimately there was nothing to protect the Jews from the king himself, by whom they were successively cherished, menaced and fleeced, and at the time of the coin-clipping hysteria of 1287/88 they underwent mass imprisonment, summary executions and an impoverishment from which they never recovered.

Those not involved in money dealing were recorded in a variety of occupations.[36] Some served the king as sergeants in his bodyguard, and a few became crossbowmen, one of whom converted in 1226, changing his name to Philip. The employment of crossbowmen was a controversial topic, particularly after the crossbow was condemned as an inhumane weapon by the Lateran Council. Although there is no evidence to suggest that Henry's use of a (very few) Jewish crossbowmen was intended to get around these strictures – he was sincerely religious but not above trying to manipulate things for his own advantage – he nevertheless employed converted Jews and got wealthy Jews to pay for the maintenance of individual crossbowmen.[37] Other Jews visible in the records taught dancing or became fencing masters.

Several Jews were involved in working with trades allied to money and metalwork, probably because they were skilled in gold- and silver-smithing. During the century rich deposits of silver have been discovered on the continent, which made it possible to issue more silver coins. Despite their Jewish-sounding names, however, it is unlikely that the moneyers 'David the moneyer' and 'Isaac of York' were Jews. There was a mint in Winchester indentified by the name 'Pinche' on the coins it produced. As we will see, a Jewish family in Winchester had apparently bore the surname 'Pinche', although it may have no connection with the actual mint. Among other craftsmen was Marleburun living in Billingsgate who painted holy images (a remarkable occupation given the iconoclasm of the Jewish faith), and of course there were gold- and silver-smiths making and dealing in jewellery and precious stones and metals.

Jewish doctors were particularly respected by Christians, who also consulted them as fortune-tellers as well as for their medical skills.[38] Jewish wet nurses and midwives were particularly sought after, being regarded as better nourished and more informed as to the best medical practices. Some Jewish women worked as scribes in their family businesses, while others were servants. The employment of servants and nurses of a different religion by families was repeatedly banned by the Third and Fourth Lateran Councils yet there is evidence of Christians and Jews defying or ignoring the ban. Both Jewish and Christian attorneys were used by everyone, regardless of religious affinity. Jewish food and everyday goods and services were produced not only for the community but also for the general neighbourhood, and we know that Gentiles used them because such use was banned by various churchmen. The poorer members of the community roamed the country as peddlers, while those who owned houses rented them out, although by the middle of the century they were confined to renting only to their co-religionists.

Many other Jews were associated with money-dealing and exchanging money as the coins became worn down or clipped for some of the precious metal they contained. An assortment of currencies was in use, but all main coins everywhere were in gold and silver, so that their value was assessed by their weight. This meant that any foreign coins were likewise assessed and used accordingly. It is not unusual to find the assorted coinage figuring in documents as a musical-sounding torrent of silver and gold marks, gold *bezants* worth between a half and one sovereign, and silver *bezants*. There were also *Obl'de Musce dinars* and half *dinars*, and Byzantine and Nicean *hyperons*, all waiting to trip the researcher looking hopefully for a simple final total of someone's resources. The coins themselves were worth more than their weight of metal content, but as they diminished in size due to wear and illegal clipping, exchangers would trade them for more legal tender. This was a source of much illegal activity, which seriously undermined the economy throughout the century and beyond. Christians as well as Jews were involved and, as will be seen in the discussion below of the coin-clipping panic of 1278/79, concerns about it caused the impoverishment of the whole Jewish community.[39] Many of the lesser moneylenders also acted as clerks or agents for the more powerful usurers, and as pawnbrokers and second-hand dealers to dispose of forfeit property.

This range of employment began to diminish by the beginning of the thirteenth century as opportunities narrowed and Jews became increasingly focused on moneylending and its associated trades. When in 1275 they were forbidden to lend money at interest, and urged to go and work on the land, they were unable to comply, even if they had wanted to. They were to be allowed to hold land for only ten years, which was not enough to invest for the long term. Additionally, living in the countryside would expose them to the dangers of attack without any protection. Realistically, the Jews could not compete as merchants and dealers because they could not offer the same credit as their Christian counterparts. Neither could they enter any guild because of the requirement of a Christian oath. The only exception, as we shall see, was Licoricia's son, Benedict who, uniquely, became a guildsman in Winchester in 1267.

CHRISTIAN–JEWISH RELATIONS

Before we begin our exploration of Licoricia's life, however, it is worth pausing to discuss the relationship between the Jewish minority and their Christian neighbours in England. It is often implied that both communities were uniform in their beliefs, with everyone slavishly following the dictates of their religious or community leaders. As we have seen already, however, despite the fact that religion played a much more controlling and central role among its adherents in the Middle Ages, nevertheless there is evidence of individuals taking more independent action. Jews could be found operating outside their own community's restrictions, or being debarred by their co-religionists from living in a town because they were regarded as suspect in their business practices. Among the Christians, there were many who allowed their avarice to succeed over their piety. Even King Edward's queen ignored the sternest warnings of Archbishop Peckham not to deal in Jewish debts and sinful usury. Other Christians were able to behave in a way more friendly to their Jewish colleagues than most of their church leaders approved. It was after all the century of eighteen popes, so there was inconsistency at the very highest levels as to whether the Jewish community offered any genuine threat to Christians.[40]

Attitudes to Jews had varied during the previous century and also across Europe. Generally, inter-religious relationships had been amiable until the onset of the Crusades, when all non-Christians came to be regarded as the enemy at home. Whenever the crusaders encountered a town with a Jewish population, they attacked and slaughtered many of them.⁴¹ Some theologians, among them Peter Abelard and Bernard of Clairvaux, deplored any attack on the Jews, pointing out that the promised second coming of Christ was expected to be preceded by the conversion of all the Jews – not when they were all dead or absent. England did not participate in any of the Crusades until Richard I led an English contingent off to the Third Crusade in 1189, and through the 'Saladin' tallage, taxed everyone heavily to finance the expedition. This raised both the enthusiastic national mood while fuelling resentment against the aliens. It led to an increase in anti-Jewish violence and a worsening situation for the Jewish population, with attacks in York, London and East Anglia,⁴² but no uniform attitude is visible.

Generally, in peaceful times Jews and Christians got on well together, even to the extent of making friends and being defended by their neighbours when they were threatened. They dealt with each other as merchants and shopkeepers. Peter des Roches, the bishop of Winchester, entertained some Jews in his castle, while another bishop threatened mass excommunication in an unsuccessful bid to stop his congregation going to a Jewish wedding. A Christian family in Chichester attempted to protect their Jewish neighbours from a violent mob, and was only forced to give them up when their own house was threatened by fire. At the time of the accusation of child-murder against the Jews of Lincoln in 1255, when many were under threat of death, the Dominicans incurred some notoriety when they attempted to intercede on their behalf.

Leaping from the records comes an account of young Christian and Jewish men illegally chasing a deer through the streets of Colchester even as late as 1290, and of cross-religious banquets and drinking parties. There is a happy account from the twelfth century of a convoy of churchmen riding up to Wales in the company of a Jewish merchant who kept them vastly entertained with examples of medieval name-play and the same self-deprecating Jewish humour that is familiar today.⁴³

But these were not the Jews of today. They were surrounded with a potentially dangerous situation, which grew worse as the thirteenth century progressed, and in a way that seems to have echoes of twentieth-century Europe; but there are also profound differences that make such comparisons questionable. Religious practices differed between the Jewish communities of the Diaspora, and at different times attitudes of the medieval rulers wavered between encouragement and tolerance only to change with successive rulers to savage intolerance. In medieval England, there were Jews who were more observant of Jewish ritual and requirement than others, just as there were Christians who ignored the strictures of their church and pope. When comparing various Jewish communities in other countries, it emerges that while some followed the new instructions and rulings of sages and religious teachers such as Rabbi Gershom and Maimonides immediately, others, who were more isolated and on the continent's margins, tended to be more conservative and slower to accept change. Nevertheless, there was an exchange of the latest religious views, either brought in by those travelling between Jewish communities or by rabbis visiting Jerusalem, such as those who attended a Maimonides synod in 1211.

Against this background, it is possible to set the story of one woman in the thirteenth century living not only within her Jewish community, but alongside her Christian neighbours in the old capital of Winchester. Her life and that of her family reflect the experiences of the Jews of medieval England during the century that ended with their expulsion to the continent, and with it the story of Jewry in this country, until their return in the seventeenth century.

NOTES

1. Joseph Jacobs, *The Jews of Angevin England* (London: David Nutt, 1893), which anticipated the publication of some records by selecting and translating many extracts; H.P. Stokes, *A Short History of the Jews in England* (London: SPCK, 1921); Michael Adler, *Jews of Medieval England* (London: JHSE, 1939); Cecil Roth, *A History of the Jews in England* (Oxford: Clarendon Press, 1941, 2nd edn, 1942, 3rd edn, 1964); H.G. Richardson, *The English Jewry under Angevin Kings* (London: JHSE/Methuen, 1960); most recently Patricia Skinner (ed.), *Jews in Medieval Britain: Historical, Literary and Archaeological Perspectives* (Woodbridge: Boydell, 2003). David Katz, 'The Marginalisation of Early Modern Anglo-Jewish History', in Tony Kushner (ed.), *The Jewish Heritage in British History: Englishness and Jewishness* (London: Frank Cass, 1992), says Roth's work was 'full of mistakes, undocumented assertions and numerous gaps'.
2. R. Davies, 'The Medieval Jews of York', *Yorkshire Archaeological Journal*, 3 (1875), pp.148–97; Michael Adler, 'The Jews of Canterbury', *TJHSE*, 7 (1911–14), pp.19–96; Cecil Roth, *Medieval Lincoln Jewry and its Synagogue* (London: JHSE, 1934); Cecil Roth, *The Jews of Medieval Oxford* (Oxford: Oxford Historical Society NS 9, 1945–46); V.D. Lipman, *The Jews of Medieval Norwich* (London: JHSE, 1967); R.B. Dobson, *The Jews of Medieval York and the Massacre of 1190* (York: Borthwick Papers no. 45, 1974), R.B. Dobson, 'The Decline and Expulsion of the Medieval Jews at York', *TJHSE*, 26 (York: 1974–78), pp.34–52; R.B. Dobson, 'The Jews of Medieval Cambridge', *JHS*, 32 (1990–92), pp.1–24; J. Hillaby, 'Hereford Gold, Irish, Welsh and English Land: the Jewish Community at Hereford and its Clients, 1179–1253', part 1, *Transactions of the Woolhope Naturalist Field Club*, 44 (1984), pp.358–419; part 2, ibid., 45 (1985), pp.193–270; part 3, ibid., 46 (1990), pp.432–87; J. Hillaby, 'A Magnate among the Marchers: Hamo of Hereford, His Family and Clients, 1218–1253', *JHS*, 31 (1988–90), pp.23–82; J. Hillaby, 'The Worcester Jewry, 1158–1290: Portrait of a

Lost Community', *Transactions of the Worcestershire Archaeological Society*, 3rd series 12 (1990), pp.73–122; J. Hillaby, 'The London Jewry: William I to John', *JHS*, 33 (1992–94), pp.1–44; J. Hillaby, 'London: the 13th-Century Jewry Revisited', *JHS*, 32 (1990–92), pp.89–158; J. Hillaby, 'Testimony from the Margin: the Gloucester Jewry and its Neighbours', *JHS*, 37 (2002), pp.41–112; D. Stephenson, 'Colchester: a Smaller Medieval English Jewry', *Essex Archaeology and History*, 16 (1985), pp.48–52; Michael Jolles, *A Short History of the Jews of Northampton, 1159–1196* (London: Jolles Publications, 1996).
3. Robin R. Mundill, 'Anglo-Jewry under Edward I: Credit Agents and Their Clients', *JHS*, 31 (1988–90), pp.1–21; Robin R. Mundill, 'Lumbard and Son: The Businesses and Debtors of Two Jewish Moneylenders in Late 13th-Century England', *JQR*, 82 (1991), pp.137–70; Robert C. Stacey, 'Royal Taxation and the Social Structure of Medieval Anglo-Jewry: The Tallages of 1239-1242', *HUCA*, 56 (1986), pp.175–249; Robert C. Stacey, *Politics, Policy and Finance under Henry III, 1216–1245* (Oxford: Oxford University Press, 1987); Robert C. Stacey, 'Jewish Lending and the Medieval English Economy', in R. Britnell and B.M.S. Campbell (eds), *A Commercialising Economy: England 1086 to c.1300* (Manchester: Manchester University Press, 1995), pp.78–101.
4. See my previous articles, above, p.x. Also Adler, *Jews of Medieval England*, pp.39–42; Pamela Fletcher Jones, *The Jews of Britain: A Thousand Years of History* (London: Windrush, 1990); most recently Cheryl Tallan, 'Structures of Power Available to Two Jewish Women in Thirteenth-Century England', in *Proceedings of the Twelfth World Congress of Jewish Studies, Jerusalem 29 July–5 August 1997, Div. B: History of the Jewish People*, Mordechai Altschuler (ed.) (Jerusalem: Magnes Press, 2000), pp.77–84. I thank Cheryl for sharing this manuscript with me in advance of its publication.
5. The most recent survey of the Jewish migration and spread in England is that of Joe Hillaby, 'Jewish Colonisation in the Twelfth Century', in Skinner (ed.), *Jews in Medieval Britain*, pp.15–40.
6. Hillaby, 'Jewish Colonisation', pp.16–17.
7. See W.C. Jordan, *The French Monarchy and the Jews: From Philip Augustus to the Last Capetians* (Philadelphia, PA: University of Pennsylvania Press, 1989).
8. Tallage was a tax periodically levied on the Jewish community throughout the thirteenth century, to the extent that it caused its eventual impoverishment: see Robin R. Mundill, 'Edward I and the Final Phase of Anglo-Jewry', in Skinner (ed.), *Jews in Medieval Britain*, pp.40–2.
9. Robin R. Mundill, 'The Jewish Entries from the Patent Rolls, 1272-1292', *JHS*, 32 (1990–92), pp.25–88, at p.34.
10. Anna Sapir Abulafia, 'An Attempt by Gilbert Crispin, Abbot of Westminster, at Rational Argument in the Jewish-Christian Debate', *Studia Monastica*, 26 (1984), pp.55–74. See also Hyam Maccoby, *Judaism on Trial: Jewish-Christian Disputations in the Middle Ages* (Rutherford, NJ: Fairleigh Dickinson University Press, 1982).
11. Roth, *History of the Jews in England*, p.14.
12. Hillaby, 'Jewish Colonisation'.
13. These were Bedford, Berkhamsted, Bristol, Cambridge, Canterbury, Colchester, Devizes, Exeter, Gloucester, Hereford, Huntingdon, Ipswich, London, Lincoln, Marlborough, Norwich, Nottingham, Oxford, Stamford, Sudley, Wallingford, Warwick, Wilton, Winchester, Worcester and York. On the Exchequer see below, pp.6–7.
14. *Select Pleas, Starrs and Other Records from the Rolls of the Exchequer of the Jews, AD 1220–1284*, J.M. Rigg (ed.) (London: Selden Society Publications 15, Bernard Quaritch, 1902), p.85.
15. Richardson, *English Jewry*, p.21.
16. Jacobs, *Jews*, p.381, says the number never exceeded 2,000; Roth, *History of the Jews in England*, p.91, says an estimate of 16,000, accepted by Stokes, *Short History*, p.41, is wildly exaggerated, and discusses the problem on p.274.
17. Paul Brand, 'The Jewish Community of England in the Records of English Royal Government', in Skinner (ed.), *Jews in Medieval Britain*, pp.73–83, introduces the problems; see also his introduction to *Calendar of the Plea Rolls of the Exchequer of the Jews* [hereafter *PREJ*], VI, Paul Brand (ed.) (London: JHSE, 2005).
18. The main records used here are those of the Jewish Exchequer: *Calendar of the Plea Rolls*

of the Exchequer of the Jews, I, J.M. Rigg (ed.) (London: Macmillan for JHSE, 1905); II, J.M. Rigg (ed.) (Edinburgh: Ballantyne for JHSE, 1910); III, Hilary Jenkinson (ed.) (London: Spottiswoode for JHSE, 1929); IV, H.G. Richardson (ed.) (London: JHSE, 1972); V, Sarah Cohen (ed.) (London: JHSE, 1992); VI, Paul Brand (ed.) (London: JHSE, 2005) [hereafter *PREJ* and volume number]. Earlier documents were published as *Shetaroth: Hebrew Deeds of English Jews before 1290*, M.D. Davis (ed.) (London: Jewish Chronicle, 1888) [hereafter *Shetaroth*]; *Starrs and Jewish Charters Preserved in the British Museum*, Israel Abrahams and H.P. Stokes (eds) with additions by Herbert Loewe, 3 vols, I (Cambridge: CUP for the JHSE, 1930); II and III (London: Spottiswoode for the JHSE, 1932) [hereafter *Starrs*]. See also *Select Pleas, Starrs and Other Records from the Rolls of the Exchequer of the Jews, AD 1220–1284*, J.M. Rigg (ed.) (London: Selden Society Publications 15, Bernard Quaritch, 1902) [hereafter *Select Pleas*]; also of use are the Charter Rolls [*Ch. R.*], Close Rolls [*Cl. R.*], Fine Rolls [*F. R.*], Liberate Rolls [*Lib. R.*] and Patent Rolls [*Pat. R.*] of the period (see Bibliography for full publication details), and the Memoranda Rolls: *Medieval English Jews and Royal Officials: Entries of Jewish Interest in the English Memoranda Rolls, 1266–1293*, Zefira Entin Rokeah (ed. and trans.), (Jerusalem: The Hebrew University Magnes Press, 2000) [hereafter *Rokeah*].
19. See below, Chapter 9.
20. Adler, *Jews of Medieval England*, pp.129–30; Jacobs, *Jews*, p.144.
21. Jacobs, *Jews*, pp.156–9 quotes Roger of Howden's account of the creation of *archae*.
22. On which see Michael Adler, 'Jewish Tallies of the 13th Century', *MJHSE*, 2 (1935), pp.8–24.
23. Stokes, *Short History*, p.16, noted that several surviving chests could still be seen in the south transept of Westminster Abbey in 1921. A group of wooden boxes known as *pyxes* can still be seen in the Abbey, although it is unlikely these have Jewish connections.
24. Lincoln F. Ashe, *The Legal Background to the Starrs* (London: Edward Goldston, 1932).
25. A recent survey is Robert C. Stacey, 'The English Jews under Henry III', in Skinner (ed.), *Jews in Medieval Britain*, pp.41–54.
26. Cecil Roth, *Essays and Portraits in Anglo-Jewish History* (Philadelphia, PA: Jewish Publication Society of America, 1962), pp.22–5.
27. *Select Pleas*, p.xv.
28. A good guide to the problems is C.R. Cheney (ed.) *A Handbook of Dates for Students of British History*, (Cambridge: Cambridge University Press, 2nd edn, 2000).
29. *Medieval Jewish Documents in Westminster Abbey*, Ann Causton (ed.) (London: JHSE, 2007), p.2.
30. Robert Chazan, 'Ephraim Ben Jacob's Compilation of 12th-Century Persecutions', *JQR*, 84 (1994), pp.397–416. Other chroniclers commenting extensively on the Jewish situation were Matthew Paris and Richard of Devizes: *Matthaei Parisiensis Chronica Majora*, Henry Richards Luard (ed.) 7 vols (London: Rolls Series 57, 1872–84). Richard of Devizes' chronicle is published in *Chronicles of the Reigns of Stephen, Henry II and Richard I*, Richard Howlett (ed.), 4 vols, vol. 3 (London: Longman, 1884–89). See also Anthony P. Bale, 'Fictions of Judaism in England before 1290', in Skinner (ed.), *Jews in Medieval Britain*, pp.129–44.
31. James Parkes, 'The Jewish Moneylender and the Charters of English Jewry in Their Historical Setting', *MJHSE*, 3 (1940), pp.34–41.
32. Robert Bartlett, *England under the Norman and Angevin Kings, 1075–1225* (Oxford: Clarendon Press, 2000), p.349.
33. Sophia Menache, 'Matthew Paris's Attitudes towards Anglo-Jewry', *Journal of Medieval History*, 23 (1997), p.154.
34. Roth, *History of the Jews in England*, pp.114–15.
35. B. Lionel Abrahams, 'Condition of the Jews in England at the Time of their Expulsion in 1290', *TJHSE*, 2 (1894–95), pp.76–105, at p.82.
36. Roth, *Essays and Portraits*, pp.32–7, discusses some of these.
37. See, e.g., *Pat. R. Henry III, 1232–1247*, p.229 (1238).
38. Roth, *Essays and Portraits*, pp.46–51.
39. See below, Chapter 9.
40. See now Michael Frassetto (ed.), *Christian Attitudes toward the Jews in the Middle Ages* (New

York: Routledge, 2007).
41. There is a substantial literature on these massacres, however, some of which argues that religious conviction was only one motive. See the relevant sources in Shlomo Eidelberg (tr.), *The Jews and the Crusaders: The Hebrew Chronicles of the First and Second Crusades* (Madison, WI: University of Wisconsin Press, 1977), and discussion in Robert Chazan, *European Jewry and the First Crusade* (Berkeley, CA: University of California Press, 1987) and Robert Chazan, *In the Year 1096: The First Crusade and the Jews* (New York: Jewish Publication Society, 1997).
42. James Parkes, *The Jew in the Medieval Community*, (London: Soncino Press, 1938; 2nd edn, New York: Herman Press, 1976), p.361.
43. Roth, *History of the Jews in England*, pp.120 and 277 respectively.

CHAPTER ONE

Licoricia of Winchester

WHO WAS LICORICIA?

We shall probably never know precisely when or where Licoricia was born. She first appears in Winchester in 1234 as a young widow with at least three sons but with enough money and business acumen to be operating a moneylending business for herself. While there are clues as to her father's name, discussed below, there are no references to her mother, or any brothers or sisters. There is no surviving evidence of when she married or at what age, and we can only guess at when her husband may have died. Despite the existence of marriage fines, levied by the king on certain wealthy individuals, there were no official registers of births, marriages or deaths in the thirteenth century. Even the birth dates of members of the royal family can be vague or inaccurate. The only reason why we know as much as we do about the English Jewry was due to their importance to the Exchequer.

Licoricia's own name is an odd one, and it reflects a fashion in early thirteenth-century England, among Christian and Jewish women, for exotic names such as Floria, Saffronia, Almonda, Preciosa, Bellassez and Comtissa, and while these names were sometimes replicated in different families, Licoricia seems not to have been such a popular choice. This partly explains why her life and career show up more clearly in the record.[1]

Two of the earliest mentions of Licoricia occur in the Close Rolls, both dated 1234. In the first:

> Rex perdonavit Hugoni Sanzaver usuram X librarum quas Peytavin et Lycorez, Judei Wintonie, ei mutuo dederunt [The king relieves Hugh Sanzaver of the interest on £10 which Peytavin and Lycorez, Jews of Winchester, lent him].[2]

The second is more informative:

> To the Jewish Justices. For William of Hamtun [Hampshire]. The

king concedes to William of Hamtun of Basingstoke that of the 27 marks he owes Josce le Prestre, Jew of London, he should repay the said Jew 4 marks per annum, namely 2 marks at Easter and 2 at the Feast of St Michael [29 September]; and of the 10 marks he owes Licoricia, who was the wife of Abraham of Kent, he repay the said Licoricia 2 marks per annum at the previously stated intervals ... Instruct the Justices and the assigned custodian of the Jews that this shall be recorded in the Rolls and be made to happen.³

This brief second reference to Licoricia provides us with valuable additional information about her, not least that she 'was the wife of Abraham of Kent'. This was the most common phrase to indicate a widow. Less frequently, a woman could be described as *veuve*, the Norman-French for widow, but this was rarely used. The document also highlights the use of toponyms – places of origin – to identify individuals, but this can be confusing. For example, in another document we meet 'Sara wife of Isaac fil Abraham of London'. Who is from London, and who is the child of Abraham? Where toponyms were used by Christians they refer to where they originated or were currently living, but for Jews, unless they had recently arrived from a different country, these were most likely to indicate where their main area of business was, and when that changed so did this part of their names. For Licoricia, Kent was where her husband's primary area of work had been, and as he is referred to as being also 'of Winchester' in an earlier document, he seems to have had business interests in both locations. Licoricia may have originated from Canterbury in Kent too, but even if not, she would have moved to wherever Abraham was from her family home, as she did on the occasion of her second marriage, when she moved to Oxford. Other Jewish women of the same period are often described as being 'of' their husband's home town, presumably because they went to live there after marriage too. Abraham of Kent was described as also being 'of Winchester' when tried for a crime there in 1225. Some of his co-defendants at that trial were from a Winchester family, which also seems to have had business dealings in Kent, along with many other places. Licoricia herself showed an attachment to the Hampshire city for the rest of her life, whether she originally came from there or not.

What of her parents? Jewish men frequently bore their father's name, or patronymic, as well as their own, for example, 'Solomon son of Isaac'. Where mothers became well-known moneylenders in their own right, the matronymic was sometimes added to the son's or daughter's name instead. Confusingly, either could be used in turn, as we shall see with Licoricia's sons. This may have been the wish to be identified with the best-known parent or the head of a well-known business consortium, who might be a woman or a man.

Women's names present further difficulties. When they operated as moneylenders before they married, they normally did so under their father's name, although unmarried women dealers might also use their mother's name. Among Christians, the matronymic was sometimes used when the son or daughter had inherited property from the mother rather than the father. In some cases, it could also signal illegitimacy. Once Jewish women married, it was their husband's name that became the wife's main identity and the parents' names vanished. When the husbands died their widows were described as having been the wife (*que fuit uxor*) of their late husband, and on remarriage they immediately used the name of their new husband, which can severely complicate investigating their subsequent careers. The result is that we rarely know the identity of their original family, their date of birth or birthplace, and therefore can only guess at their ages or origins at any one time. If a Jew converted it became even more confusing because they were renamed after their sponsor or royalty, and converts frequently 'disappear' from the records: only occasionally can a reference to the previous name re-establish contact.

Two possible clues survive as to the identity of Licoricia's father. In a bond found in a chest at Wilton in 1272, there is a document originally belonging to 'Licoricia daughter of Isaac'.[4] That this reference is dated many years after she first married has in itself little significance: the original names on the bonds continued to be used regardless of changes in the creditor's circumstances. Sometimes bonds would reappear some thirty or forty years after the original creditor had died. Thus, the Licoricia whose document was found in the Wiltshire chest could have been our widow, the bond perhaps bought on her behalf by her father before she married. It is also possible that there was another Licoricia, perhaps even named after the widely celebrated woman from Winchester, although I have found no others mentioned in the records.

The other reference to a possible father is found among papers relating to the efforts to assess the wealth of Licoricia's second husband, David, for estate purposes after his death (for David, see Chapter 3). Here the father is referred to as 'Lumbard', but it is unclear whether this refers to Licoricia or to her husband, David. Indeed, tracing David's patronym illustrates further problems of identifying individuals in the records, for Licoricia's second husband's father was also referred to as Asser in a different reference.⁵ There was an Asser Lumbard living in Lincoln paying towards the Northampton Donum in 1194,⁶ and David is known as David of Lincoln in his earliest business ventures, and occasionally after he moved to Oxford in 1216.⁷ However, there was another David, also called David Lumbard, living and dealing in Northampton in the first half of the thirteenth century. He may have been the one related to the Asser Lumbard who appears to have moved to Winchester in the early 1200s, and stands as a surety for one of the accused in the 1225 trial in that city, referred to above. There was yet another Lumbard living in Winchester in the early thirteenth century, as well as several Isaacs at the same period. It may be significant that our David's only son was called Asser, as grandsons were often named for grandfathers. There may indeed be some family connection between all of these individuals, which does not show up in the record.

Another way to try to work out the name of a father is through grandsons' names, as indicated by David's son Asser. The records of the times show that there were families who repeated the same names for generations. There is, for example, a court case that has Samuel son of Sampson and Sampson son of Samuel appearing together jointly with Saulot son of Solomon and Solomon son of Saulot. Other families did not repeat the same name twice. Plainly there was no fixed convention for naming children amongst Jewish families, and using the grandfather's name as a way of identifying the father is not without its problems. Licoricia's three sons by her first husband, for example, were named Isaac, Lumbard and Benedict, so either of the first two names suggested could be that of her father. One of her sons could also have been named for their paternal grandfather. The order of the birth of her sons could have given another clue, but as we do not know any of the birth dates, this avenue is closed to us. Isaac was the first to have a record of a business deal under his own name, and while this might just be a chance survival from the records, he was also the son who worked most closely with his mother, not only sometimes acting as her agent, but still living in part of her house some forty years later when she died. Again, this might simply be a reflection of her relationship with her other sons, or of their usefulness to her business activities, as much as an indication of the order of their birth.

While some Jewish men exclusively used their Hebrew names on documents, some only used the more easily recognized English equivalents, while others alternated between them. Licoricia's son Isaac was known as Cok or Cokerel, Baruch was only ever referred to as Benedict, while Lumbard used no alternative. Further, there were no conventions governing the spelling of names, which can lead to some confusion as to how many individuals were involved.[8] Benedict in one single-sentence record had his name spelt three different ways: Benettus, Beneton as well as Benedict.[9] The competence of the clerks varied considerably and instances of mistaken spellings or misunderstanding of court procedures can be found. Sometimes they used the wrong names or, at a stroke of their quill pens, changed the sex of the person concerned. This was more likely to happen in the case of women, who may not have appeared in court in person and were represented by male attorneys. With unfamiliar names perhaps spoken in a foreign accent, clerks could easily become confused. This seemed to occur more rarely with the women using the unusual names cited above, but there are also those who appear under simple Hebrew names such as Sarah, Hannah and Malka, and while the spelling of these can vary a little, Sarah becoming 'Sarra', and Hannah 'Henna', they are still recognizable and therefore traceable. Bellassez is an exception to this rule. She can be called Belia or Bella, while Antera or Anchera was also recognized as Chera; one Antera is identified under both of these alternatives. On the whole, Jewish women can be easier to trace than their menfolk because there are fewer of them in the records, and those with distinctive names are even rarer. Men are referred to as *filio* and women as *filia* of their parents, both abbreviated to *fil*.

To return to Abraham of Kent, Licoricia's first husband: what is known about him and when did he die? The records are sometimes confused and incomplete, and in places contradictory. As we saw above, Abraham first appeared in Winchester in 1225 when he was accused with five others of murdering a Christian child. The co-accused are listed as another Abraham, Samarian, Benedict-cum-barbe, Abraham Pinche and his brother Elias of Winchester. Abraham of Canterbury and Winchester, Samuel or Samarian and Benedict were found guilty and their detained chattels were confiscated. The other Abraham and the two Pinches were found innocent on their own submissions and their goods were returned to them.[10] The question always arises as to how much bribery played a part in the seemingly inexplicable sentence in this and other cases of the day. All the accused would surely have pleaded their innocence, but perhaps their different treatment related to whether they had local connections, or powerful patrons. Equally unclear is what followed from this judicial finding. Samarian, purportedly found guilty, seems to have survived, and is still being mentioned in the records in 1244.

A second version of events is recounted by the seventeenth-century historian, William Prynne, who states that only four Jews were accused, who were all tried in front of the king and twenty-four jurors, half of whom were Jews. Prynne states that they were all acquitted and their property restored.[11] He may have deduced this from the same original records that yielded the version of events given above, but he may have had access to many more surviving records, and it could be that this is a correct account of what happened. If so, Abraham of Kent may have lived a little longer. There are also cases recorded throughout the century where powerful figures intercede before or after court cases, resulting in a wholly unexpected outcome such as a finding of innocence. Another possibility is suggested by later cases in Winchester and elsewhere in the country, when the real murderer of the child was found or the case collapsed for other reasons, such as the child being discovered alive and well. There were also undoubtedly instances where we can suspect that a substantial sum of money changed hands and contributed to the eventual result.

No Abraham of Canterbury, Kent or Winchester appears in subsequent rolls, yet nor is there any reference to his having been hanged. If he was, Licoricia's marriage to him and the births of her sons pre-dated 1225, but even if he survived for a longer period she was certainly widowed nine years later when she first makes her appearance as a moneylender in Winchester. If he had been executed, all of Abraham of Kent's chattels would have been confiscated, in which case the money she had for business purposes would have been her own, perhaps invested successfully in the intervening years. The amount mentioned in her first recorded debt of ten marks is a not insignificant amount. She possessed not only the money but also the competence and contacts to be in business for herself, and on her own. From where did she acquire this knowledge? A clue about her having her own money is the Wiltshire bond in which she appears unmarried and her father is named.

The Wiltshire bond, if we accept that it does refer to our Licoricia, would have predated any marriage, since a husband, past or present, would have been named. Most of the Jewish women dealing on the money markets of the day learnt their trade from their families and their husbands. Some of the men treated their womenfolk as partners, allowing them to deal for themselves as well as helping in the family business. A rabbinical writer of the eleventh century remarked on the custom of men to appoint their wives as 'masters over their possessions'.[12] In other families the women were invisible in the records but handled their husband's business when he was absent, becoming skilled enough to emerge immediately at his death as a dealer in their own right. There were clearly also families where the wife's role was confined to that of housewife and mother. Some widows as inheritors of their husband's business were swept off into remarriage by fortune hunters within days of his death. There were also the unmarried daughters who dealt in partnerships with their mothers, but women were best accommodated within family consortia, which were a feature of the thirteenth-century Jewry. Individual women could enter into their own business agreements outside of the family, or deal jointly with some or all of the other members on large-scale transactions. This granted these women the freedom to carry on their business activities while advice, legal representation and support were easily available. Membership could include the extended family, or even outsiders. Often it was a matriarch who headed these groups, and, as we shall see, Licoricia later became such a matriarch. There was in Winchester from the beginning of the century an extremely powerful family consortium that figured in Licoricia's early business dealings, dominated by an older woman called Chera. It is worth pausing to examine her activities in detail.

CHERA OF WINCHESTER

Chera was the head of a large family business consisting of her current husband, four sons and what may have been four daughters, and which would have included daughters-in-law and stepsons at various times (see fig. 2). According to many sources, women in medieval England were not supposed to have any legal standing, but this has been disputed.[13] Of the thirteenth-century married woman, Pollock and Maitland state 'she had a recognized legal position. Theoretically her lands and goods were under the control of her husband, but she was his equal in private law'. Further, 'A woman can hold land ... can own chattels, make a will, make a contract, can sue and be sued ... without the interposition of a guardian; she can plead with her own voice ... a married woman will sometimes appear as her husband's attorney'. This legal principle would have applied to both Christian and Jewish women and they are found appearing in courts on their own behalf, as well as representing their families or consortia, as witnesses, or *mainpernors*, that is guarantors standing bail for others.[14] Attorneys were employed to represent those who were unable to appear for their own cases, and both Christians and Jews supplied this need on behalf of others of any

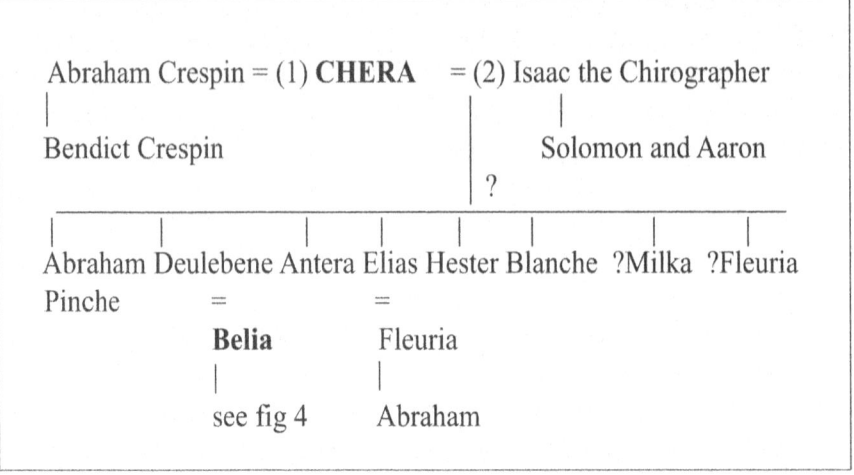

Figure 2. The Family of Chera of Winchester

faith. Benedict Crespin, Chera's stepson, was a very successful attorney, representing others in this capacity in courts across the country. Jewish women frequently were represented or accompanied by a relative.

Chera was married at least twice. She had a close and mutually respectful relationship with her stepson, the hugely successful Benedict Crespin, whose father was Abraham Crespin. She may have had children by Abraham, and this could account for her having two sons called Abraham, the older one having a different father from the younger one.[15] Two daughters, Antera and Hester, also appear in the records.[16] Chera herself is recorded as having loaned twenty pounds to Hyde Abbey in Winchester in 1206, and is securely recorded there in 1207.[17] Her closest family partner was her son, Abraham Pinche, possibly by her second husband, who was referred to as 'the younger'.[18] This was the same man who with his brother, Elias, escaped the accusation of child-murder in 1225. He had various business deals in Kent in the early 1200s, and it is conceivable that he knew Licoricia's Abraham. Nowhere are his wife or child mentioned. The surname Pinche is most unusual and is used mostly by him, although his is not the only example. Two more of her sons, Deulebene and Elias, seem also to date from early in this marriage, since they are mentioned as dealing from early in the century.

Chera's second husband, Isaac the Chirographer, son of Solomon, was located in Winchester by 1191, when he is recorded there living in a house worth eighteen pounds in Shorten St with his then wife, Flora of Beverley, but he was also operating as a businessman in London.[19] Isaac had three brothers, Sampson, Jacob and Deulebene, who were all moneylenders. That he was actually always called 'the Chirographer' seems to indicate that he may have been one of the first appointed, probably in London in 1194. By 1205 Isaac seems to have retired from the post, possibly on moving his main business to Winchester. King John had rewarded him for his services by granting him Bakewell Hall in St Lawrence's parish, London.[20] This had originally belonged to Josce of York, who had been killed in the 1190 coronation riot in York, and Samuel Hoppecole, who had been convicted for coin-clipping. The property had therefore passed to the king who gave it to Isaac, free of all exaction tax, except to pay Henry of Cornhill, the Lord of the Fee, one pound of cumin seed yearly. In 1220, Solomon, Isaac's son, was sued by Hugh Neville for ten years' arrears of rent, but Solomon successfully claimed that it had been granted to Isaac and his heirs rent-free on payment of the cumin seed.

Isaac was a wealthy widower when he married the widowed Chera. While it is possible that the Isaac referred to as Licoricia's father in the 1272 Wiltshire debt was this same man, it is unlikely. It would explain her location in Winchester and her association with this family, but she would surely have been recorded as being a member of the consortium in the tallage records, whereas it seems that she only dealt in partnership with members of the family once, in 1236. Unless she was born of his marriage to Chera, which must have been about 1210, she seems to have been too young to have been his daughter. If she had been Chera's daughter, she would have been noted in the records along with Chera's other children, unless not yet born (Licoricia is not listed among the family members liable to pay the tallage, or Jewish tax, in 1211). The consortium headed by Chera, was assessed in the 1211 tallage as having to pay £1,336 9s 6½d, the largest sum of any family in the country.[21] Needless to say, they had trouble meeting this demand, so along with many of the leading Jews they were imprisoned by King John, Isaac in Winchester and Chera in Bristol.

There they stayed while King John was engaged in civil war, and Winchester was twice occupied and sacked by the rebel armies led by Prince Louis of France, who installed the notoriously savage Comte de Nevers in charge of the garrison. The most ferocious attacks were focussed on the Jews and their property, and many were killed. Winchester Castle, where the imprisoned Isaac and others were kept, resisted and in the ultimate rout it was reported that a witness saw the bodies of a hundred of the French, whom the English slew between Winchester and Romsey, eaten by dogs. Chera too was safe in her prison in Bristol, and with the death of King John and the accession of his son, Henry III, the wars ended. The prisoners were permitted on payment of a fine to return home to Winchester, and to search for evidence of their missing debts. Many of Chera's debtors appeared in the records, pleading that they had settled the debts 'before the broils', and some of them were still being pursued and appealed some twenty years after these wars ended.

The lives of Licoricia and Chera share notable similarities, even if we cannot prove a family relationship between them. Both were married more than once and had several children. In both cases, the records do not tell us all we should like to hear about them. What they share is their common location in Winchester. Let us now explore their environment in a little more detail.

NOTES

1. On naming, see Simon Seror, 'Les nommes des femmes juives en Angleterre au moyen age', *REJ*, 154 (1995), pp.295–325.
2. *Cl. R. Henry III, 1231-1234*, p.362.
3. *Cl. R. Henry III, 1234-1237*, p.27.
4. *PREJ*, IV, p.15.
5. Osseney Cartulary: 'Starrum David filius Asseri' in *Cartulary of Oseney Abbey*, ed. H.E. Salter (Oxford, Clarendon Press, 1929-36, 6 vols), VI, p.79.
6. I. Abrahams, 'The Northampton *Donum* of 1194', *MJHSE*, 1 (1925), pp.59–74, at p.67.
7. Robert C. Stacey, 'English Jews under Henry III', in Patricia Skinner (ed.), *Jews in Medieval Britain: Historical, Literary and Archaeological Perspectives* (Woodbridge: Boydell, 2003), p.45.
8. *PREJ*, III, p.xxx: Rigg comments that 'the spelling of anything but Latin was at this time . . . almost incredibly un-regulated . . . It is nothing for a writer to give even his own name three or four different spellings in as many lines.'
9. *Pat. R. Edward I, 1272-1281*, p.113.
10. *Rotuli Litterarum Clausarum in Turri Londinensi Asservati*, T.D. Hardy (ed.), II (London: Records Commission, 1844), pp.50–1.
11. Avram Saltman, *The Jewish Question in 1655: Studies in Prynne's 'Demurrer'* (Ramat Gan, Israel: Bar-Ilan University Press, 1995), p.138.
12. Rabbi Gershom, cited in I. Epstein, 'Pre-Expulsion England in the *Responsa*', *TJHSE*, 14 (1935-39), pp.187–205.
13. Dobson thought Jewish widows were the most liberated, independent and influential of women with more protection than their Christian counterparts: R.B. Dobson, 'The Role of Jewish Women in Medieval England', in D. Wood (ed.), *Christianity and Judaism* (Studies in Church History, 29) (Oxford: Blackwell for the Ecclesiastical History Society, 1992), pp.145–68.
14. F. Pollock and F.M. Maitland, *History of English Law before the Time of Edward the First*, I (Cambridge: Cambridge University Press, 2nd edn, 1968), p.482. Michael Adler, *Jews of Medieval England* (London: JHSE, 1939), p.38, says that a woman could not write or sign a starr, nor represent their community as a talliator (one who accounted for payments of tallage), but that these were 'practically the only differences between her and the financier of the opposite sex'.

15. An unpublished Winchester document (42), membrane 13, mentions 'Abr primog. Chere' [Abraham, firstborn of Chera], owed a debt of 6s 3d by Hugh son of Cler. De Odiham. [Editor's note: I have not been able to find the source of this reference in Sue's notes.]
16. Antera: Helena Chew, 'A Jewish Aid to Marry, 1221', *TJHSE*, 11 (1924–27), pp.92–111; Hester: *Cl. R. Henry III, 1231–1234*, pp.10 and 103. Two further daughters, Blanche and Milka, paid 18d and 7d into the One-Third Chattels tallage at Winchester in 1240/01: Robert C. Stacey, 'Royal Taxation and the Social Structure of Medieval Anglo-Jewry: The Tallages of 1239-1242', *HUCA*, 56 (1986) p.219; a 'Fluria fil Chere' paid £10 into the same tallage, ibid., p.221, but we do not know where, and so she cannot be securely linked with our Chera.
17. *Starrs*, I, p.6; *Great Roll of the Pipe for the 8th Year of King John*, D.M. Stenton (ed.) (London: Pipe Roll Society, 1942), p.46.
18. *Cl. R. Henry III, 1234–1237*, p.28: 'Abrahe Pinche iuniori, filio Chere'.
19. Joseph Jacobs, *The Jews of Angevin England* (London: David Nutt, 1893), p.154.
20. Ibid., pp.234–6.
21. H.G. Richardson, *The English Jewry under Angevin Kings* (London: JHSE/Methuen, 1960), p.173.

CHAPTER TWO

Winchester:
'The Jerusalem of the Jews'

THE MEDIEVAL CITY

The city in which Chera and the Pinches now resumed their lives, and which Licoricia would make her home, had been the capital of Wessex and England, and continued to be of prime importance for some years after the Norman Conquest, but gradually began to lose its commercial and political status to London. By the thirteenth century, Winchester was simply the capital of the County of Southamptonshire, as Hampshire was called then. This causes much confusion in the records where *Southton*, the abbreviation of its full title, is used, and which can be misinterpreted as the city of Southampton, when it is clear that the county is meant.

The city itself had grown up between two steep hills pierced by the fast flowing River Itchen, running from north to south in the valley between, and on to the sea at Southampton. It had three walls: the city wall, which was constantly needing repair and, within it, the castle wall at the western end and the walled cathedral close. The Bishop's Palace of Wolvesey was also enclosed by a wall, most of which can still be seen bordering the river in the east following the original circuit, before turning north towards the King's Gate, its masonry containing the orange Roman bricks that were incorporated by the frugal medieval builders. Apart from the usual four main gates at the points of the compass, there were two smaller gates in the walls, a postern in the Durngate for pedestrians, and another cart entrance at the King's Gate with a porter's lodge and chapel over the entrance. The latter gate, which survives today, is adjacent to another within the walls that still serves as an entrance to the precincts of the cathedral. Tolls were levied at these gates on carts and certain goods, such as a halfpenny for loads of corn or hay, and fourpence for fish or leather; at the times of the St Swithun's Fair the toll for an ape, falcon or bear was also fourpence. The two main roads that ran between the North and South gates intersected at a dog's leg of a crossroads in the centre, which is still visible.[1] Elsewhere in the city, other fragments of walls and towers can be found, while the circuit that stood alongside the West gate is marked out in the road by modern tiles. The West gate itself, built in the thirteenth and fourteenth centuries, still exists, as does the Great Hall built in the 1230s, so it is still possible to see buildings that Chera and Licoricia would have used and known (see Figure 3).

A sign of Winchester's continued importance to the English kings is the fact that the royal treasury had been housed there, and to which Henry I raced in order to claim it on the death of his brother, William Rufus. Winchester had also been one the main minting centres, but by the beginning of the thirteenth century the mint was considered redundant and the building housing it leased to the city. In 1207 King Henry III was born in a green-painted chamber in Winchester Castle, and the city retained a special place in his affections throughout his life. His early years had been insecure, growing up surrounded by mounting

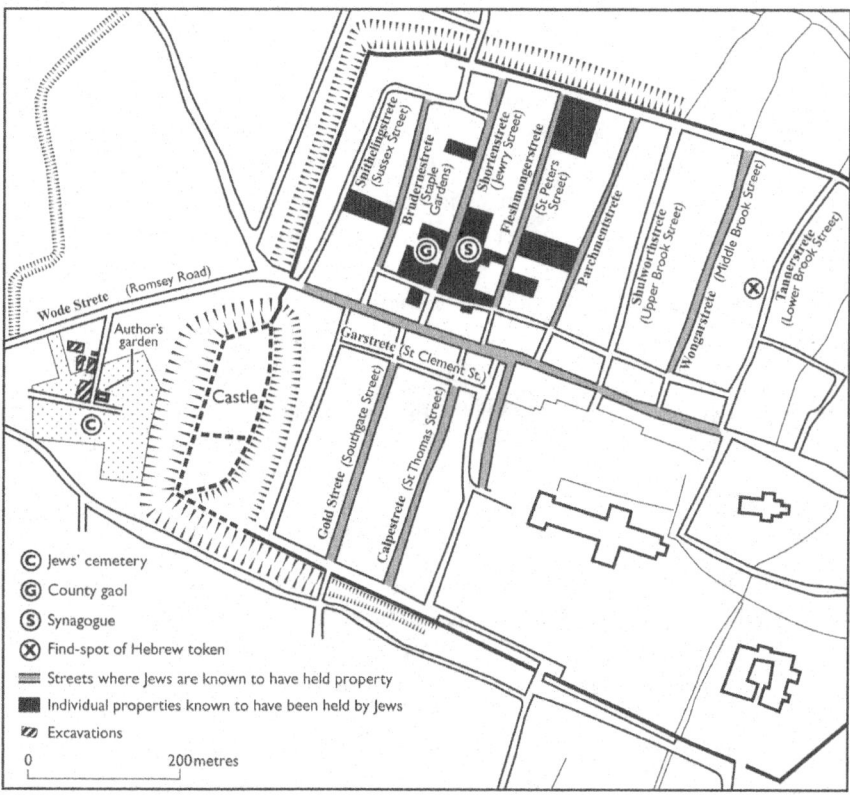

Figure 3. The Medieval Winchester Jewry. After Keene, *Survey of Medieval Winchester*, Fig. 46, by kind permission of the Winchester Excavations Committee.

hostility towards his father, King John, leading eventually to civil war. He was moved round the country separately from his sisters and brother until he was nine when his father died, it was said, from eating too many peaches and drinking too much cider, although it was more probable that he was worn out by the seemingly endless conflict with his barons and churchmen. Henry's mother, Isabel of Angouleme, had returned to France almost immediately on the death of King John, abandoning her children. She had hoped to become regent for her nine-year-old son, wielding power until he came of age, like the widowed French queen, Blanche of Castile, but she was firmly denied this by the ruling triumvirate of William Marshal, Chancellor Hubert de Burgh and the bishop of Winchester, Peter de Roches.

Henry brought his court to Winchester as often as he could, and spent most of his Christmas celebrations in or near the city. As a result, for the duration of his reign, the continued decline in the city's fortunes was suspended. Within this walled city there had been two palaces, the king's and the bishop's, but the castle became the king's residence in Winchester as Henry began a rolling programme of building and enhancement that lasted throughout his reign. The Bishop's Palace at Wolvesey was noted for its comforts and tasteful furnishings, and as the bishop, Peter des Roches, was the king's tutor, it is not surprising that Henry acquired his interest in architecture and decoration from the bishop, and viewed any improvement or embellishment at Wolvesey, the bishop's palace, as an inspiration and a challenge.

There were also two abbeys at Winchester, resulting from an earlier church dispute. St Swithuns was in the centre of the city and became the cathedral church. Hyde Abbey moved into the suburbs outside the North gate; they were frequently opposed to each other and this conflict sometimes gave way to violence. Other religious foundations were established and housed as the century brought in various groups of friars: the Dominicans or 'Black' friars, the 'White' friars or Carmelites, the Austin Friars in Southgate Street, and the Franciscans. There was an older establishment of Benedictine nuns at the convent of St Mary's or Nunnaminster, as well as two other Benedictine foundations with their own churches. As in all medieval cities, there were also many small parish churches within and just outside the city walls.

The city was dominated by the castle, which loomed over it from the western hill and housed not only the king and his family and courtiers when they were in residence, but also a permanent garrison overseen by a warden. While the castle shared the protection of the city walls to the south and west, it had its own huge walls towering over the houses beneath it to the east, while the castle gate to the city was positioned next to the West gate. It also had its own main gate that was accessed from outside the city walls to the west by a bridge that ran over the deep city ditch. Most of the castle has long vanished, but still standing is the Great Hall built by King Henry III. In this huge medieval hall the king held his court, justice was administered, court celebrations were staged and Licoricia and the Jews of Winchester met with some of their wealthier clients. It is likely that some of the money paid by the English Jews at this time was used to fund its building.

Henry continued refurbishing and improving various parts of his palace, building and decorating extra accommodation and chapels, and making weatherproof various open areas. There is reference to a roof being built over a passage used by the queen alongside the 'Jews' Tower',[2] which was employed in times of danger to harbour the threatened members of the Winchester Jewry, as well as to imprison them on other occasions. Nothing remains of it today, but the base of the huge Round Tower, which the Jews may have passed through to enter the castle at these times, has been excavated and can now be seen.

During the reign of King Edward I, a fire broke out that seriously damaged the royal living quarters as well as endangering the queen as she slept. Although the king ordered repairs, he was never as fond of Winchester as his father had been. Henry is known to have come to the city at least a hundred times in his fifty-six-year reign, while Edward was only at the castle eleven times during his thirty-five years on the throne. After the fire in 1302, he tended to stay at the Bishop's Palace at Wolvesey or the prior's lodging at the cathedral. There is one impressive reminder of his presence that hangs in the Great Hall. It is believed that the so-called King Arthur's Round Table, which can be seen there to this day, dates from a tournament held by Edward in Winchester in April 1290.[3]

The High Street ran west-to-east steeply down to the bridge that spans the river outside the East gate, and led through to the suburb called the Soke to St Giles Hill where the St Swithun's or St Giles Fair was held every September. The Soke housed those cloth workers who wished to escape the commercial regulations imposed on their trade within the city. During wet weather the water would have run down the hill to flood the bottom of town, which is still liable to flooding in winter. Some houses had their own channels, and clean water was available to the wealthier houses further up the hill, most of which had their own wells. Before draining into the river, streams ran through the city, supplying water and waste drainage for domestic and industrial use. All the industrial waste from the leather-working, dyeing and butchery industries was dumped into the streams at the bottom of town, added to which there was a large and open public urinal called the Merewynhay, which must have added to the stench that pervaded the lower part of the city. The river was bordered by nine water mills used for grinding grain and fulling cloth, the production of which was the major industry of the area, apart from agriculture. Because of the mills, it is thought that the river could not have been used for transport except for relatively light loads and it does not seem to have provided deep river access to the south and the sea.

The St Giles Fair was making Winchester internationally famous by the thirteenth century, and drew considerable numbers from beyond the city to trade. A transitory township of tents, stalls and booths offered everyday products such as cloth from all over the country, as well as more exotic imports of silks, velvets and furs, pottery and glass, spices and peacock feathers; luxury livestock included bears, falcons, game hawks and pet monkeys. The Fair was divided into retailing sections such as pottery, spices, and drapery, while foreign dealers such as the Flemings, Genoese and Limousins were housed in their own sections. A permanent building housed the Fair Court, which enforced and policed the regulations. The Bishop of Winchester collected the tolls and rents, amounting to over £100 each year, and was constantly trying to lengthen the duration of the Fair from its sixteen-day limit in order to enlarge his income still more. Winchester tradesmen, by contrast, wished to reduce its duration, because while it was being held, local trading in anything other than necessary and perishable food was not allowed. Traders coming from elsewhere in the country had to be safeguarded from attack by those, like the earl of Salisbury, who resented being by-passed by all this wealth. There were also the dangerous robbers and footpads who based themselves in the surrounding countryside; guards and toll collectors were posted on all the major roads.

THE WINCHESTER JEWRY

Winchester, also called *Winton*, was the focus for Jewish administrative matters in the county.[4] The first Jews are recorded as living in Winchester in 1148, Deulecreise, Urselin and Samuel, residing in

Sowrtenestrete or Shoemakers Street, sometimes also called Shorten Street.[5] This was the main street from the North gate towards the central crossroads where it met the main commercial High Street, before continuing towards the South gate. Although its name indicates the original focus of the occupations it accommodated, the importance of its position so close to the commercial centre and the through traffic from outside the city made it attractive to moneychangers and dealers. The Jews increasingly settled there but it never became a ghetto. Despite having always had a mixed population, after the Expulsion of the Jews in 1290 it came to be called Jewry Street, its name today.[6] The street probably came to be identified as such at the time, but there were also Jews living in other properties elsewhere in the city. Licoricia's son Benedict, for example, had a house on the Romsey road that may have served as the entrance to the Jewish cemetery behind it, like the similar access to the Jewish cemetery in London. In 1177 when Jews from communities outside London were permitted to have their own cemeteries beyond city walls, a large plot of land was rented from the Priory of St Swithuns. It was outside the West gate, bordering the far side of the castle ditch, and covered a large area, probably because it was intended to serve for communities across a large part of south-east England for a long period. It was by no means crowded or filled some 113 years later in 1290, when the Jews were expelled from the country, owing a considerable amount in rent for it to the Priory.

Jews tended to live as close to the royal castles or the gaols as possible, because at times when they were under attack the king had promised them his protection, and they were entitled to seek sanctuary in his designated secure places. Winchester was no exception. Here the Jews' Tower, on the south side of the castle, was supposed to offer protection at such times, but its position raises many questions.[7] To access it from the city side would have required Jews to make their way to a wicket gate reputed to be beside the West gate, which for most of them would have meant a dangerous journey across a hostile city. While this would have been safe enough when the attacks came from outside the walls, the fact is that they were in greater danger from inside the walls, most frequently from their fellow citizens. On the west side of Shorten Street itself there was a gaol, which would have given better protection to those living nearby. More ominously, Jews saw the insides of both these places when they were imprisoned awaiting trial, or in advance of a particularly heavy tallage. The castle was also the focus of the king's administration so the leading Jews would have frequented it in pursuit of their business activities, to see the king or members of his court, or to appear before local tribunals.

Winchester had a reputation for good relations with its Jewish population. This rests on an account by the monk Richard of Devizes of the 1190 coronation massacres, when most of the Jews in other towns in the north and east of the country were attacked and killed by their Christian neighbours. Richard wrote, 'Winchester alone spared her vermin' and then went on to deplore the slowness of the Wintonians. It is from Richard that we have the phrase 'Jerusalem of the Jews', describing the city, but it is clear, as we shall see, that his description is a hostile one. It was not strictly true that Winchester was alone in not attacking its Jewish population on this occasion, as most of the other *archa* towns of the south and west did not witness massacres at this time, but if they escaped in 1190 they were not spared in the following century.

There were at least three or maybe four accusations of child-murder perpetrated by the Jews during their stay in Winchester. The least credible is a near fictional account of a case in 1192 when a French apprentice disappeared and his friend accused a Jewish shoemaker in Shorten Street of his murder. Versions of this story inspired several writers, the first being Richard of Devizes, who wrote a long account including the advice given to the boy in France about the English towns to avoid. Winchester was described as 'a Jerusalem to the Jews of England', although the advisor also accuses its citizens of lying like watchmen.[8] This recommendation would make sense if the apprentice himself was Jewish, although this is not stated in any account. If this were the case, however, the subsequent accusation of child-murder would be inconsistent with earlier cases such as that of William of Norwich in 1144, where the victim was clearly not portrayed as Jewish. Perhaps for Richard, the friendliness of Winchester's citizens towards their Jewish neighbours, and their lying ways, were two sides of the same coin. Geoffrey Chaucer certainly knew versions of these stories, and drew on them for his *Prioress's Tale* in the *Canterbury Tales*. It appears that in a subsequent trial the judges found no evidence of any crime having been committed. Certainly there seemed to have been no finding of guilt against any accused Jews in this case, and this account seems to have owed more to the imagination of the author, perhaps inspired by the Norwich story, than any grounding in fact.

Of all the other child-murder accusations,[9] only one seems to have resulted in a finding of guilt, that of Abraham of Kent and the five co-defendants in 1225, and none of them appears to have provoked riots. This may have been due to the quick intervention of succeeding sheriffs, who at the first signs of potential danger took vulnerable or leading members of the community into the safety of the castle and the prison until the threat had passed. Certainly, the Jewish community suffered attacks from outsiders during the two civil wars, and from fellow citizens whenever there were armed disputes between the factions of the commonalty and the churchmen.

Perhaps it is true to say that the Jews of Winchester enjoyed a better relationship with their neighbours than elsewhere in the country, their continuous stay in the city lasting as long as Jews were allowed to live in England. Although it was such an important community by the thirteenth century, when it ranked sixth among all the English Jewries in wealth, the actual number of Jews in Winchester at that time is difficult to assess. The amount of the estimated tax to be levied on the Jews would be a reflection of the wealth of the richest only, not the community as a whole. The peak figure for the Jewish population in all England has been estimated at 5,000 in 1200, after which it generally diminished with some fluctuations to the 2,000 thought to be the number expelled in 1290.

Throughout the 1230s, pressures on the Jewish population elsewhere in the country had knock-on effects for those in Winchester. The Jewish community of Southampton was expelled in 1236, and probably moved to Winchester then. Four individuals, including Benedict of Winchester, his son, Lumbard and Deudonne, the other Winchester chirographer, are named as paying for permission to visit Southampton to carry on servicing their debts, and were allowed to hold houses there while they did this. When the Jews of Romsey were expelled in 1264 they also moved to Winchester. The city attracted Jews from further afield as well: the Warwick Jews evicted by Simon de Montfort in 1234 are reputed to have moved here, as the Jewish community became more concentrated into fewer *archa* towns. In some cases, when they did return to their businesses they had to be escorted by the sheriff or his representatives to defend them from attack, and to protect the king's interest in their financial dealings. There is a graphic account of the attack on Deudonne the Chirographer and the sheriff's escort at Southampton in 1274.[10] The nuns of Romsey are recorded as selling permits to those Jews who needed to revisit the town in pursuit of debtors, almost as soon as they had managed to have them expelled.[11] There are also references to individuals paying for licences to move to towns without *archae*, such as one of Licoricia's sons who paid to move to Basingstoke in 1273.[12] As the century progressed, evictions elsewhere in the country brought others to Winchester from more distant places, some of whom would have moved there to be closer to family members or friends, although there would have been others moving elsewhere in England or abroad. It seems probable that there could never have been more than about 200 Jews living in the city at any one time during the thirteenth century.

CHERA'S DEALINGS

This, then, was the city that Chera, her husband Isaac and the other imprisoned Jews returned to on their release in 1216.[13] They were frequently in court after this in disputes with their previous clients, caused by the disappearance or destruction of the written evidence of debts during the war.[14] Some of their clients took advantage of the lack of evidence to the contrary and claimed that they had paid off their debts in full, while among the moneylenders were those who were also trying to benefit from the loss of official records, by claiming again for debts that had already been settled. There was also genuine confusion arising from the lack of any written evidence and the length of time since they had last had any dealings.[15] Some of the cases kept reappearing in court over many years. Henry of Brayboeuf, the prior of Southwick, was still disputing his £30 debt in court long after Chera herself was dead. Another woman, Emma, a convert, was in conflict with both Chera and Isaac over six *messuages* or small properties in Winchester.[16] At that time, all the chattels of converts went to the Crown, which undertook to maintain the new Christians with food and clothing in the House for Jewish Converts (Domus Conversorum) in London. When it became obvious that such a loss of their property was no way to encourage conversion, the rules were changed to ameliorate converts' situation in 1280.

The records show that there were also several disputes over property in Kent from an earlier time, but it seems unclear whether it was Chera or Isaac the Chirographer who was first involved there. Chera's areas of business deals would include all those places where she had lived with her previous husbands, as well as where her agents operated. Business interests could take women dealers travelling to London, Kent and wherever they saw a need. It seems that Chera and her son Abraham Pinche acted as agents of Isaac of Norwich, as did other Jews across the country. At her death a disputed debt proved that one of her clients had been William de Warenne of Wormegay, a cousin of the earl of Surrey based in Norfolk.[17] Chera sometimes attended the Exchequer in London at the Tower, representing the Jewish community with Benedict Crespin and Isaac of Norwich, a position of some importance for a Jewish woman. She was accompanied by the Bishop of Winchester's agent, John of Herriard, during 1218/19, presenting the record of a debt in which the bishop had an interest.[18] She was creditor to many churchmen, and to abbeys and monasteries. In 1206, as we have seen, her earliest recorded loan was to Hyde Abbey, although subsequent chirographs refer to much earlier transactions.[19]

Chera had probably lived in London during her marriage to Abraham Crespin, and before that, possibly during an even earlier marriage, she may have had connections in Kent, as evidenced by some of the debts that she was still dealing with in Winchester in the early years of the century.[20] Another demand for repayment from Helto Fauciliun ultimately involved the sheriff of Essex,[21] and she had other business interests in Bedford and Devon, but this may not have necessitated her ever going to these places, as she may have acquired them from other Jews, and only dealt with them at a distance. This could be done through attorneys at their places of origin, through the local courts or at the Winchester *archa* if she had registered them there. Chera often acted with her sons.[22]

Chera's husband Isaac must have died some time in 1220,[23] and she may have died soon after, as an entry in the Fine Rolls dated 1221/22 sees Deulebene son of Chera with his brothers, Samson son of Isaac the Chirographer and Benedict Crespin, fining for the debts formerly of Chera and Isaac. A further entry in the same year includes Aaron, Samson's brother, alongside the others, the group agreeing to pay 100 marks a year for the debts.[24] Her multiple marriages ensured that her business affairs took some sorting out.[25] Widows could keep their *ketuba*, the agreed dowry, till they died, even if they married again, but on their death it reverted to the children of the dead husband. As some of the most prosperous widows remarried several times, different parcels of property needed to be disentangled.[26] The Crespins, the Pinches and Chera's children from any other marriage, were all involved in the settlement of her estate along with Isaac the Chirographer's sons. Most of them were members of the family consortium at some time, but the resulting knot of business affairs must have taken some untying. Nevertheless it seems to have been accomplished fairly quickly and apparently amicably, for all of them appear to have acted for each other in their later business interests at various times. Indeed, the group of step-siblings continued to act as a consortium,[27] and their dealings brought them into contact with Licoricia.

We have already seen that Licoricia first appears in Winchester in the 1230s, when she can be traced through her business activities and seems to have been living in the city with her three sons. Her first loan of £10 to Hugh Sanzarer was a huge sum, the estimated cost then of a new, fully fitted ship.[28] She was clearly a wealthy woman, with money to lend and with business connections to the most important of her co-religionists. She sometimes dealt through male attorneys, mostly her sons when they began to operate their own business ventures, and occasionally with other partners. Her third recorded debt in January 1236 links her firmly to the Chera Pinche consortium. The partners here are Chera's son Elias, and his newly widowed sister-in-law, Belia. Licoricia's clients at this time seemed to come from local minor gentry and landowners, but she clearly still kept on her Kent connections as well, as the document recording the loan refers to her as 'Lyquiric' de Cantuaria'.[29]

By this time, however, another prominent member of Chera's family was dead. There had been another accusation of child-murder in Winchester in 1232, when all the leading Jews had been locked in the gaol as a defence against attack from the rest of the population. They had stayed there for several months while the child's mother had first reputedly fled to the shelter of Abraham Pinche's house opposite the gaol in Shorten Street, and then had left Winchester altogether. An official enquiry had decided upon her guilt and the men were released in 1234 after payment of twenty marks, the fine usually to be paid at the end of a prison sentence.[30] Abraham Pinche (who, as we have seen, was one of the accused men in 1225 as well) was immediately re-arrested and charged with having stolen two shillings from a shop some two years earlier, a plainly trumped-up charge, and hanged for felony.[31] This is possibly indicative of a sustained campaign against him by persons unknown. The reasons for his unpopularity might be found in his involvement in some rather questionable business practices, and more probably in the fact that he seemed to have got away with them and to have been hugely successful. He and his mother had worked as agents for the great Isaac of Norwich and, through Benedict Crespin, had been involved in some of the shadier dealings of the bishop of Winchester and sometime chancellor of England, the unpopular Peter des Roches.

Peter des Roches figures prominently in the story of our families. Like many other churchmen, he was concerned with collecting land to establish monasteries, in particular at Titchfield and Selbourne.[32] One of the cheaper methods of doing this was either to encourage or take advantage of local landowners' financial difficulties to persuade or otherwise encourage them to borrow money from Jews. Upon the debtors' failure to meet the stringent demands for repayment, or foreclosure, des Roches would offer help in settling the debt, possibly accompanied by a little extra money, in exchange for the pledged land. Another method was to buy the land cheaply from the Jews after they had seized it as forfeit, since they were legally unable to keep it for longer than a year and a day. He could also negotiate the payment of the Jewish creditors' tax debts in the land pledges they held. He had one of his clerks, his private attorney, John of Herriard, help Chera with one of her debts, although this may have been one of those involving the land in which he was interested as security. After Chera's death, Benedict Crespin also paid the fine for his share of the inheritance tax through the bishop, thereby obtaining a discount. During the early thirteenth century, the abbeys and monasteries managed to accrue vast estates in this way, to the detriment of the previous landowners, and powerfully stoking their resentment. This was one of the grievances of the barons that would subsequently fuel civil war.[33] Peter des Roches certainly did not hesitate to use Jews for some of his business interests. There is a record of his entertaining Jews at his Fareham castle, although none are identified by name.[34] He also appears to have encouraged some Jews to move to his Taunton estates.

Abraham Pinche's unpopularity, therefore, may have stemmed from his own and his family's close relationship with the bishop, and association with the prelate's sharp practice. Vincent calls Chera and Abraham 'two of the most active usurers in Hampshire'.[35] The questionable accusation of theft following his release from prison in 1235 resulted in his being sentenced to death. Not only was he drawn through the town, either at the tail of a horse or at the back of a cart, to the gallows erected in the street outside his own house and opposite the jail, but uniquely he was denied burial in the Jewish cemetery. There seems to be no other instance of this; a Jewish burial was a fundamental requirement of the religion, exceeding even the need for a synagogue in importance. Until 1177, when they were granted permission to have cemeteries in some of the towns in which they lived, Jews had taken their dead to the only Jewish cemetery that had allowed them up till then, the cemetery located in London. There are accounts of special pontages or bridge tolls to be paid for the passage of the Jewish dead and their corteges, and there is even an account of one Jewish procession being trailed by barking dogs on its way to the capital. The stipulation that Abraham Pinche was to be denied this vital ritual and was to be buried in the street under the gallows, despite the pleas of the Jewish community, seems exceptionally severe for the mere theft of two shillings.[36] Plainly, something much more serious was involved, but there is no clue as to what this might have been. All his chattels were forfeit and his house was given to one of the king's cooks.[37] This resulted in another appeal from the Jews, as their synagogue was in the grounds of his house. After some dispute and some vacillation by the king, the house stayed in the hands of the new owner.[38] It seems likely that he may have hung on to the property in order to dispose of it back to the Jewish community at a ransom price, because there is no firm evidence of the synagogue being relocated away from Shorten Street.

BELIA OF WINCHESTER

It is unclear whether Chera's son, Deulebene, was spared witnessing his brother Abraham's execution, as we cannot be sure of the date of his death.[39] His widow, Belia, certainly emerges into the records by 1236, when she paid 200 marks to the king for her late husband's chattels and loans.[40] Within three months of her husband's death she was working with her brother-in-law Elias, who was Licoricia's partner, in a loan to Roberto de Bello Alneto of eighteen marks.[41] Belia also negotiated the right to buy back at some 200 marks, from Jerman the king's tailor, some of the houses that Deulebene had held in fee, which is evidence that she had access to money.[42] She had clearly been involved in her late husband's business, for she showed immediately that not only had she considerable financial capability, but also she seemed to have money of her own, as the estate would not be settled for some time. It may have been that Chera and the family helped Belia out, and in some of her earliest deals she was in partnership with her brother-in-law, Elias.

Intriguingly, Belia seems to have had a close relationship, or perhaps it was a friendly rivalry, with Licoricia. There is circumstantial evidence to suggest that they may have been related in some way, because even after Belia moved away from Winchester on her subsequent remarriage, they seemed to have stayed in contact. More tellingly, some of their sons and grandsons shared names. Belia's four sons included a Lumbard and a Benedict, as well as Jacob and Moses. Licoricia certainly had a daughter called Belia, who is only mentioned at Licoricia's death in 1277, but the dates suggest that Belia of Winchester (later of Bedford) and Licoricia's daughter were not the same person. More likely, Licoricia named a daughter after her friend. There is plenty of evidence that their grandsons frequently worked together until 1290, and the names Cokerel, Lumbard and Benedict appeared among both families (see Figure 4 for Belia's family, and below, Chapter 5, for Licoricia's).

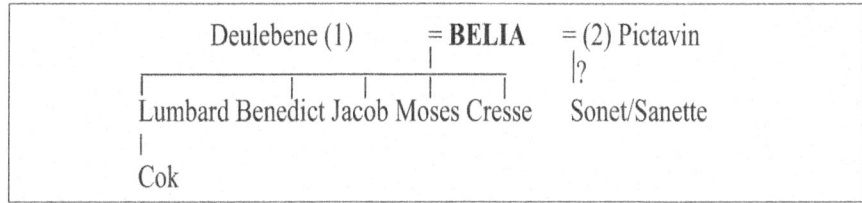

Figure 4. The Family of Belia

Belia continued dealing successfully, becoming increasingly wealthy, until by 1239 she equalled Licoricia in the assessment for the One-Third Chattels tallage, although Licoricia still seemed to have been regarded as the more successful of the two.[43] Belia, however, was the only woman allotted a special legal responsibility following the so-called 'Worcester Parliament' in 1240, which was a special meeting of representatives from all the Jewish communities to decide the allocation of tallage payments. While no woman actually took part in the discussions, Belia was the only woman given a specific responsibility in the arrangements following the Parliament's decisions. She was delegated to ensure her brother-in-law Elias reported at the Tower of London, as hostage for the local tax.[44]

The end of the 1230s found both Licoricia and Belia successfully carrying on their business deals in Winchester,[45] but the next decade began with profound changes in their personal lives.

NOTES

1. On the city's history see the survey of Barbara Carpenter Turner, *A History of Winchester* (Chichester: Phillimore, 1992), and on its Jews, Barbara Carpenter Turner, 'The Winchester Jewry', *Anglo-Jewish Association Quarterly*, 1, no. 4 (March 1956), pp.120–5. A more detailed study of the medieval city is Derek Keene, *Survey of Medieval Winchester*, Winchester Studies 2, 2 vols (Oxford: Clarendon Press, 1985), I, Part i, from which much of the following discussion is drawn.
2. *Lib. R. Henry III, 1245–1251*, pp.235–6 and 369.
3. Martin Biddle, *King Arthur's Round Table: An Archaeological Investigation* (Woodbridge: Boydell, 2000), pp.361–75.
4. Despite its relative wealth and importance, the Winchester Jewry has not yet formed the subject of an extensive study. Malcolm Gomersall, 'The Jewish Population of Medieval Winchester', *Winchester Museum Service Newsletter*, 15 (July 1992), pp.3–6 is extremely brief and repeats some earlier misunderstandings, particularly with reference to Licoricia's son Benedict.

5. Keene, *Survey*, I, p.385.
6. See now Tony Kushner, *Anglo-Jewry since 1066: Place, Memory, Locality* (Manchester: Manchester University Press, 2009), Chap. 3.
7. *Rokeah*, p.77.
8. *The Chronicle of Richard of Devizes*, John T. Appleby (ed.) (London: Nelson, 1963), p.386, for the accusation of child-murder. See also Anthony P. Bale, 'Richard of Devizes and Fictions of Judaism', *JCH*, 3 (2001), pp.55–72.
9. Keene, *Survey*, I, p.387, says there were three episodes, in 1225, 1232 (*Cl. R. Henry III, 1231–1234*, p.80) and 1235.
10. *PREJ*, II, p.216. For further details on this attack, see below, p.107.
11. H.G. Richardson, *The English Jewry under Angevin Kings* (London: JHSE/Methuen, 1960), p.21 note 5.
12. *PREJ*, II, p.104 (Lumbard).
13. *Pat. R. Henry III, 1216–1225*, pp.59–60 (1217): Chera is to be released and allowed to come to Winchester because 'the king has made peace with her'.
14. See Chera's long-running pursuit of Adam of Corhampton for a debt recorded on a chirograph 'lost in the war': *PREJ*, I, pp.19, 40 and 41.
15. See *Documents Illustrative of English History in the 13th and 14th Centuries: Selected from the Records of the Department of the Queen's Remembrancer of Exchequer*, Henry Cole (ed.) (London: Eyre and Spottiswoode, 1844), pp.286–7, 289–93, 302, 306, 314–15, 318 and 320–1 chronicle Chera's battles in 1218/19.
16. Henry: Chera initially brings the demand for repayment against him in 1220: *PREJ*, I, p.24 and it reappears as a debt regularly thereafter: *PREJ*, I, p.37; *Cl. R. Henry III, 1234–1237*, p.307 (1236); Emma: *Curia Regis Rolls of the Reigns of Richard I and John, VII: 1213–1215* (London: HMSO, 1935), p.245. This document gives the name of Chera's former husband, Abraham, and her stepson, Abraham.
17. *Select Pleas*, pp.12–14.
18. *PREJ*, I, p.4. This may have been related to the bishop's acquisitions of land in Hampshire to establish monasteries, discussed below, p.42.
19. *Great Roll of the Pipe for the 8th Year of King John*, D.M. Stenton (ed.) (London: Pipe Roll Society, 1942), p.46.
20. See her demand for sixteen marks from Simon of Cray, leading to a counterclaim by his mother, Margaret, in 1220: *PREJ*, I, p.26.
21. *PREJ*, I, pp.6 and 33.
22. For example, with Deulebene in 1220, when acting against Andrew the chaplain: *PREJ*, I, p.36.
23. *Starrs and Jewish Charters*, I, p.19. See also *PREJ*, I, p.19, describing him as 'late'.
24. *Calendar of the Fine Rolls of the Reign of Henry III*, I, 1–8 Henry III (1216–1224), Paul Drybergh and Beth Hartland (eds) (London/Woodbridge: National Archives/Boydell, 2007), pp.238–9, entries 48 and 51. This means that the Chera recorded in *Shetaroth*, pp.280–3, no. 140 cannot be our Chera, as this undated document is linked to two others dated 1262 in Nottingham, where she and her still-living husband Abraham are old enough to have a grandson. M.D. Davis, 'Early Winchester Jews', *Jewish Chronicle*, 16 September 1892, erroneously dates Chera's death to 1244.
25. The 'co-parceners of the inheritance of Isaac the Chirographer and Chera of Winchester' are summoned in a case of 1244/45: *PREJ*, I, pp.105 and 110, and *Select Pleas*, p.13. A payment by Deuelebene 'and other heirs' is recorded in 1233: *Cl. R. Henry III, 1231–1234*, p.197.
26. Elias is recorded individually paying for some of his mother's debts in 1239: *Lib. R. Henry III, 1226–1240*, p.380.
27. For example, *Cl. R. Henry III, 1231–1234*, p.120: Elye filio Chere and Abraham fratre eius et filio Duelebeneie are called to account in 1232 for a loan to John de Everesly and ordered to return half the land pledged to them for John to live on, so that the loan might not incur usury (*non currant usure*). In the same year the interest on Abraham Pinche's loan to Richard of Grunested is suspended by the king whilst Richard's heir is underage: ibid., p.47
28. Margaret Wade Labarge, *Mistresses, Maids and Men* (London: Phoenix Press, 2003), p.163.
29. *Cl. R. Henry III, 1234–1237*, p.230.
30. Original imprisonment of 'omnes Judeos de Wintonia': *Cl. R. Henry III, 1231–1234*, p.80 (1232). See also Keene, *Survey*, II, p.667. Z.E. Rokeah, 'Crime and the Jews in Late 13th-Century England: Some Cases and Comments', *HUCA*, 55 (1984), pp.95–197, at pp.154–5, reproduces the account of the case dated 1236.

31. Rokeah, 'Crime and the Jews in Late 13th-Century England', p.101.
32. See Nicholas Vincent's study of the bishop, *Peter des Roches: An Alien in English Politics, 1205–1238* (Cambridge: Cambridge University Press, 1996).
33. See below, Chap. 6
34. Nicholas Vincent, 'Jews, Poitevins, and the Bishop of Winchester, 1231–1234', in D. Wood (ed.), *Christianity and Judaism: Studies in Church History 29* (Oxford: Blackwell for the Ecclesiastical History Society, 1992), pp.119–32, at p.122.
35. Vincent, *Peter des Roches*, p.289.
36. *Cl. R. Henry III, 1234–1237*, p.341 (1236): 'the viscount of Southampton is ordered to allow the Jews of Winchester through the king's licence to bury Abraham Pinche, that Jew who was previously drawn and hanged at Winchester, but that they are not to bury him anywhere except under the gallows on which he was hanged'.
37. *Cl. R. Henry III, 1234–1237*, p.239: the king grants houses which were Abraham's, 'qui nuper suspensus fuit pro felonia', to one Adam, the king's *salsario* in 1236. Cf. *Ch. R. Henry III, 1226–1257*, p.218.
38. Joe Hillaby, 'Beth Miqdash Me'at: The Synagogues of Medieval England', *Journal of Ecclesiastical History*, 44 (1993), pp.182–98, at p.194.
39. *Cl. R. Henry III, 1234–1237*, p.271, refers to a 'Deulebene judei, qui nuper obiit', but it is not stated if this is Chera's son. It is, however, likely that a scribal slip explains Deulebene's (rather than Elias') appearance in a case in 1244/45 between William de Chinham and Belia of Winchester, Deulebene fil Chera and Deulebecoc fil Ursell: *PREJ*, I, p.95.
40. *Cl. R. Henry III, 1234–1237*, p.277.
41. Ibid., p.230.
42. *Lib. R. Henry III, 1226–1240*, p.329 (1238). She is referred to simply as 'Belia, a Jewess of Winchester', with no mention of Deulebene. This pattern is repeated in other rolls, for example *PREJ*, I, pp.59, 62, 83, 87, 95, 101, 102, 111.
43. *Lib. R. Henry III, 1226–1240*, p.472, records her paying £10 into the king's Wardrobe in 1240 for her One-Third Chattels tallage. Robert C. Stacey, 'Royal Taxation and the Social Structure of Medieval Anglo-Jewry: The Tallages of 1239–1242', *HUCA*, 56 (1986), p.220, notes that both women paid the same amount.
44. Stacey, 'Royal Taxation and Social Structure', p.247.
45. For example, Licoricia's £10 loan to St Swithuns, Winchester: *Lib. R. Henry III, 1226–1240*, p.440.

CHAPTER THREE

David of Oxford and Marriage in the Jewish Community

Some time in the early 1240s Belia remarried, to a widower called Pictavin, and in 1244 they moved to Bedford, where a new Jewry was being allowed to settle.¹ On her re-marriage Belia took three of her sons, Jacob, Benedict and Cresse, with her to set up her new consortium, but left two others, Moses and Lumbard, to continue the activities of the Winchester branch.² She sometimes travelled back there to oversee some of her earlier debts, but she became more rooted in Bedford. After Chera's death, Belia seems to have taken over something of her role, protecting the family interests in court. In 1244, following an announcement in the synagogue that all who were owed money by the son of Robert of Chineham should present themselves at court, she appeared as an attorney for 'Deulesant fil Chera' and also for Pictavin of Lincoln and Bonamy son of Samarian, as well as on her own behalf for a debt of £54.³

Jacob and Benedict's proximity to their stepfather led to them taking his name for some of their transactions, particularly later, after his death.⁴ A daughter may have been born to the marriage, named Sanette, who emerged much later, in the 1280s, as a seller of salt, and although there is a little confusion over her sex in the records, she was also a moneylender in her own right.⁵ Belia soon became a leading member of the Bedford community and a very successful dealer who worked with her husband as well as independently. By 1266 Belia was being referred to as the widow of Pictavin, but continues to appear regularly in the records.⁶ Later on, her sons and Licoricia's often shared business transactions or sponsored each other over various legal affairs. As we have seen with Chera, serial marriages to older wealthy business men may have been as good as a career move for many Jewish women in the Middle Ages. Belia's marital history and more extensively that of Licoricia, provide an opening onto the world of medieval Jewish marriage.⁷

JEWISH MARRIAGES IN ENGLAND

The records of the fines that had to be paid by most women, whether Jewish or Christian, for permission to change their marital status, give some indication of the variety of circumstances in which marriage could take place. Most fines were just for permission to marry, but in the case of wealthy widows, it was not quite so straightforward. Where the new couple combined their business ventures, the death of one would not bring the expected windfall to the royal treasury of one third of all their wealth, if the survivor could claim that they had an equal right to it. One request for permission to marry between two widowed moneylenders refers to their having made an agreement to do so. Another woman paid to *not* marry a man who had requested permission from the king to do so. A rather colourful dispute, between the widow Milla and Samuel of Bolum, had to be decided by the masters of Jewish law. Samuel caddishly insisted that they were virtually already married 'by reason of contract and commerce between them'. Milla did not deny anything except to dispute that such activity would mean that they were married. The nub of the disagreement then emerged. Samuel had used this as a basis for trying to get hold of her property and control her business activities. He had insisted that she could not dispose of her chattels without his consent. The justices agreed with her and she did not marry Samuel, although she may have regretted it when she subsequently got into financial difficulties.[8]

We have a substantial amount of information about Jewish marriage, both in legal treatises and in practical documents. Children were generally betrothed, sometimes in infancy, but more commonly girls were betrothed at eight or nine, and married at around eleven or twelve. One father betrothed his infant daughter only to find later on that he had not actually specified which one of his three girls was involved in the agreement. The potential groom had to release all three to avoid the charge of bigamy, and ultimately did not marry any of them. An extant betrothal agreement of 1271 between Belassez of Lincoln and Benjamin fil Josce Yechial, concerning her daughter Judith and his son Aaron, shows some of the specific elements of a marriage contract. She promised a wedding gift of twenty marks and a precious Hebrew bible written on calfskin. The groom's father undertook to maintain and clothe the children, and Bellasez gave a further twenty marks to be invested on behalf of the young couple. The *ketuba* or dowry was specified as £100 'as is the custom of the isle', revealing that a specifically English practice had grown up.[9] This is a notional amount, but was intended to make some provision for the bride should she survive her husband. Frequently this sum was covered by the provision of a house for her use. The wedding was to be deferred for four years as the children were too young, but safeguards were included should the marriage not take place. It may in fact never have occurred, because Judith is named as someone else's wife in a later court case. In it she asked for permission to remarry when her then husband disappeared on the road to Lincoln, carrying £10 of her money, and a Christian reported that he had killed him in the course of a robbery.[10] Another agreement by a father, Yomtob ben Moses, promised his daughter's compliance to marriage 'as far as he can sway his daughter's actions',[11] which seems to indicate a degree of freedom of choice was possible for some girls.

The records also refer to the sort of difficulties that arose when a widow remarried. As we have seen, theoretically she could carry her *ketuba* from each husband with her until she died and then the children of her various marriages could claim their share, which inevitably led to many legal disputes. Unlike Chera, who seems to have got on well with most of her sons and stepsons, other widows seemed to be locked in legal combat with their own children over their rights to her *ketuba* and the property left by the deceased husband, and some seem to have been left destitute by their son's actions. Conversely, there are also instances of the children making generous provision for their mother or sister.

If women used marriage as an opportunity to advance their fortunes, it was also true that men took the same road to improving their own financial interests. Widows were sometimes spirited away into another marriage immediately on their husband's death. The children could find that their mother and their share of their father's property had disappeared, with their new stepfather having taken both away to another part of the country, avoiding the assessment of the estate and payment of the king's fine. For example, Isaac of Berkhamsted not only seized Porun, the widow of Abraham of Worcester, and took her back to Berkhamsted, but also even managed to get his hands on her previous father-in-law's estate, while evading payment of the inheritence fine.[12]

Licoricia was, as we have seen, a wealthy widow and thus may have attracted similar attention. Her status may be indicated by the fact that the matrimonial market now yielded her a major prize. Her second husband, David of Oxford, was among the six wealthiest Jews in England, and has been the subject of significant historical research. Davis describes him as 'a pinnacle towering above his contemporaries'.[13] He is unusually well documented, allowing us to see the calibre of man Licoricia now married.

DAVID OF OXFORD

David started his business activities in Lincoln, his probable birthplace, at the beginning of the thirteenth century. His father is identified as Asser of Lincoln, who appeared in the records of those paying into the Northampton Donum there in 1194.[14] As discussed above, an Asser Lumbard is recorded as living and dealing in Winchester in the 1220s.[15] It is not certain if this is David's father, although there are many points of possible connection between them. Both David and Asser Lumbard are recorded as owing tallage in Lincoln in 1210. By 1216 David had moved to Oxford to service the need for credit from the new and growing university and its students, and his toponym had changed from being 'of Lincoln' to 'of Oxford',[16] and also 'David of London' on occasion. He travelled the country in pursuit of his business and community interests, which took him to Warwick and Berkshire as well as London.[17] In 1221 he had to pay part of Winchester's tallage allocation as well as Oxford's, which demonstrates he had extensive business interests in both cities. He quickly prospered and was soon beginning to accumulate properties in Oxford. In 1227 he acquired a stone-built house with stone vaults for the safekeeping of his goods and wealth in the very centre of the town, as well as other houses, and witnessed an exchange of properties to secure one for use as a synagogue. In 1228 he could be found in Worcester as witness to the purchase of a house to be used as a synagogue.

There are at least sixty separate mentions of David's business activities in the records.[18] He was dealing with landowners and the monasteries as well as the students and university, 'lending as little as one mark and as high as £300',[19] and soon had a reputation for ruthless dealing.[20] Henry de Oilly, whose family had built Oxford Castle and founded Oseney Abbey, borrowed 300 marks and found himself unable to meet David's demands for repayment and interest. He complained of David's 'hard hand' to Pope Gregory IX, who in turn asked the archbishop of Canterbury to use his influence to curb David's 'immoderate usury'.[21] The subsequent complaint to the king seems to have coincided with a strategic 'gift' of £100 to him from David and nothing more was done. Oseney abbey bailed out Henry de Oilly in return for which they gained his manor of Weston.[22] The abbey may well have been playing a double game, benefiting from David's loans to acquire property cheaply. From another loan of David's, to William de Hampton, Oseney also acquired his pledged watermill and other property at Hampton Poyle. As we have seen from Peter des Roches' use of Jewish debts in Winchester, this was how the abbeys and monasteries amassed huge estates cheaply at the expense of the landowners and barons, who deeply resented it.

David dealt with some of those at the highest levels of society. His clients included senior churchmen, judges, local landowners, and members of the nobility. He began to be involved with some of the king's personal finances, and could be found brokering loans for him from his brother, Earl Richard of Cornwall. Among his clients were the king's illegitimate cousin, Stephen Lungspee, and the king's sister Eleanor, the countess of Pembroke, who subsequently became the wife of Simon de Montfort. She relieved a debtor of David's, acquiring his pledge of a manor before persuading her brother to pardon the debt.[23] Between 1230 and 1244 David had some thirty of his debts pardoned or cancelled by the king. They could be pardoned in their entirety, that is, both capital and interest, or of just the interest element. This was usually a reward for services to the king, or absence on a crusade. The king issued the pardons in lieu of wages or as gifts, and sometimes the creditor could be partly compensated by other debts from the Treasury. In 1230 John Talbot was excused an entire debt of £15, while 'Fighting Judge' Roger Clifford was excused both usury and repayments of the loan, which was suspended during his service to the Crown.[24] Sometimes the pardoned debts could be reinstated; Simon de Montfort was pardoned some debts to David, worth £110 11s, that he had acquired on behalf of two of his tenants in 1244. But after his defeat and death at Evesham in 1265, the debts re-emerged from the treasury and were imposed on de Montfort's heirs.[25]

At times of war or crusade a moneylender was vulnerable, in that his services were urgently required by those needing to equip themselves for battle, while the creditor would have known there was a high probability that at least part of the debt or the interest could be cancelled by the king. At times, he was commanded to raise money for particular projects. In 1237, David was commissioned with Aaron and Leo of York to raise 3,000 marks for Richard of Cornwall's pilgrimage, and when they found some difficulty in raising such a sum, they were ordered to get tough on their debtors.[26] In these circumstances it was the Jewish creditors, not the king, who became the focus of the hatred and resentment of those subjected to the resulting financial pressure. In 1238, a trio of David, Aaron of York and the ubiquitous Benedict Crespin (Chera's stepson) were ordered to maintain a servant of the king's, Simon the crossbowman, in the manner his status deserved. As we have seen, at least some, if not all, of Henry's crossbowmen were converted Jews.[27]

As one of leaders of the Jewish community, David acted as an assessor to decide the allocation of the target set for the tallage or Jewish tax between the Jewish communities, but he also represented them and would try to serve their interests at court. He complained when the level of tax was falling too heavily on his co-religionists. In 1238 he was part of a group of eight Jews, including Benedict Crespin, who requested the king to hold an enquiry into coin-clipping.[28] The clipping or filing of silver coins was a constant threat to the currency, and the chronicler Matthew Paris commented, 'Neither the inhabitants nor even foreigners could contemplate [English coin] with a serene eye or an even temper'.[29] The coins themselves were meant to be at least equal in worth to their metallic content, and clipping or wear reduced their value. The resulting devaluation of the coinage was the bane of the medieval economy, necessitating repeated reissuing of new money. Some of the money-dealers made a profit by substituting light coins for the full-value money. Others dealing in cash, such as the moneylenders, suffered as much as anyone from the devaluation, and the enquiry team toured the country accompanied by two Christian Justices of the Jews, enquiring into not only clipping, but also the receiving of stolen goods among the Jewish communities. The local legal officials were ordered to produce any witness they needed to question. One of the more severe punishments they requested to deter the falsifiers of the realm's coinage was that they should be banished from the country.[30]

One of these Christian Justices of the Jews, William de Breton, was later instructed by the king to deal fairly with David, described as 'an ante-majore exceeding his brothers in opulence', which can be read as being favourable to David but could equally have a more sinister emphasis.[31] Targeting an 'opulent' Jew may have meant that he could have afforded to pay more and quicker. As David was *not* the richest, this might also imply that he was more ostentatious than the others.[32] He is recorded as riding through Wallingford on 'a black palfrey with a better bridle', and he presented one to the king, a costly gift, the equivalent today of an expensive sports car. Plainly, David was a lover of horse-flesh, and kept a well-stocked stable. He gave the king two palfreys as part of his contribution to the Tewkesbury tallage in 1241. David also gave the king strategic gifts of cash, usually stated to be £100 when it is clear the exact worth is not known, in advance of a specific request for favours. On another occasion he paid £59 10s towards the king's expenses into the Wardrobe, which was the king's personal account. The king would also demand sums of money called *prests*. In 1241, on the eve of the so-called Worcester Parliament, he demanded that David, Aaron and Leo of York and Benedict Crespin pay him an instant 'loan' of 400 marks, threatening that they would 'lose everything' if they failed to oblige. In this case it is recorded that the king repaid the loan.[33] These sudden demands reveal that the king's attitude was never consistent, and he regarded Jews as monetary 'cows' he could milk on demand.

In 1241 the king summoned the 'Worcester Parliament'. All Jewish communities were instructed to elect representatives to attend a meeting in Worcester, the purpose of which was to decide new ways of allocating a large tallage demand that would be more efficient, fairer, but above all quicker in producing the total amount demanded by the king. Up until then, the decision as to where the burden of the tax fell had been decided by the most powerful and richest Jews, some of whom had a tendency to emerge paying something less than their fair proportion of the total. David of Oxford had paid £14 5s, that is 52 per cent, of the Oxford total of the 1221 Aid to Marry tallage. In 1223 he paid 49 per cent, but in 1241 his share totalled 2,200 marks, while Aaron of York had to pay 6,000 marks,[34] and their combined total was over 50 per cent of the entire tallage. It has been stated by Robert Stacey that this sudden shift in apportionment spelt the beginning of the eventual ruination of English Jewry.[35] The new allocation took a much heavier percentage from the richest, without changing the king's expectations of the usual additional 'gifts' and payments he exacted at will. This was on top of tallage debts from earlier demands, as well as the additional funds that the king expected at other times. The new system set up an elaborate network of assessors from within the community, with hostages from each Jewry to be taken to the Tower of London and held until their share had been paid. Individuals were made responsible for producing the hostages. In Winchester, the hostage was Chera's son Elias, and as we have seen, a woman, his sister-in-law Belia, was responsible for producing him. Not just wealthy, powerful and astute, David was also very well read, reputed to possess an extensive library of Jewish books as well as those precious ones he had accepted as pledges; at his death he left forty-nine books. While many of these would have been acquired as pledges, he was known as a collector of books for himself. Compare the extent of his library with that of King Edward III, who left twenty books, mostly tales of chivalry, when he died in 1377.

DAVID AND LICORICIA

David travelled all over the country, including Winchester, where he had probably first encountered Licoricia, a young widow with three sons and an admirable record as a businesswoman in her own right. He may have known her for some years, or at least would have heard favourable accounts of her. It is even possible that the outcome of the 'Worcester Parliament' had some influence on what David did next, namely marry Licoricia and pool resources with her. But David was already a married man. His wife of many years was one Muriel, whom he had married in Lincoln before coming to Oxford. She came from a respectable family: her brother Peytevin was a well-known lawyer who had been operating in France before moving to Lincoln. She is occasionally mentioned in the records as helping in her husband's business.[36] What is noticeably missing from the records is any mention of children, although a nephew is a witness in one transaction. In 1242, Jewish society was shocked to hear that David had suddenly divorced Muriel.

Divorce was an extremely rare occurrence in medieval England. For Jews, with their emphasis on the value of the family, it was not regarded favourably. There was an established procedure for the Beth Din or rabbinical court to hear divorce cases, although the grounds for so doing were very limited. One of the few grounds for divorce among Jews was childlessness after ten years, and it seems highly likely that David's case was based on his wife's barrenness. In the absence of any of the divorce details, there is much speculation about what might have happened. It seems that the case was heard and decided by the English Beth Din, and that possibly the first that Muriel heard of it was when the decision was presented to her by a member of the tribunal, Jacob of Oxford, a colleague of her husband. She instantly began to fight the decision with the help of her lawyer brother. She was not entitled to any further appeals in England, so with the support of her brother, nephew and other family friends from Lincoln, she petitioned the Paris Beth Din, which had previously been a senior body to the English court. Her appeal may have been based on the teachings of Rabbi Gershom, (960–1028) who in his book, *The Light of Exile*, had stipulated that a wife could not be divorced without her assent.[37]

But if Muriel was unhappy with the divorce, so was David. It is commonly believed that his subsequent dispute with her concerned the size of the *ketuba* he was ordered to return to her as a divorce settlement. I believe it was a totally different stipulation that he contested, for Gershom had also ruled that a divorced person could not remarry, as that would constitute bigamy. This is borne out by what followed. David appealed to the king, who was in France at the time, no doubt accompanying the request with a strategic gift. The king caused to be issued two letters, the texts of which still exist, and which form much of the evidence we have for the divorce itself:

> To the Masters Mosse of London, Aaron of Canterbury and Jacob of Oxford, Jews, greeting. We forbid you from henceforth holding any plea concerning David of Oxford and Muriel who was the wife of the same. You are not to distrain him under any circumstances either to take or retain her or any other woman as his wife. Know for a certainty that if you do otherwise, you will incur grave punishment.[38]

The named trio were the members of the adjudicating English Beth Din. The stipulation restraining them from forbidding him to remarry freed David from what must have been for him an unacceptable restriction.

The second letter was signed by William, the archbishop of York, who was acting as regent, in the king's absence and on the king's instructions. It is dated 27 August 1242:

> Whereas by the counsel of the venerable Archbishop in Christ, W[illiam] of York, and sundry of the King's Council, it was provided that henceforward no tribunals might be held concerning the Jews in England. And whereas the justices assigned to the custody of the Jews are firmly enjoined on the part of the king to see with regard to all the Jews of England that no chapters should henceforth be held throughout England. Consequently Peytevin of Lincoln, Muriel who was the wife of David of Oxford, Benedict son of Peytevin of Lincoln, Vaalin and Moses of Banbury, Jews, are to appear before the aforesaid Archbishop and others of the Kings Council on the Octave of St Michael, wheresoever they may be in England, to show cause why they sent to France to hold a chapter concerning the Jews of England. And the aforesaid Justices are ordered not to suffer David of Oxford to be coerced by the Jews to take or hold any woman to wife except of his own free will.[39]

The archbishop would have been happy for any excuse to suspend the Beth Din, which had the right to arbitrate on Jewish matters such as marriage that the church would have liked to control. It may have been necessary to intervene to prevent the Beth Din from confiscating all of David's property, as it was entitled to do if he defied their instructions to stay with Muriel and not remarry. The second stated intention to hold an enquiry into the appeal to Paris was because such appeals to a foreign court were forbidden: the English Jews were subject only to the English king. David was now free to marry Licoricia, which he probably did in 1242, and she would then have moved to Oxford. There is nothing to indicate whether she took her sons with her, or if she left them in Winchester.

Muriel was given the use of one of David's houses in Oxford, on a repairing lease, perhaps a contribution towards her *ketuba*. If she was childless, it would have reverted to David, or whomever he stipulated as his heirs in his will, on her death. In fact, there is evidence that she subsequently suffered financial difficulties, or it may have been that she just could not cope on her own. She had difficulty meeting a tallage demand of twenty marks and eighteen shillings even after she was given easy terms in 1248,[40] and she fled Oxford. Her chattels were confiscated to offset this debt, the king giving 300 marks of it to Vincent, the teacher of his half-brother, Aymer de Lusignan, to defray his expenses as nuncio to Rome.[41] Muriel evidently had chattels that she could have sold to offset her tallage, and the question arises as to why she had not paid the initial twenty marks demanded. She then returned to Oxford, but the following year the council issued an order for her to repair her house, and by 1253 the house was in the hands of Licoricia and David's little son, Asser.[42] This may have been on the death of Muriel, or perhaps Licoricia may have been less than sympathetic to her plight and reclaimed the house.

Licoricia's marriage to David lasted barely two years. They named their son Asser after his paternal grandfather, but he was also called Sweetman, which may have been a family pet name for 'the son of Licoricia', whose own name referred to a sweetmeat.[43] She was very much involved in her husband's business, accepting repayments, and even negotiating easy terms for those in difficulties.

In February 1244 David suddenly died. All the chirograph chests across the country were locked in preparation for the search for every one of his bonds needed for the assessment of his estate and the fine that would accrue to the king.[44] Those coffers found to contain his bonds were taken to Windsor, along with all those Oxford Jews who could help in tracing and identifying his concerns. Among the places where his chirographs were found were London, Oxford, Warwick, Northampton, Berkshire, Bedfordshire and Buckinghamshire. Although the practice was for the king to take one third of the estate, on occasion he would keep it all, as Henry II had done with Aaron of Lincoln's entire fortune in 1187.[45]

On her husband's death, Licoricia was taken to the Tower of London. This happened when the windfall to the Crown was expected to be huge, and to prevent interference from the heirs who might have spirited away prized belongings. There is evidence in the records of this occurring, just as there must have been genuine fear concerning the choice items selected for the king. Widows and heirs would be allowed to buy back property from the king. Not every newly bereaved widow was imprisoned in this way, and it may have been a reflection on how the king or his officials viewed Licoricia's acquisitiveness, the amount involved, or he may have been particularly interested in some of the deceased's possessions. In David's case, the king seemed to be attracted to his library, for he asked that it be searched for any books that were regarded as against the teachings of the Christian or Jewish faiths. This has been seen as a reference to the famous work by Maimonides, the *Guide for the Perplexed*, written about 1190, which outraged some of the most conservative Jews. It might also have referred to the Talmud, which was regarded as being anti-Christian and had been ordered burnt by the pope. The king finally kept three of the books for his own use: a bible, a decretal and a psalter with a glossary. These would originally have been pledges for loans that were not repaid, and would probably have been richly illuminated and bound. The Fine Rolls state that they were eventually returned.[46]

A special account was set up to collect all of David's wealth as it came in. His best house in Oxford was taken to maintain the Domus Conversorum in London, the establishment set up on the order of the king to house those Jews who converted to Christianity. The income from some of David's other houses contributed to its upkeep.[47] Houses for the converted survived in England for some 300 years, long after there could have been any English Jewish converts from the period before the 1290 Expulsion. There may have been a trickle from some later immigrant converts arriving from Spain or Portugal.

David's other houses in Oxford and elsewhere appear to have stayed in the family's ownership. Licoricia and Asser Sweetman not only repossessed Muriel's house in 1253, but seem to have still owned others in Oxford, one of which was disposed of in 1283. On David's death, a flood of his debtors disputed recorded debts and repayments.[48] The commonest contention would have been that a debt had been repaid but the repayment not recorded. Many realized they could be asked by the Treasury to settle the whole debt at once or lose the pledged items, which they may have found very difficult. If the Crown acquired the debt, the king could not collect interest, as it was usury. While this could be regarded as an advantage to the borrower, they were as likely to find that the king had given their debt to someone else, who could be much more severe in their demands for a full settlement, with loss of their pledge when unable to comply. If the loan was underpinned by their land and the new creditor was a Christian, they might permanently lose it.

Licoricia was kept in the Tower until September 1244, and while she was there, six of the leading Jews were ordered to oversee her business interests. This was obviously an onerous duty on top of their own concerns, and Aaron of York immediately paid a contribution of £100 towards the approaching war with Scotland (which in fact never took place) to be freed of this obligation, his place being allotted to Bonami of Canterbury.[49] There were further delays caused by the absence of the other guarantors, among them Benedict Crespin, who was engaged elsewhere on important court and Exchequer business with the barons and Justices of the Jews.[50] By September 1244 the estate was settled and an agreement about the payment of the king's share of the total was reached. The final amount was 5,000 marks,[51] which compares with the 6,000 marks and 7,000 marks that the heirs of Hamo of Hereford and Leo of York respectively had to pay that same year. From this it might be suggested that David was not the wealthiest of his co-religionists, but we cannot discount the possibility that other unspecified (and unrecorded) arrangements were made that were preferable to the king.[52]

Of that 5,000 marks, the king earmarked 4,000 for his own pet scheme, the building of a rich shrine and chapel to Edward the Confessor at Westminster Abbey. A special chest was established for the collection of donations, voluntary and otherwise, and Licoricia's further forced contribution of over £2,500 was by far the biggest single donation at that time.[53] How did she pay it? She could have liquidated some of her share of David's assets, but it becomes clear on reading the settlement concerning future tallage payments that it was agreed that she did not have to do that:

> Licoricia, for a fine of 25 marks per annum that she should have all the charters, monuments and debts late of David of Oxford wherever they may be found, whether in the Treasury or elsewhere, and she might pay her tallage to the king by her own hand, and that she might not be part (without the king's special order) of any tallage as long as she pays 25 marks per annum.[54]

There are some very curious features about this document. Licoricia was to have all of David's chattels and bonds wherever they could be found. Usually the king's third was taken in money, chattels and bonds, but it seems that Licoricia was able to keep it all. She also seems to have been able to strike an amazing bargain over her tallage, only having to pay twenty-five marks per annum, which considering the extent of her wealth was very small. This would not have been a loss to the king, of course, because the shortfall of the target total which had been assessed as the tallage due from the entire Jewish community, including her own wealth, would have to be made up by the rest of the community. The phrase 'by her own hand' could have merely meant that it was to be paid into his personal account rather than the Exchequer, but similar agreements made with other individuals did not always have this stipulation. This was an example of the king's use of Jewish funds for his own purposes, which gave him a measure of independence beyond the control of his ministers. For the barons, this proved yet another source of resentment against the Jews. It may be that Henry was so anxious to have Licoricia's contribution towards the construction of the shrine that he was willing to be generous in the terms of her settlement. Moreover, the Exchequer enforced the collection of some of her debts and forwarded the money on to Licoricia, provided that she continued to pay her twenty-five marks each year, and gave her licence to distrain her debtors, having made a fine with the king.[55] Certainly, she did not figure in the tallage payments for many years.

David was buried in the Jewish cemetery in Oxford, in the section that has since become subsumed in the Physic Garden of Magdalen College. The death duties settled, in September 1244, Licoricia, now the wealthiest Jewish woman in the country, was released from the Tower[56] and returned to live in Winchester with her baby, Asser, and with her three older sons, who were reaching an age to begin dealing for themselves.

NOTES

1. Belia paid her contribution of £14 6s 8d to the 20,000 Mark Tallage at Winchester in 1241/42. Her future husband paid just 17s 9d into the same Tallage at Bedford. Belia may well therefore have been the wealthier partner: Robert C. Stacey, 'Royal Taxation and the Social Structure of Medieval Anglo-Jewry: The Tallages of 1239–1242', *HUCA*, 56 (1986) pp.235 and 222 respectively.
2. Evidence that Cresse was Belia's son not Pictavin's: *PREJ*, III, p.14, 'Cresse son of Belia and Pyctavinus of Bedford mainperned her [Belia] and had her not, therefore *they* [my emphasis] are in mercy': the plural verb shows that Cresse and Pictavin acted together, but Cresse is identified only as Belia's son.
3. *PREJ*, I, p.75.

4. For example, *Select Pleas*, p.48 (1268). See Mundill, 'The Jewish Entries from the Patent Rolls, 1271–1292', *JHS*, 32 (1990–92), p.79.
5. *Rokeah*, p.156, entry 611 mentions a 'Sonet son of Bella' in 1275.
6. Widow of Pictavin: *PREJ*, I, p.136, and *Select Pleas*, p.35. In numerous entries from the Memoranda Rolls from 1264 onwards she is seen being pursued for the fine owed for gaining access to her late husband's goods and business interests: *Rokeah*, pp.31 (entry 130), p.45 (entry 188), p.88 (entry 360) and p.129 (entry 514, where she is imprisoned in the Tower of London). In the last entry, ibid., p.72 (entry 303) dated 1271, she finally receives the goods on an agreement to pay by instalments. Debts owed to her in the 1260s and 1270s are mentioned in ibid., pp.19, 60, 77, 81, 82, 163 and 375 and in *PREJ*, I, pp.137, 224 and 288 (this last in 1272, with her son Jacob).
7. An earlier version of this discussion appeared in my article 'Women in the Medieval Anglo-Jewish Community', in Patricia Skinner, ed., *Jews in Medieval Britain: Historical, Literary and Archaeological Perspectives* (Woodbridge: Boydell, 2003), pp.113–27.
8. *PREJ*, I, p.152.
9. The contract is reproduced in Michael Adler, *Jews of Medieval England* (London: JHSE, 1939), pp.43–5 and facing plate.
10. Judith: Cecil Roth, *A History of the Jews in England*, (Oxford: Clarendon Press, 3rd edn 1964), p.116, note 5, citing *Shetaroth*, p.298.
11. *Shetaroth*, p.33.
12. *PREJ*, II, p.21.
13. M.D. Davis, 'An Anglo-Jewish Divorce', *JQR*, 5 (1893), pp.158–65 at p.159.
14. The Northampton Donum was the donation made by the Jewish community towards the ransom paid for King Richard's release from imprisonment. The English Jews paid 5,000 marks: I. Abrahams, 'The Northampton *Donum* of 1194', *MJHSE*, 1 (1925), pp.59–74.
15. See above, Chapter 1 note 6. He stood bail for Abraham Pinche in the 1225 child-murder case.
16. In the tallage list for Oxford in 1241 he is listed as 'David de Linc': *Cl. R. Henry III, 1237–1242*, p.355. Intriguingly, a debt found in the Nottingham *archa* in 1262 refers to a debt owed to Licoricia, 'widow of David of Lincoln', which suggests that the toponym persisted in the Midlands: *Medieval Jewish Documents in Westminster Abbey*, Ann Causton (ed.) (London: JHSE, 2007), pp.98–9, document 235.
17. Warwickshire: *PREJ*, I, p.72. David's business interests extended also to Northamptonshire (ibid., p.71), Staffordshire (ibid., p.84), Berkshire (ibid., p.59), Gloucestershire (ibid., pp.76 and 103) and Buckinghamshire (ibid., p.78).
18. Davis, 'Anglo-Jewish Divorce', p.159.
19. Roth, *The Jews of Medieval Oxford*, (Oxford: Oxford Historical Society NS 9, 1945–46), p.46.
20. *Pat. R. Henry III, 1232–1237*, p.228 terms David and others 'receivers and thieves'.
21. H.P. Stokes, 'A Jewish Family in Oxford in the 13th Century', *TJHSE*, 10 (1921–23), pp.193–206 at p.195.
22. *Ch. R.* I, p.49, copies and confirms the grant to Oseney.
23. *Cl. R. Henry III, 1242–1247*, p.195 (1244).
24. Roth, *History of the Jews in England*, p.48.
25. Margaret Wade Labarge, *Simon de Montfort* (New York: Norton, 1963, repr. London: Eyre and Spottiswoode, 1975), p.70.
26. *Cl. R. Henry III, 1237–1242*, p.4, *Pat.R. 1232–47*, p.173.
27. *Pat. R. Henry III, 1232–1247*, p.229.
28. *Pat. R. Henry III, 1232–1247*, p.228.
29. *Matthaei Parisiensis Chronica Majora*, H.R. Luard (ed.) 7 vols (London: Rolls Series 57, 1872–83) V, p.15.
30. This has a particular resonance in 1278 when Licoricia's son was convicted of this offence: see below, p.128.
31. Davis, 'Anglo-Jewish Divorce', p.160.
32. Nonetheless, he paid the significant sums of over £160 into the One-Third Chattels Tallage in 1240/01, and £1,000 (by far the largest amount) into the 20,000 Mark Tallage of 1241/42: Stacey, 'Royal Taxation and Social Structure', pp.218 and 232 respectively.
33. *Pat. R. Henry III, 1232–1247*, p.246.
34. Stacey, 'Royal Taxation and Social Structure', pp.202, Table 4.

35. Stacey, 'English Jews under Henry III', in Skinner, (ed.), *Jews in Medieval Britain*, p.46.
36. It is also possible that she is the 'Muriel of Oxford' who paid 9½ d into the One-Third Chattels Tallage in 1240 at Canterbury: Stacey, 'Royal Taxation and Social Structure', p.211.
37. I. Epstein, 'Pre-Expulsion England in the *Responsa*', *TJHSE*, 14 (1935–39), pp.201–2.
38. *Cl. R. Henry III, 1237–1242*, p.464.
39. Ibid.
40. *Cl. R. Henry III, 1247–1251*, p.57.
41. Ibid., p.143.
42. *Cl. R. Henry III, 1253*, p.455.
43. He appears as 'Sweteman' in most Jewish Exchequer, Patent Roll and Close Roll entries, but the Fine Rolls have references to him as Asser: *Calendar of the Fine Rolls, I: Edward I 1272–1307* (London: HMSO, 1911), pp.162 and 164 (both dated 1282). *PREJ*, II, p.90 (1273) uniquely has him referred to as Sweteman, son of Licorice, and Sweteman, son of David of Oxford, in the same entry.
44. *Lib. R. Henry III, 1240–1245*, p.223: all the sealed boxes were to be brought to Winchester. Cf. *PREJ*, I, p.72.
45. *Rokeah*, p.65 entry 276, mentions debts of David in the Bedfordshire and Buckinghamshire accounts long after David's death.
46. Cecil Roth, *The Intellectual Activities of Medieval English Jews* (London: British Academy/Oxford University Press, n.d.), p.7.
47. *Cl. R. Henry III, 1242–1247*, p.174 (1244); this was upheld in 1274: *Rokeah*, p.137 entry 536.
48. Some succeeded in proving they were not debtors: *PREJ*, I, pp.76–7, 96, 101.
49. *Cl. R. Henry III, 1242–1247*, p.260.
50. *Royal and Other Historical Letters Illustrative of the Reign of King Henry III*, W.W. Shirley (ed.), 2 vols (London: Longman, 1862–66), II, p.46.
51. Not £5,000, as given in *Select Pleas*, p.25.
52. In 1244 Queen Eleanor pardoned a debt owed to David of Oxford for £100, possibly part of the settlement payment: *Cl. R. Henry III, 1242–1247*, p.195.
53. *Pat. R. Henry III, 1232–1247*, p.478.
54. *Cl. R. Henry III, 1247–1251*, p.198 (1249): 'per manum suum' and *Pat. R. Henry III, 1247–1258*, p.6.
55. For example, *Cl. R. Henry III, 1247–1251*, pp.196 and 402.
56. *Royal and other Historical Letters*, Shirley (ed.), II, p.46: she was to be released in the presence of three Jews, and the justices were to make them hurry.

CHAPTER FOUR

Licoricia the Widow

Now Licoricia came into her own. She moved back to Winchester, to Shoemakers or Shorten Street where she had probably lived before, and where her oldest sons may have remained while she was in Oxford. So many Jews lived there that it was probably called 'Jewry Street' by the locals at the time, but it was officially renamed only after the Jews were expelled.[1] Living here, Licoricia was at the heart of the business community, for it was the road that ran from the North to the South gates and was bisected halfway by the High Street running from the West to the East gates, and was therefore in an ideal position for travellers, merchants and others seeking the services of the moneylenders. It was also very close to the royal castle, which King Henry had been preoccupied with rebuilding and refurbishing since coming to the throne, and as we have seen, Licoricia seems to have had a special relationship with the court. It is worth pausing, therefore, to examine in more detail this king from whom she had received the extraordinary document in 1244.

THE ROYAL CONNECTION: HENRY III

What was this king like? His effigy on his tomb at Westminster is of a serene and noble man with flowing hair and beard (see Figure 5). Matthew Paris, who saw him often when he visited St Albans Abbey, describes him as 'fox-like, squint-eyed, silly and impotent. More like a woman than a man, with penetrating eyes' – presumably when they weren't squinting.[2] It should be remembered that Paris shared the hostility felt against the king by most of the church establishment. Another contemporary account by Nicholas Trevet describes him as about five and a half feet tall and of strong build, with a drooping eyelid. A word that is also used in contemporary descriptions of the king describes him as *simplex*, which Carpenter points out could mean stupid, or more likely naïve, and speculates that his isolation when growing up afforded

Figure 5. Henry III's Effigy. Photo © Dean and Chapter of Westminster Abbey, used by kind permission.

him a poor political education.[3] He also describes him as having a warm-hearted personality, and Henry was certainly a fond family man, although he had the usual monumental Plantagenet temper tantrums. He loved a luxurious life, as reflected in the provisions ordered for his visits to his many castles. In 1248 he arrived at Whitby Abbey bringing 2,560 gallons of Bordeaux wine for himself and his court. He rode on to Pickering Castle, adding 2,500 gallons to his stocks, presumably replacing that which had been consumed. He spent Christmas at Clifford Tower in York, by which time he had accumulated some 30,720 gallons (190,000 bottles). In 1251 he is reported to have had three tons of roasted swan and 300 boars served to his guests as part of the Christmas celebrations. In his appetite for food and drink, therefore, he resembled his father.

It is generally agreed that King Henry was profoundly devout in an open and generous manner, feeding as many as 50,000 paupers on one occasion.[4] He attended as many as four masses a day and loved the rituals and rich trappings of church ceremonies, which chimed in with his lifelong preoccupation with architecture, sumptuous decoration and embellishment. This was not considered admirable at a time when the ideal monarch of the period was someone martial, determined and strong, like the king's uncle, Richard the Lionheart. But Henry had inherited the throne as a boy of nine, at the end of a civil war which had left the country divided and impoverished. As a result, the king preferred a peaceful life. He was not interested in hunting or tournaments, and although he did undertake campaigns to try to regain some of the lost Plantagenet possessions in France, he was indecisive and, consequently, unsuccessful. He preferred visiting and improving his castles in the south, which included Windsor, Clarendon, Marlborough and Woodstock, as well as Winchester. Here he was in friendly competition with his old tutor, Bishop Peter des Roches, who was continually refining and embellishing his own Wolvesey Palace, while Henry tried to outdo him across the city at Winchester Castle. Amid many improvements, there was the building of the Great Hall which stands to this day, completed in the mid-1230s. There are also records of chambers painted green and decorated with rich wall paintings, a roof to cover the outside passage from the queen's chamber to her chapel, glass for the windows in her room, new chapels elsewhere in the castle and a new tower. His building and improvements frequently demonstrated an interest in practical matters that was ahead of his time; he commissioned the first public conveniences to be built since Roman times, and also installed underground drainage in Westminster Palace.[5]

Henry revered and admired his patron saint, and ancestor, Edward the Confessor, and his ambition was to build a golden shrine covered in precious stones to be housed in a 'Temple of Honour' at Westminster Abbey. In 1245 he had the old Westminster Abbey torn down and, prompted by a royal visit to his brother-in-law, the king of France, when he was dazzled by the newly built church of Sainte-Chapelle and the cathedral at Rheims, he rebuilt Westminster Abbey to house the rich and bejewelled shrine for St Edward. That shrine is still there, though stripped of all the precious casings during the Reformation (see Figure 6).

For all this extravagance, the king required a private source of funds outside the control of his council, and his private treasury, called the King's Wardrobe, was expanded. Although some of its accounts survive, there were also 'invisible sources' that came in the form of gifts – both solicited and freely given, and a siphoning of the income from the Jewry.[6] This was probably one of the reasons for the close working relationship between Licoricia and the king in Winchester.

By 1244 Henry was 41, and his queen was Eleanor of Provence, whom he had married some eight years earlier, and by whom he had five children. An influx of ambitious relatives had accompanied Eleanor, sister of the queen of France, when she arrived in England in

Figure 6. The Shrine of Edward the Confessor. Photo © Dean and Chapter of Westminster Abbey, used by kind permission.

1236, and others followed. Her uncles were hungry for their own advancement, and the English barons saw some of what they considered to be their rightful gifts and benefits from the king going to these interlopers, whom they called the Savoyards. In 1240 Peter of Savoy became earl of Richmond while his brother, Boniface, was appointed to the see of Canterbury. Worse was to follow when Henry's half-brothers and yet more of his mother's relatives began to appear in 1247. Henry, who had grown up with no real family life, was particularly keen to foster his new relations. These two groups became the focus of resentment and xenophobia for the English barons, some of whom had been forced to sever their own connections with France at the beginning of the century, and who still resented the loss of those lands and estates across the Channel. King Henry encouraged intermarriage between these two groups and his English nobility, but while he was providing himself with the happy family life he had missed, he ignored the possible consequences for himself and his kingdom.

THE WIDOW LICORICIA

As her late husband David had been involved in the king's personal financial activities, so Licoricia as widow now fulfilled the same role. She was in and out of court whenever Henry was present at Winchester and London, and probably pursued her business interests with the members of the court when he was absent, as she was also well known to the king's officials.[7] Among her connections were the king's brother-in-law, Simon de Montfort, and Henry's cousin, Peter D'Albeyon.[8] The king's bastard half-brother, Stephen de Lungspee, had been pardoned a debt of £95 that had been David's, even while the king had promised not to interfere with any of Licoricia's bonds.[9] Certainly, the court employed her for their money transactions, and the king put pressure on them when they were slow to repay their loans, as when he ordered the countess of Devonshire, Margaret de Riparis, to pay back what she owed Licoricia immediately.[10]

Not surprisingly, therefore, the Jewish community saw Licoricia as its representative and turned to her with its various concerns, sometimes asking her to intercede on their behalf with the king. In addition to her own business interests, she now possessed all of David's considerable enterprises. Demonstrating amazing confidence, she preferred to handle it all herself, although she seemed to have used her son Isaac, known as Cokerel or Cok, as her main agent from about 1248. She may have employed others across the country to cover the most distant of David's debts, although there is plenty of evidence that she could deal with any repayments or renegotiations of debt locally, wherever they originated.

It was common practice to use agents in other towns to oversee or arrange new loans locally, particularly because of the difficulties of travel for most people, as well as actual restrictions on the poorest leaving their immediate surroundings. Chera and Abraham Pinche had acted as Isaac of Norwich's agents in Winchester at the beginning of the previous decade. Licoricia's two other sons, Lumbard and Benedict, may have been acting in her interests at this time for they only begin to figure in the Pipe Rolls in their own right in the late 1240s, although they must have been adult. She certainly appeared in court very often in pursuit of her business interests and wrangling over financial issues: she presented, as Rigg comments, 'a great figure as a litigant'.[11]

Licoricia is known to have undertaken quite lengthy journeys, a precarious undertaking for a Jewish woman. The roads throughout the country were of poor quality. In Winchester the roads were surfaced in flint, but apart from any surviving surface on the Roman roads of England, mud, ruts and dust confronted travellers of the thirteenth century. Horses could manage twenty-four miles a day, and pack horses half that. A trip to London from Winchester would have taken three or four days, and one to the northern capital of York, about 215 miles as the crow flies, could take as much as two to three weeks.[12]

When travelling on her own business, Licoricia would have to provide herself with an escort for protection from attack and robbery on the dangerous roads; she might have waited to travel in the company of others. As we shall see, she probably went in person to see her dubiously retained estates in Warwickshire.[13] She travelled on horseback, or more probably in a special cart that could be hired for the purpose, assuming she did not possess one. She may have acquired some of David's love of expensive horses and might have owned many high quality mounts of her own. Overnight stops would most likely have been with co-religionists, or with some of her far-flung family members. Where there were no relatives or friends, every synagogue complex included accommodation for Jewish travellers. This not only catered for special dietary and religious requirements in affording them a secure place to stay, but provided a source of information and cultural stimulation for the resident Jews.[14] Someone as wealthy and as well known to the Jewish community as Licoricia would have been a welcome and honoured guest. Some of her journeys, however, were under arrest when she was either accused, or taken to the London Jewish Exchequer at the Tower. She would then have ridden with an escort of guards and officials.

It must also be remembered that all money had to be carried and was of considerable weight, as there was no paper currency. Jews could offer a valuable service on occasion by contacting fellow money-dealers at a distant place for actual money to be supplied there. In the previous century, three Winchester Jewish money-dealers had transferred a large sum of credit by this method to pay the king's soldiers in Carlisle. Even in the following century in Avignon, the pope paid the mercenaries he was employing in Italy through the services of Issarmeda, a local Jew who arranged the payment in Italy.[15] Whenever large amounts of coins were to be transported, armed escorts needed to be hired. There are records of excuses from sheriffs for the late delivery of collected taxes to the Exchequer in London, pleading that they could not afford the cost of hiring the guards that such a valuable transport needed.

LICORICIA'S DAILY LIFE

What must life have been like at this time? Although we have very little information about medieval Jewish social life in England, we can attempt to build a picture of Licoricia's environment and actions. As a wealthy widow, she would have had many servants, some Christian, despite the fact that Jews were not supposed to employ Christians; one of them would die with her in 1277.[16] Other servants would have been Jewish. Her *messuage* or house and grounds might have covered almost an acre of land, sloping down to Fleshmonger Street that ran parallel behind Jewry Street. It would have included a large stone house with a secure cellar in which to store her money and valuables, there being no banks for security. Other buildings might have enclosed the property on three sides, and would have housed family members and servants; they may also have surrounded a garden and orchard, or a courtyard with domestic animals.

If Licoricia occupied the house that had belonged to Abraham Pinche, the community synagogue was located within her own courtyard. She might have possessed her own private *mikveh*, or ritual bath, for the ablutions required weekly before prayers and once a month for women: there is no evidence of a public *mikveh* in the city. The private bath that Benedict Crespin had built in his opulent house in Milk Street, London, was excavated in 2002. It was beautifully constructed from green sandstone brought from Kent, the joints fitting so closely that they were watertight, and it had steps going down into the water.[17] Benedict Crespin had figured often in Licoricia's life, and she had known him for many years. She would have known about his private *mikveh* and she was wealthy enough to possess one for herself. Her house was served by a spring or well of fresh water from the chalk of the western hill.

Licoricia required a room to conduct her business, where clients or aspiring debtors were received, serviced by clerks or perhaps her sons acting as secretaries who kept the records of her deals. Jewish life was multi-lingual. Licoricia may have been able to read Hebrew and sign her name, but the spoken language of the court was Norman French, and the vernacular spoken by her friends and neighbours was English. She may have been taught to write too, as there were no impediments in Jewish law to the education of women or their employment as clerks.[18] The official written language and the language of law was Latin, and she seems to have been able to conduct her own cases in law courts.

There was little official education for Jewish girls, although some were taught privately or by their parents. The better-off Jewish boys were expected to be educated for several years at the religious schools attached to the synagogues, but religious requirements meant that they were also provided with tutors by parents who valued a more extensive syllabus. Licoricia's sons would have been well educated, and Benedict and Cokerel's interest in books is demonstrated in the detailing of them in the records. They may have acquired some of their late stepfather's considerable collection.

Kosher food was provided by other members of the community and in some cases it was popular enough for the surplus to be on sale in the street to their Christian neighbours. There are references to various edicts forbidding the purchase of food from Jews, one as late as 1281.[19] Conversely the Jews did not manage their own livestock, grain or other basic foodstuffs, and so were reliant for their purchases on Christian merchants and farmers. In the 1270s, such dealing was forbidden, and the Jewish community had to petition King Edward to cancel this order, or else they would face starvation.

Jews also dealt in the many spices essential during the winter months when so much meat was salted and, by late winter, tainted. Spices themselves were a precious commodity – they could function as a substitute currency – and there were also dealers who specialized in them; one spice-seller lived on the corner of Jewry Street. Licoricia's son, Benedict, sometimes rented out his property for a 'spice rent', and at one time a tenant of his living in nearby Micheldever was in arrears for sixteen pounds of peppercorns to cover sixteen years' rent.[20] A 'peppercorn rent' in the Middle Ages, therefore, did not mean an extremely low amount, but a speculative investment. The value of spices fluctuated from year to year depending on how transport was affected by wars and civil unrest in the countries that had to be crossed, or in England itself. While the stated rent could be quite a reasonable sum for the tenant in one year, it could also be a profitable return for the landlord in another. Evidently, the Micheldever tenant had found difficulty in meeting the rent for some sixteen years.

Benedict, in addition to all his other business deals, became a wine merchant in later life along with some of his fellow guildsmen, whom he probably joined in their drinking sessions at the Guildhall. Jacobs quotes a comment in a thirteenth-century manuscript by Rabbi Elchanan that expresses surprise at the amount of strong drinking in England on the part of the Christians and the Jews who drank with them. The rabbi states that this was in spite of the Jewish law that forbade drinking with Christians, on the grounds that it might lead to intermarriage. However, he goes on to say that as refraining might cause ill feeling, 'one must not be too severe upon them'.[21] Kosher wine is mentioned in some of the records, and Belia was paid with two barrels of cider for a debt in Winchester.[22]

The dress of Winchester Jews would have been much the same as that of their Gentile neighbours. Only one illustration of an Anglo-Jewish woman survives from around this time, and it is problematic to say the least. She figures in a doodled caricature by a bored and clearly anti-Jewish clerk, at the top of an Exchequer document of 1233, in which devils are shown tormenting three Jews. She is Abigail, the wife of Isaac of Norwich's bailiff, Mokke, who is also depicted. While the sketch only shows her head and shoulders, she is wearing a fancy coif over a cap, her hair flowing down her back. The top of a tunic is visible; over this she would have worn a supertunic, and a cloak as an outer garment.[23]

Lists of clothing appear in the records, frequently in disputes where those who had undertaken to safeguard Jewish property during threatening times were reluctant to return it afterwards. Most claimed they had never taken the clothing, or that it was theirs in the first place. The descriptions of robes of richly coloured velvets and brocades, trimmed with fur, may well have been articles that were pledged against debt, but could also have been the clothes of the Jews themselves. From the records, it seems that a vital part of dress throughout the Middle Ages was the girdle, which could be simple or of precious metals, of silk beaded in gold or silver, or encrusted with jewels. In any list of personal property, either the belongings of executed Jews or of items given as pledges, girdles figure large, a reflection of their universal use and as items of value. Other jewels mentioned were mostly brooches or buttons, which could be accepted as payment or as pledges for debts. Among the stones left by Benedict, garnets and peridots are mentioned, the latter used almost exclusively on church vestments and sacramental cups and crosses, and reputed to have been brought back by crusaders.

That Jew and Christian were difficult to tell apart simply by their dress is indicated by the introduction of the most notorious distinguishing mark. The Fourth Lateran Council meeting in 1215 demanded that Jews and Saracens everywhere in Christendom should wear either an item of clothing like a pointed straw hat called a *pilum*, or a badge of cloth stitched to their outer garment called a *tabula*, or some such distinguishing item of clothing. The expressed purpose of this was to ensure that no Christian should accidentally enter into undesirable friendship with a non-believer, and that any potential sexual relationship (because of non-recognition) would be prevented. The exact phrase was 'a prevention against miscegenation', which was a concern to both Jews and Christians. The *pilum* had not been worn by English Jews for some time, although the two men in the Norwich caricature are shown wearing them. It had probably become an artistic device to identify Jews, although elsewhere on the continent the *pilum* was still actually worn, and continued to be for some time.

It is postulated by Kisch that England was the first country to adopt the instructions of the Lateran Council because the Jews had assimilated here more than elsewhere and there was therefore a need for some distinguishing mark.[24] The English badge was a length of yellow cloth, 'two fingers wide and four fingers long', cut into the shape of two Mosaic tablets. The pope excused travellers or doctors from wearing the badge on the grounds that it could endanger their lives. Almost immediately, English Jews began buying permission to be excused from wearing the badge, and we know that there was little enforcement between 1218 and 1253.[25] Jews could buy exemption from the church either for themselves or for their entire community. The church regarded this as a welcome source of additional funds and several times during the thirteenth century saw to it that the instruction was re-imposed, thereby collecting another tranche of exemption money. Jews regarded the cloth as a badge of shame and bitterly resented wearing it.

LICORICIA'S DEALING: THE CHARLECOTE CASE

Among David's many clients there was one longstanding debtor, a landowner from Warwickshire whom Licoricia herself had dealt with while her husband was still alive. This was Sir Thomas de Charlecote, who appears to have been in considerable financial difficulties. He had negotiated several debts from David and had trouble meeting the repayments. In these circumstances it was sometimes advantageous to reschedule all the debts together as one loan, perhaps with easier instalments agreed, and Sir Thomas had negotiated this more than once. He had paid off one of his debts with a casket of jewels handed to Licoricia, who had issued a starr of acquittal, but there was still a considerable amount outstanding. After David's death in 1246, Sir Thomas reached an agreement with Licoricia to cover a loan of £180 with a new agreement. He would repay the loan over a period of six years at the legitimate rate of 2d per pound per week, against the security of his estate, rents and chattels. The final total was to be £400, and this was to be paid by the estate if he did not survive the term of six years. In 1248, Sir Thomas was found drowned in a lake on his own estate; it was generally accepted that he had been murdered, allegedly by some servants, but no further investigation took place, and it seems just as possible that it was either an accident or suicide. In these circumstances, the creditor was entitled to take possession of the pledge. However, a Jew could not take permanent possession of the land, and was only allowed to sell off the mortgage after a year and a day,[26] in the meantime receiving the income from rents, the produce of the land, and the chattels thereon. At the end of that period, the land could be sold on to a Christian or restored to the heir. This did not happen at Charlecote. Licoricia took possession with the king's approval, and installed her own agent, one Isaac (who might possibly have been her son, Cok). She should have given Thomas's underage heir, or his representatives, the chance to offer repayment of the debts, but it seems that this was not done. For the stipulated year, therefore, the income from the estate was ruthlessly creamed off. There is evidence from similar practices elsewhere that this could involve the selling of all the livestock, the destruction and sale of the materials in farm buildings and the felling and sale of all the trees. Some debtors who knew they were to lose the custody of their pledged land were just as likely to pre-empt their creditor by spiriting away their own crops, livestock and chattels before it was lost to them.

What distinguishes Licoricia's rapacity, however, is that she was still in possession of the Charlecote estate three years later, and with the agreement of the king. This is one of several occasions when the king seemed to be using Jews to bypass the feudal laws of his own country or the demands of the church. It may have been at the suggestion of Licoricia herself, or perhaps Henry saw it as a way to obtain the required payments towards his project to build St Edward's shrine as quickly as possible. Whoever initiated the extension, in 1250 the king granted to Licoricia

> seisin[27] of all lands, rents and tenements late of Thomas de Cherlecot [sic], which are in her pledge, and that she shall not be disseised

thereof till the debts for which they are pledged were paid or until she be disseised thereof by judgement of the court. Grant to Master Simon, Archdeacon of East Riding, that he will keep the said lands, if the said Licoricia is willing, until she has been paid her debts on condition she be answerable to all the Jews who are able to prove that the said lands were pledged to them.[28]

By 1252 the heir, young Sir Thomas, saw his income, which was supposed to be protected under the stipulations of the Magna Carta, severely eroded and his resentment grew accordingly. His bailiff, Lucien de Fresl, severely attacked Isaac, Licoricia's agent, and was forced to pay compensation of five marks as damages to Licoricia.[29] This was the final straw and the heir took Licoricia to court, accusing her of illegal occupation beyond the stipulated period, misuse of the laws governing Jewish moneylending, and falsifying the charter of agreement.[30] She was aiming to collect the full £400 that would have been due had his father lived six years, rather than two; she was also charging compound interest, which was illegal.

Licoricia's conduct in court shows her acting aggressively in defence of her interests, not afraid to attack her accusers, confident and able to conduct her own case. Many of those writing of medieval Jewish women allege that they had no legal standing and had to be represented by male attorneys, but specialists in medieval law take a very different view. They state that a woman could own chattels, make a contract, sue and be sued, could plead for herself, appear in court, be a witness and could act as a guarantor or *mainpern* for others.[31] They could certainly negotiate their own business agreements without the need of a male agent, although many relied on their relations for backing. There is plenty of evidence that this applied in practice. Belia, for example, had appeared in court on behalf of members of her mother-in-law's consortium, and acted as agent for other Jews at the same time.

Licoricia replied to young Thomas de Charlecote's accusations by counterclaiming that his father had been murdered by his seneschal, another Thomas, to help the heir to settle the debt earlier, which he might have negotiated if he had been given the chance. Young Sir Thomas alleged that she had persuaded the chirographers to agree a false settlement, and that his father's signature was forged, but this was rebutted. Sir Thomas had indeed agreed the terms of his debt, but may not have fully appreciated all its ramifications. He was obviously desperate about his mounting debts by this time, and may have been senile.

The heir's final claim was that over the four years Licoricia had been in occupation, she had already collected all the money outstanding.

The court, held in Hampshire, decided in favour of the heir, and ordered Licoricia to pay rent for the time during which she had occupied the estate. The king was furious, and he immediately took the case from the local court for it to be retried in his own court at Westminster, on the grounds that Jews were supposed to be answerable only to his jurisdiction. Licoricia was held in the Tower of London during the retrial, but her agent was presumably still in possession of the Warwickshire estate, because the king had restored it to her while awaiting the outcome of the Westminster hearing, so allowing her to continue to receive the profits. Henry then carefully chose five judges to try the case, three of them being newly reinstated after some years' suspension for corruption. The five were headed by his brother, Richard, Earl of Cornwall, who was the more capable of the two royal sons, having a clearer awareness about what was acceptable among the nobility. Despite the king's best efforts, the judges again found for the heir. Henry pre-empted them by immediately announcing the penalty, ordering Licoricia to pay half a silver mark, a derisory amount when compared with the five marks that the bailiff had been ordered to pay for the attack on Licoricia's agent. The king would have overturned the verdict if he could, but apparently the earl of Cornwall prevented him.

Another case, similar to Licoricia's, was awaiting the outcome of this trial, that against Warin of Bressingham, but following the Charlecote verdict it was settled out of court in 1253. Had Licoricia won this case, the way would have been open for similar asset-stripping to increase the income from pledged lands, which would then have been available for the king's use.

LICORICIA'S DEALINGS: OTHER CLIENTS

With the ending of the Charlecote case, Licoricia returned to Winchester, but from this point the records grow patchy as many of them vanished or were destroyed in the various attacks, raids and civil upheavals that began to erupt across the kingdom from the mid-1250s onwards. Licoricia's local Hampshire clients included many landowners and churchmen, while among the bonds she had inherited from David were those of Roger de Clifford, the 'Fighting Judge', the abbots of Thame and of Beaulieu, the prior of St Frideswide in Oxford, Walter de Lucy and Simon de Montfort, the king's brother-in-law, whose debt was cancelled some six months after David's death, to be re-imposed on his heirs after his death at Evesham in 1265.

Licoricia continued her extensive dealings from her Winchester base, and her fellow Jews still used her as an intermediary on their behalf at the royal court. In 1259 she became embroiled in a court case when accused of stealing a ring which her old friend, Belia of Bedford, who probably still continued her Winchester business through her sons, had left to the king in her will ('quem Belya Judea in ultima sua voluntate regi legavit'). Licoricia's neighbour Ivetta accused Licoricia of having stolen it, and she was again arrested and taken to the Tower of London to await investigation and a possible trial. A few months later, it was found that Ivetta herself was the thief, and Licoricia was released, and her possessions, which had been seized, were returned to her on 7 June.[32] Whether the outcome was based on a confession by Ivetta or a hefty payment by Licoricia is unclear, since we have no more information about the episode, but it is hard to conceive of a motive for Licoricia to steal the object, and particularly one destined for the king. Although there is no more apparent communication between Belia and Licoricia, there was plenty of mutual and joint business activity between their two families. Perhaps this was unavoidable in such a small and isolated community, but it seems to demonstrate that there were no lingering resentments.

Licoricia seems to have been taken to the Tower once more in 1260, when there is a record of her being handed over to the Constable of the Tower by the Exchange Marshal.[33] This may have involved overdue payment of the agreed fine for David's estate, or perhaps an investigation into some irregularity in her business activities. Although she was still not figuring in the tallage lists that survive, she could have been involved in the king's business interests and may well have influenced the king to issue an instruction to his treasurer, William de Breton, to ensure that 'My Winchester Jews be not taxed beyond their means and that they should pay their taxes in sums convenient to them'.[34]

NOTES

1. See above, Chapter 2.
2. Quoted by Rebecca Reader, 'Sweet Charity and Sour Grapes: The Historical Imagination of Matthew Paris', *Medieval History*, 4 (1994), pp.102–19, at p.102.
3. D.A. Carpenter, *The Struggle for Mastery: Penguin History of Britain 1066–1284* (London: Penguin, 2004), p.340.
4. *Lib. R. Henry III, 1240–1245*, pp.124, 220, 281.
5. Winchester: *Lib. R. Henry III, 1240–1245*, pp.127 and 131; London: Stephen Smith, *Underground London* (London: Little, Brown, 2004), p.47.

6. Ralph V. Turner, *King John* (London: Longman, 1994), p.91, refers to money that passed through the Exchange that went unrecorded in the Pipe Rolls. In 1246 Edward son of Odo, Keeper of the King's Works at Westminster, received £100: *Lib. R. Henry III, 1245–1251*, p.24.
7. For example, *Lib. R. Henry III, 1245–1251*, p.270, records 100 marks credited to Licoricia's account towards her fine of 200 marks, when the debts of William of Lancaster granted to her were given by Henry to his brother William de Valence.
8. *Cl. R. Henry III, 1253*, p.326.
9. *PREJ*, I, p.120; *Cl. R. Henry III, 1256–1259*, p.229.
10. *Cl. R. Henry III, 1247–1251*, p.402.
11. *PREJ*, I, p.xvi.
12. Richard Fletcher, *Bloodfeud: Murder and Revenge in Anglo-Saxon England* (London: Penguin, 2003), p.31.
13. See below, p.73.
14. There is also an account of a Jew, Abraham f. Deulecresse of Norwich, staying on two separate occasions at the house of a Christian customer, Isabel de Greynvill the wife of Simon, with two of his servants and two horses: *Select Pleas*, p.89.
15. Frances Stonor Saunders, *Hawkwood: Diabolical Englishman* (London: Faber and Faber, 2004), p.164.
16. See below, p.109.
17. I. Blair, J. Hillaby, I. Howell, R. Sermon and B. Watson, 'The Discovery of Two Medieval *Mikva'ot* in London and a Reinterpretation of the Bristol *Mikveh*', *Jewish Historical Studies*, 27 (2002), pp.32–4.
18. Judith R. Baskin, 'Jewish Women in the Middle Ages', in Judith R. Baskin (ed.), *Jewish Women in Historical Perspective* (Detroit, MI: Wayne State University Press, 1991), pp.94–114.
19. *Cl. R. Edward I, 1279–1288*, p.176.
20. *PREJ*, III, pp.151–2.
21. Joseph Jacobs, *The Jews of Angevin England* (London: David Nutt, 1893), p.269.
22. *PREJ*, I, p.59. It is unlikely that this was for her consumption.
23. Cecil Roth, *Essays and Portraits in Anglo-Jewish History* (Philadelphia, PA: Jewish Publication Society of America, 1962), p.23 and Figure 5 following p.82.
24. Guido Kisch, 'The Yellow Badge in History', *Historica Judaica*, 4.2 (1942).
25. H.G. Richardson, *The English Jewry under Angevin Kings* (London: JHSE/Methuen, 1960), pp.179–80. In 1281 an order was made for *Jewesses* to wear the mark, suggesting that women may not have been targeted as much before this: Ada Corcos, 'Extracts from the Close Rolls', *TJHSE*, 4 (1899–1901), pp.202–19 at p.212.
26. A law dating back to King John: *Select Pleas*, p.2.
27. *PREJ*, I, p.xv, defines *seisin* as 'possession entitling the holder to quiet enjoyment until it be shown that another has a better right'.
28. *Pat. R. Henry III, 1247–1258*, p.58.
29. *PREJ*, I, p.120.
30. The case is set out in detail in *Select Pleas*, pp.19–27.
31. F. Pollock and F.W. Maitland, *The History of English Law before the Time of Edward I*, I (Cambridge: Cambridge University Press, 2nd edn, 1968), p.462. It is unlikely that Pollock and Maitland were thinking of Jewish women. Under Jewish law, a woman could plead provided the property was legally hers. See discussions in Michael Adler, *Jews of Medieval England* (London: JHSE, 1939), pp.18–20 and R.B. Dobson, 'The Role of Jewish Women in Medieval England', in D. Wood (ed.), *Christianity and Judaism: Studies in Church History 29* (Oxford: Blackwell for the Ecclesiastical History Society, 1992), pp.145–68.
32. *Cl. R. Henry III, 1256–1259*, pp.229–30. That Belia had made a will, however, does not mean she had died, or was about to – perhaps she made the bequest known as a 'sweetener' to the king, or as advance payment for a favour. As we shall see, she remains visible in the documents well after 1259.
33. V.D. Lipman, 'Jews and Castles in Medieval England', *TJHSE*, 28 (1981–82), pp.1–19, at p.17 n. 33.
34. *Cl. R. Henry III, 1259–1261*, pp.398–9.

CHAPTER FIVE

Licoricia's Family

Although Licoricia is prominent in the records, her family members, too, feature regularly in the rolls in the mid-thirteenth century (see Figure 7). Her three sons by her first marriage to Abraham, Isaac (Cokerel/Cok), Benedict and Lumbard, begin to figure in the Exchequer Rolls within two years of her return to Winchester. They probably started being involved in the business interests of their mother while she was living in Oxford, and perhaps lived with their mother and stepfather there, learning through managing some of David's deals. Alternatively the eldest sons may have remained in Winchester, beginning to build up their own businesses. Unlike Chera's clan earlier in the century, Licoricia's sons did not act in a family consortium with their mother. It may have been that Licoricia was too difficult or dominant a personality to work with, or that she had a less-than-perfect relationship with her sons. While she sometimes used Asser/Sweetman, her son by David, as an agent, particularly in managing her more far-flung debts, occasionally used Benedict as an attorney, and Cokerel most frequently as a combination of the two, she seems to have preferred working for herself. Her elder sons worked together only rarely, and the fact that they tended to live in different towns implies a wish to distance themselves from their forceful and powerful mother. Perhaps her second marriage and the birth of a half-brother had loosened the family bonds, allowing them to establish their independence.

A clue to this distancing is in the use of their parents' names with their own. Early on in the records of their individual deals, they used their matronymic, for hers was a well-known and reputable name. Soon Benedict started to change that part of his name to his father's, and he was known as 'fil. Abraham', while his mother's was rarely used.[1] Cokerel, who worked most closely with Licoricia, and lived within the boundaries of her Winchester house, always used his mother's name, while Lumbard gradually changed to using his patronymic in his later life.

This change in naming, from their mother to that of their long-dead father, may have reflected their initial need for financial respectability

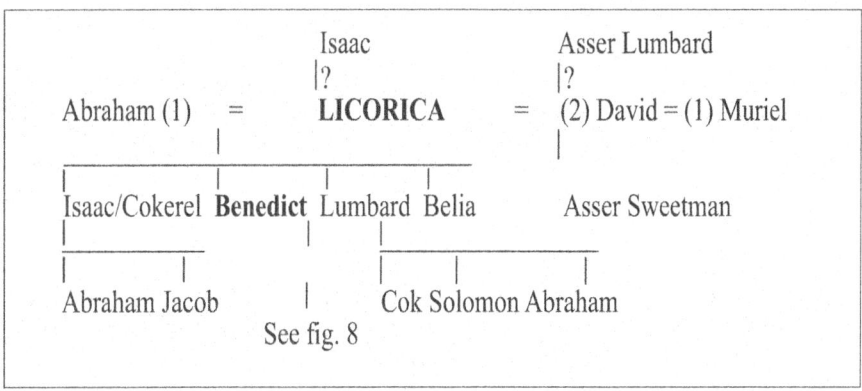

Figure 7. The Family of Licoricia

to support their emerging business enterprises, which then, having been established, was succeeded by the wish to honour their father as a mark of retrospective respect. All three of Licoricia's sons by her first marriage named one of their sons Abraham. So this was never a close family, although Cokerel was heavily involved in her business and still living in the grounds of her property at her death. Asser/Sweetman used both his parents' names and on one occasion he is recorded as being 'fil Licoricia and fil David'.[2] Being her youngest son, however, Sweetman appears only in the latter part of Licoricia's story, and we shall meet him again, calling for an inquest into Licoricia's death.[3]

ISAAC/COKEREL

That Cokerel features most regularly in the records alongside his mother might have been a reflection of how well they got on, or may indicate that he was her eldest son.[4] Cokerel was based in Winchester all of his life. As well as his house within Licoricia's messuage, from which he carried on his business, he also owned another house in Gold Street, on which he is recorded as owing *landgable* in 1285, and he may have moved there after his mother's death in 1277. He married, but we do not know his wife's name; this may have been because she was never involved in business matters or she may have died young. They had at least two sons, Abraham and Jacob, and a daughter whose name is unknown but whose husband, Josce, appears as a fellow juror with Cokerel at a later date.

Cokerel's earliest appearance in the records is in 1245, the first mention of any of her sons, which adds to the likelihood that he was the eldest. Four years later, the king pardoned a debt from Enrico de Sacy to Cokerel of twenty-five marks.[5] This was probably as a reward to De Sacy for services rendered, such as carrying out a successful diplomatic mission or a particularly courageous exploit as a soldier. Cokerel may have received in exchange a confiscated bond or bonds from the Exchequer, or perhaps was excused tallage to the same amount, but equally he might have received no recompense at all.

Some idea of how much Cokerel was involved in Licoricia's business is shown by the records of 1253. He had been very much in court on her behalf during the Charlecote case, and had to take care of all her loans during the times she was in prison. He may indeed have been the 'Isaac' installed at the Warwickshire estate who was attacked by the bailiff, but as he is never otherwise referred to by his Hebrew name 'Isaac' in the documents, but only by the name of 'Cokerel', this must remain uncertain. In any case, he was far too important to his mother's business to be spared to go and live there permanently. In 1253 he also represented Licoricia in court over her loan to one Thomas Bigge, and may also have been involved in the settlement of one of his mother's loans when Baldwin de Wayford repaid Licoricia by paying for Lumbard's and Cokerel's shares of the tallage.[6] It might have included hers too, although Licoricia was supposed to be exempt from tallage following her settlement of David's estate in 1244. Baldwin voided his debt, paying instead the tallage owed by other family members. Cok was also in court in 1253 on his own behalf, when he sued Bonamie fil Samarian, seeking the return of a book valued at twenty shillings, clearly a very expensive volume, and which might have been one of those he inherited from David of Oxford.[7]

In 1255 the sheriff of Hampshire was ordered to take Cokerel, Benedict and Isaac fil Hester, whose mother may have been Chera of Winchester,[8] to the Tower of London as hostages for the amount of tallage due from the Winchester Jewry. This sum was to be paid to Richard of Cornwall who had been given custody of all English Jews as security for a loan of 5,000 silver marks that he had made to his brother the king. This may have been the loan that David had originally brokered and is another example of how the Jews were used by royalty to fund their personal needs.

Richard was to raise this tax income from their fines and whatever else he could harvest as repayment of the loan he had made to his brother. He was given permission to take those bonds from the official

Exchequer chests of all those Jews who owed taxes. King Henry used this method of raising money on more than one occasion, as it exerted the most pressure on Jewish lenders to force immediate settlement of these debts so that the rest of their bonds would be handed back, but it also fired the resentment and fury of their debtors. Yet the income from taxes took a good deal of time to collect, and often never reached the target amount. Handing the custody of the Jews over to his dependents and friends gave the new owners the opportunity to raise more than the sum owed by other means, but for the Jews this could put very heavy pressure on them to liquidate some of their bonds at considerable loss to themselves. They were forced to agree much smaller sums in settlement of the debt, while incurring the hostility of their creditors forced to find the money at once. Some of these new 'owners' did not hesitate to use force, imprisonment or the threat of it to extort money from them. Prince Edward, the future king, built a special prison to house 'his' Jews. Richard of Cornwall, however, seems to have been one of the more considerate of the financial custodians of Jews, who took seriously the need to protect them and the income he made from them. McCall underlines that this apparent concern was not entirely disinterested: 'Princes and barons who owned Jews ... as long as were able to provide them with a decent income, continued to do what they could to protect them both from mob violence and religious interference'.[9]

Cokerel again managed Licoricia's business when she was accused of stealing Belia's ring in 1258, and in 1260 when she was in the Tower of London, possibly over tallage default or an infringement of the rules of the Exchange. The Exchange Marshal handed her over to the keeping of the Tower constable, but it is not clear how long she was imprisoned before she had paid the overdue amount.

One of Cokerel's biggest loans, dating from around 1260, was a very complicated case involving the prior and brothers of Reigate Hospital and Beatrice Duvall, who owned land and tenements in Southwick in Hampshire, and who had borrowed £32 against the security of some of her property. She had entered into some sort of agreement with the convert, Henry of Winchester, by which she deeded him part of the same land on condition that he undertook to settle the corresponding part of her debt for it. Henry went on to make a further arrangement with Thomas of Warblington, who owed him money, to settle his obligations concerning Beatrice. The prior of Reigate seemed liable for the rest, but all those involved kept trying to pass the payment on to someone else. Eventually the king had to summon all those involved to try and resolve this debt and finally, in 1275, the prior was ordered to pay off fifty shillings of the debt and £14 interest, while Thomas and Henry had to pay the rest.[10]

Other clients of Cokerel included Robert of Rogate, Thomas de Heesebeech, Nicholas Blundell, and Robert de Harnhull and his wife. A grant of 1262 illustrates the complexity of some business transactions, as Cokerel agreed to the transfer of a debt of 40s per annum owed him by William Lanceleve to one Ingram de Percy. The sums he lent varied between 12½ marks to £32.[11] Cokerel seems to have kept a low profile all his life, never amassing the riches of his brother Benedict. In 1278 he appeared on a Jewish jury inquiring into the property left by Isaac fil. Isaac. He may have survived till the 1290 Expulsion when there was evidence of property and of some his debts left behind, but by that time these may have been his sons' inheritance, rather than evidence of his own survival.[12]

BENEDICT: EARLY YEARS

Undoubtedly the most successful Jew of his generation was Licoricia's son Benedict, or Benedict of Winchester as he was soon to become known.[13] As we have seen, he initially used his mother's name with his own, but as he became wealthier he reverted to his patronymic and thereafter was known as Benedict fil Abraham. His name first appears in the records in 1253, acting as one of his mother's attorneys together with Cokerel in the Bigge case referred to above, and perhaps in another the same year following the verdict on Charlecote. This was a similar case where the debtor, Warin of Bressingham, was complaining about Licoricia's behaviour on his pledged land, and following on the Charlecote verdict, the dispute was settled out of court.

Benedict sometimes acted on behalf of his mother but overwhelmingly it was his own transactions that he pursued, some with considerable ruthlessness and deviousness. An instance of this can be found in the Patent Rolls in 1261 where an entry reads,

> Benedict fil's Licoricia has satisfied Prince Edward of his debt. All sheriffs and bailiffs to destrain debtors of Benedict by land and chattels so that no further clamour reach [the king's] ears of their default.[14]

Such services by the king's officials in support of his business dealings would have been suspended while he owed his taxes. Other cases are from his debtors, complaining of his confiscation of their pledged property when he had no right so to do. He could legally cull the income for a year and a day, and as we have already seen, there are many instances in the records of other creditors carrying off household goods, the very stones of the house and felling all the wood on the estate. If Benedict was indeed this harsh, he must surely have had a model in his mother's activities at Charlecote. We shall return to his story later.

LUMBARD

Licoricia's son Lumbard appears to have been the least successful of the siblings, if prominence in the fiscal records is any indication. He married but his wife is not named, and he had three sons, Cokerel, Abraham and Solomon. He is first mentioned in the Exchequer Rolls in 1254, some nine years after Cokerel's first entry, and this might be a clue to his position in the family in that he may have been the youngest of Licoricia's sons by her first husband.

Lumbard rarely appears as a dealer after that. An added complication in tracing his story is that another Lumbard appears extensively in the records, dealing in Hampshire at around the same time, Lumbard of Petersfield. His parentage is never mentioned, so we cannot assume they were one and the same man, despite our Lumbard moving to Basingstoke (closer to Petersfield) in 1273 and paying four shillings and eight pence to do so.[15] Solomon moved to nearby Odiham the following year.

Lumbard's apparent lack of activity or success may be due to the difficulties of identifying him securely among the many other Lumbards in the records. His move to Basingstoke and his son's to nearby Odiham might have been in order to set up an independent branch of business separate from that of his mother. Odiham was a royal castle that had been occupied by the de Montfort family, and was the scene of the last reunion of the whole family for Easter in 1265 before disaster overtook them at Evesham in September (see below, Chapter 6). When Solomon moved there in 1274 he would have been trying to attract potential clients among the new occupants, but there seems to have been nothing in the way of recorded business resulting from his relocation.

In April 1278 the sheriff of Wiltshire was instructed to obtain forty marks from the chattels of Lumbard for an exchange trespass.[16] This was the beginning of the deluge of accusations of coin-clipping that culminated in the autumn with the wave of arrests and executions that decimated and finally ruined the Jewish community. By then Lumbard had moved to Devizes in Wiltshire. While Lumbard apparently distanced himself from the rest of the family he seemed to have a closer relationship with his more successful half-brother, Sweetman, who had moved to Devizes after being expelled from Marlborough by the queen mother, Eleanor of Provence, with the rest of the Jewish population in 1275. Lumbard had adopted the use of his father's name and was known only as Lumbard fil Abraham by then. He still possessed a house in Winchester by the time of the Expulsion. His son, Solomon, seems to have been fairly successful in that he paid a two-shilling fine for permission to own a mansion. The final view we have of Lumbard at the Expulsion reveals him to have little wealth or property.

NOTES

1. Editor's note: Sue believed that Benedict, son of Abraham and Licoricia, was the same man as the 'Benedict of Winchester' who features so prominently in later records as a guildsman of Winchester, in contrast to earlier scholars (for example, Cecil Roth, *A History of the Jews in England* [Oxford: Clarendon Press, 3rd edn 1964], pp.54 and 75), and worked on that assumption in the following discussions. There is in fact no conclusive evidence to believe that these were two separate men. *Rokeah*, p.173, entry 656, note 86, cites the main reason for thinking they are two people, but at p.359, note 12, accepts their common identification; *PREJ*, II, p.131 refers to Benedict with both forms of his name.
2. *PREJ*, II, p.90.
3. For more on Asser, see below, pp.105–8.
4. *Cl. R. Henry III, 1247–1251*, p.249, has an order to the justices in 1249 to permit 'Kokerelleum' to be Licoricia's attorney.
5. *Excerpta è Rotulis Finium in Turri Londiniensis Asservatis, II (1246–1272)*, C. Roberts (ed.) (London: Public Records, 1836), p.55.
6. *PREJ*, I, p.115; *Select Pleas*, p.28 (1253).
7. *PREJ*, I, p.120. This could have been the same Samarian as the man accused together with Cokerel's father, Abraham, in the 1225 child-murder trial in Winchester.
8. *Cl. R. Henry III, 1231–1234*, pp.10, 103.
9. Alexander McCall, *The Medieval Underworld* (London: Sutton, 2004), p.280.
10. *PREJ*, I, pp.2, 35, 89, 204, 219 and 231.
11. *Cl. R. Henry III, 1261–1264*, p.103. Ingram also received the £6 per annum owed by Alan de Brembilhang to 'Belie qui fuit uxor Isaac de Bedford', possibly our Belia? Cok is also recorded as in possession of a certain Samarian fil. Lumbard's property in 1273: *PREJ*, II, p.2. In the same year he pledged to pay three bezants for an inquest into whether he was owed anything from the estate of the late Samarian of Winchester: his brother Benedict stood surety: *PREJ*, II, p.13.
12. In 1287 the sheriff of Hampshire was ordered to produce Abraham son of Cokerel and Lumbard 'le Petit' to do the king's command: *Rokeah*, p.343, entry 1124. A house of 'Sampson fil Cok' in Winchester was sold after the Expulsion.
13. See above, note 1.
14. *Pat. R. Henry III, 1258–1266*, p.299.
15. *PREJ*, II, p.104.
16. *Rokeah*, p.220, entry 812.

CHAPTER SIX

The Barons' War

In many of the late-thirteenth century armed uprisings against the king, the Jews were identified as his agents and resented for extorting high levels of interest, or demanding early settlement of debts, usually in response to the specific and heavy tax demands made by the king. That the king had a measure of financial freedom through his access to Jewish wealth was another reason for the hatred and resentment of the Jews, who suffered as a result. The church likewise disliked the king's independence and his special protection that kept Jews out of the ecclesiastical courts and beyond their jurisdiction, and so was becoming increasingly intolerant, stoking the fires of anti-Jewish hatred through sermons that exacerbated the xenophobia of their congregations. The result was an increase in the incidence of blood-libel accusations, attacks on the Jewries and, in particular, deliberate destruction of the chests containing records of debts.

These tensions form the background to the history of Licoricia and her family in the latter part of the century, and are worth investigating in more detail. The unrest and uncertainty caused by the Barons' War of 1265/66 have already been alluded to above, but dissatisfaction and disagreements had already begun to rise in the 1250s. Hostility towards the king also manifested itself in sporadic attacks upon those whom he protected, the Jews. In order to understand what impact this had on our families, this chapter will explore the local tensions which affected Winchester and, to a lesser extent, other centres.

WINCHESTER: THE IMPACT ON LICORICIA AND HER FAMILY

In Winchester in mid-century there seem to have been permanent disputes centred around the priory of St Swithuns and its cathedral church, as well as between St Swithuns and Hyde Abbey outside the city walls. The city and its inhabitants were caught up in the resulting turmoil, taking sides between the disputants and suffering as first one, then the other side appeared to triumph. Royal intervention, however, often increased rather than defused tension.

For some thirty years from the beginning of the century, the bishop's throne at Winchester had been occupied by the powerful Peter des Roches, who defied the pope by staying loyal to King John when he had been excommunicated and an interdict placed on the kingdom. All the other bishops chose exile and went to Rome or to France. As a result of his support for King John, Peter was rewarded with the position of chancellor under his son. At the accession of the nine-year old King Henry, des Roches became one of the three protectors, joining William Marshal and Hubert de Burgh. As bishop, Peter was a powerful protector of Winchester and a strong supporter where the interests of cathedral, city and self all coincided. He grew very rich, and his eventual displacement and exile in 1238 pleased some of those left in charge at the priory.

The king had control over choosing Peter's successor with the agreement of the monks,[1] and with royal and papal mandates in 1240 they proceeded to an election. Their choice fell on William de Rayley/Raleigh, the then bishop of Norwich, who had also served as an advisor to the king. Matthew Paris, however, reports that Henry objected strongly to William's translation, seemingly as a result of William's honest and often forthright behaviour when counselling the king, and appealed to the pope in 1243. Henry, it must be said, had a vested interest in the see remaining vacant as long as possible, since in the meantime its revenues found their way into royal coffers. Innocent IV, however, rejected the appeal. Henry reluctantly agreed to the monks' choice, and William was confirmed in office at Winchester in 1244. One of the monks' grievances had been that Peter had appropriated some of the diocese income, which should have been theirs. Initially Rayley, an efficient and honest administrator, seems to have straightened out Winchester's finances, but by 1245 he, too, was quarrelling with the monks. He died in 1249 or 1250, and the battle over the bishop's mitre recommenced.

As we have seen, Henry increasingly favoured his own or his wife's relatives. This time the king was determined to place his half-brother, Aymer of Lusignan, on Winchester's throne as bishop-elect, despite the fact that he was only aged 29 and therefore not only too young and inexperienced but under the canonical minimum age. Yet this time the monks agreed to his election, because they had suffered as a result of the king's displeasure for the past ten years. The Lusignan family, also called the Poitevins, was regarded by the English barons as a drain on all the most profitable and prestigious posts. Their resentment was increased, therefore, when Aymer was nominated by the king as bishop-elect of Winchester, following William de Valence's installation as earl of Pembroke in 1247.

On a local level, Aymer was not welcomed as the choice for Winchester's bishop. Aymer may have been a good administrator and put the finances of St Swithuns back on a good footing again, but the disputes that continued between the bishop-elect and his prior, Andrew, on the one hand, and the monks on the other, led to great disturbance. As a result, the monks began to appear at other priories and monasteries across the country in search of succour and charity. Finally in 1255, the king issued an edict prohibiting all other ecclesiastical establishments from receiving Winchester monks without special letters from either Aymer, the bishop-elect, or from Prior Andrew the Breton of Winchester.[2] There are reports of the monks debarring their bishop-elect from the cathedral; even though he came to the doors dressed simply and barefoot, he was still not admitted. Eventually he excommunicated not only all the monks and clergy but also the citizens, bailiffs and the mayor, which indicates how much support there was for the cathedral monks in the city at that time.

Aymer remained bishop-elect until 1258 when the barons got the upper hand with the Provisions of Oxford, demanding the expulsion of the Poitevins, who were designated as the hated foreigners in this case by the Savoyards and their English followers under the leadership of the Frenchman Simon de Montfort. William de Valence, Aymer and two younger Lusignan brothers fled to Wolvesey, the bishop's palace in Winchester, where they were besieged by the townspeople before making their escape to France. In 1260 Aymer was consecrated bishop of Winchester while in France, but soon died before he could claim his bishopric. The Provisions of Oxford imposed severe restrictions on the king, and in 1261 the pope released Henry from his oaths, made under pressure, to uphold the agreement. An appeal by Simon de Montfort to his overlord, the French king, Louis IX, who upheld his case in 1264 at Amiens, precipitated the civil war that raged on from 1264 to 1265, with intermittent outbreaks of violence which blighted Henry's reign.

The war had repercussions on the ecclesiastical politics of Winchester. After Aymer's death the monks chose Ralph Nevill, another of the king's favourites, as bishop. Andrew the Breton, who had been prior, was not popular with the monks and there followed a series of disputes with subsequent priors and their supporters. There had already been confrontation between the priory and the townspeople over the maintenance of the walls and gates round the cathedral where they were contiguous with those of the city, and the citizens were forced to pay for access through the cathedral gates to reach the market place. In 1258 two gates had been blocked by the monks, led by Prior Valentine, allowing access for pedestrians only through a smaller gate, which meant that those bringing bulky goods had to pay more to use those gates where the priory could levy tolls. Similar disputes were taking place elsewhere in the country, and violence was never far from the scene, a sign perhaps of the mounting sense of insecurity that was infecting society during these decades.

Such a volatile atmosphere never boded well for the Jews. They were always identified as royalist supporters because they were protected by the king, and this further alienated his opponents. During any onslaught by the barons and their supporters, attacking the Jewry was a high priority, not only for the prospect of rich pickings, spiced by a burning religious and xenophobic zeal, but also by those clients of the moneylenders anxious to wipe out the evidence of their debts, and the creditors themselves, where possible.

Such was the turmoil that preceded the war that the king resorted to an earlier procedure to safeguard the Jews, following an attack on them in Winchester by the churchmen and their supporters in May. In June 1264 he appointed twenty-four leading citizens to be their guardians.[3] This was the second time that the king had resorted to this form of protection for the Jews. The first had been during upheavals that led up to the Civil War in 1215–16, when leading citizens in each of the relevant cities were appointed to defend their Jewries. The list of names in 1264 are those of the guildsmen, the leading merchants and those serving as minor town functionaries, such as bailiffs and coroners and as the Christian chirographers overseeing the business recorded in the *archae*.[4] As such they would have been well known to the Jewish dealers.

It is not clear who were the Jewish chirographers at this time, but Licoricia and Benedict would have known the guardians very well, and from subsequent events after the war, Benedict was deeply involved with them, and with the mayor, Simon Draper, in particular.[5] They were also supposed to be protected by the king's garrison led by the castellan in the castle. During the war in 1265, Winchester was attacked and looted for three days by de Montfort's son, Simon, on his way to support his father in the coming crucial battle at Evesham. Prior Valentine, who led the monks in support of the barons, was accused by the townspeople of letting Simon into the city through the gates controlled by the cathedral, against the wishes of those citizens who were the king's supporters. During the attack on the Winchester Jewry, the *archa* disappeared and was probably destroyed, leaving the businessmen without trace of their debts. Of Winchester, it was reported that the Jewry was entirely destroyed in the raid, and everyone there killed. This near-contemporary account reads, 'All the gywes of the town he let slay echon / That me in eni stede fonde he ne leude alive none'.[6] Although many must have died in the attack, the wealthiest emerged alive when the troops departed. Other members of Licoricia's family were attacked and lost their records.

His diversion to pillage Winchester, and his subsequent loitering in Kenilworth, meant that the younger Simon only arrived at the battlefield in time to witness the defeat of his father, with his dismembered body being paraded by the victorious troops of Prince Edward.[7]

The upheavals in Winchester re-ignited division not only between the ruling clique and the general community, but also between the king's supporters and the defeated and disinherited followers of de Montfort. Prior Valentine was once again at the centre of several disputes, both at the monastery of St Swithuns and with the Winchester citizens. He and his supporters had been attacked by the populace, several monks were killed and the cathedral damaged. Faced with such hostility, the prior resigned, but the papal legate Ottobuoni reinstated him and excommunicated the Hyde monks and others who had attacked Valentine in 1268. Valentine's difficulties did not stop there, for the new bishop, Nicholas of Ely, promptly sacked him, describing him as 'a very worthless man'. Riots and violence were not confined to Winchester. The previous year had seen a massacre of London Jews where as many as 500 were reported to have been killed; one de Montfort follower strangled his Jewish creditor with his bare hands. The chests containing the records of debts were rifled, the bonds destroyed or spirited away. The raids on the Jewish communities could be savage, and many Jews were killed or severely injured.

When Simon de Montfort briefly captured the reins of government and the keys of the Exchequer after the battle of Lewes in 1264, he had cancelled Jewish debts, and plainly all money-dealing was halted. Records of Jewish debts were impounded, but Simon underwent a gradual conversion to the idea of gaining access to these funds for his own purposes, and began to encourage a return to money-trading. This was against a background of continuing attacks on Jewries and the bond chests by his followers and family members, with the result that the records of pre-war debts and whatever transactions could be carried on during the hostilities mostly went missing in many of the *archa* towns. After Evesham, the reinstated king granted Licoricia the right to search other chests across the country for evidence of her business deals. In 1269, Queen Eleanor interceded on behalf of Benedict to obtain for him a grant of five years' freedom from any interference with his debts. Prince Edmund, Edward's brother, had secured for him freedom to examine any *archae* elsewhere in the country to find any other records of bonds that had been in the lost Winchester chest. This freedom was subsequently granted to both Benedict and Sweetman.

Peace was not instantaneous following the defeat and death of de Montfort. There were continuing skirmishes, sieges, and attacks, with unrest continuing for the remainder of King Henry's reign and beyond. The Earl of Gloucester marched on London and occupied the city. Those on the losing side lost all their estates to the Crown. Initially these were given away or occupied by the victorious supporters of the king, but in view of the resentment and hatred fermenting among the dispossessed, the papal legate Ottobuoni brokered an agreement, the Dictum of Kenilworth, whereby the defeated baronial supporters could receive their lands back on the payment of a fine of up to seven times the annual rent, depending on their degree of involvement with the losing side.[8] Many of them had been impoverished by the war and had to borrow from Jewish and other moneylenders. This went some way to restoring the wealth of those Jews most damaged by the war. At this period there was a dramatic increase in Christians and Jews working together over Jewish debts, the creditors foreclosing on debts and the Christians acquiring the pledged land for resale. The records are full of court cases where many of the barons' supporters are pardoned for the murders they carried out during the hostilities. The winners, of course, were not accused of any murders.

BEDFORD: BELIA AND THE WARS

The unrest caused by the continuing aggression between the barons and the king particularly affected Bedford in the early sixties, before the final eruption into the war of 1265/66. The Bedford Jewry was one among several that were attacked across the country, and Belia lost some of her bonds.

Belia had been widowed around 1261, at the outset of the upheavals culminating in the Barons' War and the de Montfort rule of 1265/66; Pictavin may have been a victim of the anti-Jewish riots that preceded it. Belia had to pay the fine of 735 marks for his debts, a sum she found much difficulty in meeting, as she still owed half of it in 1270. Perhaps as a result of her widowhood and perceived vulnerability, some of her Jewish neighbours took advantage to poach and otherwise interfere in her debts.[9] They underestimated their woman; Belia did not take this offence lying down. In 1262 she paid ninety-three bezants into the King's Wardrobe account to have the brothers Isaac and Bonenfant and their families expelled from Bedford for five years.[10] The huge fine she paid demonstrated the extent of the damage they had done, as well as the depth of her feelings of outrage. For the exiled brothers this may have been a blessing in disguise, since they were absent when Bedford was attacked and the Bedford *archa*, together with that of Cambridge, was spirited away by the de Montfort supporters to the fastness of the Isle of Ely and looted.

By the time of the restoration to power of Henry III after Evesham, Belia emerged with her business having been hard hit. She and her son Jacob were among those members of the Bedford Jewry mentioned by name who were given permission to search for evidence of the missing bonds in other chests across the country, and being freed by the king from interference in the operation of whatever business could be salvaged.[11] This resulted in many disputes over whether debts had been settled or if they had existed at all. Some of her lost debts subsequently re-emerged some years later in the hands of James Lovel, who had been sheriff of Cambridge and Huntingdon and was also Lord of the Fee. He was one of the several sheriffs who seem to have been reluctant to deliver to the Jewish Exchequer the tallage money they had collected from the Jews. In 1270 he claimed to have bought Belia's Bedford debts in the open market, a most unlikely story, seeing that Christians were not supposed to be able to do this without the king's permission.[12] Perhaps Belia did not raise any objections because she acknowledged the hopelessness of arguing against such a powerful figure, or she willingly joined partnership with him in a practice that was becoming all too common. The Jewish partner could continue to run the debt, collecting the interest with official backing, while the Christian could acquire the forfeited land pledged as security, land that the Jewish creditor could only hold for a year and a day. Another deal with a leading member of the aristocracy was in 1268, when Belia, acting through her sons Jacob and Benedict, sold bonds worth 1,000 marks to Gilbert de Clare, the earl of Gloucester, who had sacked the Jewry of Canterbury in 1264, and who had continued his armed attacks on the restored king by seizing London in 1267.[13]

The debt Belia owed for the fine for Pictavin's chattels, as well as her accumulating tallage payments, continued to dog her for the rest of her life. She was clearly unable to pay the huge amount of 735 marks, even in instalments of forty marks,[14] and there is some evidence to suggest that she struggled to raise funds. In 1271 she agreed to absolve Ralph de Bello Campo of a debt of £30 owed to her late husband, provided that he repaid £10 owed to her, clearly a desperate measure to raise at least some money.[15] As a result, she went into prison both in Bedford and then in the Tower of London. In 1273 the sheriff of Bedford was ordered to release her if she was imprisoned for debt. Part of the fine for her release was paid by one Isaac of Bedford, who was probably her son. The records still show her pursuing debtors and lost bonds well into the 1270s, and a search of the bonds in the chest there showed she had none.[16] She still had sons operating in Winchester, and Jacob had moved to London, where she joined him. Perhaps they were carrying on the family business for her, although the last impression of Belia is that she was living in reduced circumstances. The remainder of the missing Bedford chirographs were released in 1285, when they went to the rapacious Queen Eleanor.

NOTES

1. This had also led to an earlier disagreement in 1173 when King Henry II ordered the Winchester monks to 'freely elect' the bishop of his choice: David Boyle, *Blondel's Song: The Capture, Imprisonment and Ransom of Richard the Lionheart* (London: Viking, 2005), p.186.
2. *Pat. R. Henry III, 1247–1258*, p.439.
3. Derek Keene, *Survey of Medieval Winchester*, Winchester Studies 2, 2 vols (Oxford: Clarendon Press, 1985), I, pp.76–9.
4. *Pat. R. Henry III, 1258–1266*, p.323.
5. Simon had a chequered career before becoming mayor in 1268, warden of the Winchester Jews in 1270, sheriff of Hampshire in 1282 and a knight in 1286.
6. Robert of Gloucester, *Chronicles*, quoted in the *Victoria History of the Counties of England: Hampshire and the Isle of Wight*, V, W. Page (ed.) (London: Constable, 1912), p.310.
7. Margaret Wade Labarge, *Simon de Montfort* (New York: Norton, 1963, repr. Westport, CT: Greenwood Press, 1975), p.252.
8. D.A. Carpenter, *The Struggle for Mastery: Penguin History of Britain 1066–1284*, (London: Penguin, 2004) p.381.
9. *Rokeah*, p.45, entry 188 and note 25.
10. *Pat. R. Henry III, 1258–1266*, p.205.
11. She paid two bezants for licence to distrain her debtors' tenants in 1266: *Select Pleas*, p.35.
12. *PREJ*, I, p.224.
13. *Select Pleas*, pp.48–50. The debts had been in the Bedford chirograph chest, 'which was taken and burnt by the king's enemies'. See also *PREJ*, III, p.248.
14. *Pat. R. Henry III, 1258–1266*, p.192.
15. *Rokeah*, p.81, entry 321.
16. *PREJ*, IV, p.15. In 1273 she and Jacob were distrained to appear: *PREJ*, II, p.6.

CHAPTER SEVEN

Benedict the Guildsman

The 1250s mark the onset of some ten years of national and civic disorder, during which time the records themselves were the object of attack, producing gaps throughout this period. Licoricia's son Benedict was influential and successful enough to be used as a hostage for the Winchester tallage in 1255.[1] He then hardly appears again until the next decade. There can be no doubt that he was building up his financial empire during this time because when the records re-emerge in 1265 the volume of his business was extensive and he had plainly accumulated an enormous portfolio of transactions dating back many years.[2] With the end of the war, he was obviously among the wealthiest, if not absolutely the richest, of Winchester's inhabitants.

Benedict seems to have been respected among his fellow Jews, and acted as attorney, witness or guarantor for them in court. He was present at the inauguration of a new synagogue in Bristol, and bought a house there in Winch Street.[3] Yet he also undertook semi-official duties for the Exchequer courts, for example escorting a fellow Jewish businessman to the Tower. On another occasion he was called with others to identify the handwriting of a Hebrew signature. At the same time, he was equally involved with Christians, appearing as their witness or attorney, and supporting the nomination of a named Christian for the post of chirographer. He increasingly mixed with his Christian neighbours, both socially as well as in business deals and partnerships, and he is believed to have come close to converting, although there is little to support this speculation. It would have been very much to his advantage to have converted during the 1260s and 1270s, although he would have initially suffered the loss of much of his business. Some of those who did convert and managed to involve themselves closely in the business of the Jewish Exchequer undoubtedly did well, but Benedict did not take that path.

BENEDICT'S BUSINESS CONNECTIONS

In 1267 Benedict and his wife Belassez, by whom he had at least seven surviving children, took possession of a large estate in the Sutton Hundreds.[4] It extended over thirty-nine acres of pasture and parkland, including the main house, and maintained a considerable amount of livestock, including pigs and 'young porkers'. Also included in the transaction was a villein's widow, Eva Broke with all her chattels, her cottage and a virgate of land. She and her husband had been tenants of John and Petronilla of Windsor, paying their rent in labour services for their landlord. The agreement was witnessed by Benedict's friend, Henry of Durngate, a member of the ruling guild of merchants, although John and Petronilla did not attend. Benedict had to promise to pay a pair of white gloves or one penny annually at Easter to the Lords of the Fee. He also paid 100 marks to Sir William de Wintershull, the sheriff of Hampshire, which may have been a fine for the transaction. The deal bears the hallmark of being a failed debt of the previous owners, and the payment might have been a sweetener to the sheriff for allowing the deal. It might also have been that the estate was a forfeit for the Windsors having taken the losing side in the Barons' Wars, but if this was the case, the estate would have been given to a loyal royalist, so this seems less likely. Belassez was named as Benedict's co-owner, possibly to meet with the restrictions on ownership of property by Jews to that for their own use or of their co-religionists. When this property resurfaced in the records in 1270 it was only in Benedict's name, with no further mention of Belassez, who had probably died by then.

Benedict did not exactly lie low during these troubled times. In Winchester he was mixing with some very powerful local people. He had been appointed one of the two Jewish chirographers serving the Winchester *archa*, and had become very much an accepted friend of the Christian chirographers. Through them he came into contact with the merchant guild, which constituted the governing council of the city, their leader being the mayor, Simon Draper.

Benedict was also a merchant dealing in wool and wine, besides his extensive money-lending ventures, an interest shared by the guildsmen, some of them being his clients. His involvement with them took many forms in the 1260s and 1270s, bringing mixed blessings to all who were involved. For example, Peter Saer had been the coroner, and Benedict guaranteed him for a debt of five marks owed to the king. Henry of Durngate, who had witnessed the transaction of the Sutton property, was another who worked very closely with Benedict, and was subsequently to take a very questionable role over Benedict's property after he died.[5] In 1266 another guildsman and client of Benedict's, Richard of Froxfield, took him to court, alleging damages and trespass. By 1280 Richard had become a debtor of Benedict's son, Abraham, and there had been a court case which resulted in the payment of a saddle.[6]

GUILD PRIVILEGES

It seems very likely that the guildsmen and Benedict cooperated on some mutually advantageous if shady deals. One such resulted in a case that trailed through the courts over several years at the end of the 1260s, and had far-reaching consequences for the city. After the war, Benedict was working closely with the mayor, Simon Draper, and enabled him to buy a bond from Dyey L'Eveske worth £105 in 1267. The original debtor was a man called Oysun, who had been the first Winchester mayor after the city received its charter in 1200. He had dropped out of the city's records by 1207, either dying or leaving Winchester. The Oysun family brought a legal challenge against the chirographers and Simon Draper for having connived in the extraction from the *archa* of the bond of a debt that they claimed their father had settled years before, and which therefore should not have been in the chest at all. They could not however produce the quitclaim document, which would have been the crucial evidence of its settlement.

The Oysun case, with allegations, defences and counter-accusations trailing on through the courts for many years, was yet another of those legal actions where various plaintiffs, witnesses and the accused, as well as jury members and those who had pledged the appearance in court of absentees, came and went erratically, making it impossible to conclude the case.[7] It is notable that Benedict attended more frequently than the others appear to have done, but his guilt seems to have been established by an interesting entry in the Exchequer Rolls dated 1271. This records his having paid twelve gold bezants to the king 'to forgo proceedings' concerning the unlawful removal of 'a certain bond from the chest', and the very high price reflects the severity of the alleged misdemeanour.[8] Court proceedings against his fellow guildsmen appear to have continued, but without any recorded conclusion. The arrest of Simon Draper, to enforce his appearance at Westminster, was ordered as late as 1275.[9] There is no sign of any final decision in this case, but Simon continued to successfully carry on his business during this time, selling wine to the king and obtaining one of the few licenses to export sacks of wool in 1273, and again at a later date when there was a general ban on exports.

The venom that arose from the Oysun case was more a reflection of how much the ruling clique led by the mayor were resented by the 'have-nots', excluded from the running of city business and its perks. These included the choice of the mayor and bailiffs from among their own ranks, the handling of various funds or tolls, and many other highly profitable rewards. Such resentments were a constantly recurring dispute between the ruling merchant-guild oligarchs and the excluded citizens in towns all over the country, and which often erupted into violence. These tensions were exacerbated by the continuing hostilities of the civil war, which had not died down with de Montfort's defeat and death at Evesham, although power returned to the liberated king and the royalists. Running skirmishes continued across the country; whole areas were still in the hands of the rebels, including London and the fenlands around the Isle of Ely, where the Bedford *archa* had been taken.

One of the accusations made against the Winchester guildsmen was that they enforced a collection of money as a gift to the king one week before the Battle of Lewes at which he was captured; there was however no evidence that they had ever paid it. Their defence was that they had spent some of the money on the necessary entertaining of visiting judges or government officers, which seems to have been a function expected of them, but which was also designed to sway the judges in their favour over ongoing law suits. As has already been stated, such corruption was an integral part of the operations of justice at that time, but it was clearly resented by those who had paid out for one thing, only to find that the money had been diverted for another, more dubious cause. The guildsmen also countered an accusation of the unlawful imprisonment of men from Alresford and Overton by pointing out that the justices had found them guilty of highway robbery. Yet another accusation concerned the appropriation of money from some foreign merchants' sequestered goods for themselves, instead of paying it into the city funds. Clearly these guildsmen were corrupt even by the standards of their own time. In 1274 Roger de Clifford, whom the king had ordered to investigate the allegations of maladministration made against the ruling council, found them innocent. Interestingly, he was an old client of David of Oxford who had then continued his debts with Licoricia, but his total debts to Jews of some £400 had been pardoned by the king in 1266, probably as reward for his support during the Barons' Wars.

BENEDICT AS GUILDSMAN

The simmering tension between guild and citizens at Winchester was made worse in May 1268 when Benedict was elected to the guild, the only Jewish guildsman in medieval England, and probably anywhere else in western Europe.[10] This was undoubtedly an indication of how close he had grown to the ruling clique. The Patent Roll confirms Benedict's election as follows:

> Know all men that I, Simon le Draper, Mayor of Winchester, with common counsel and assent of all bailiffs and citizens of the said city have received our beloved and faithful friend, Benedict fil Abraham, the Jew into full society of our liberty as a fellow citizen and fellow Guildsman.[11]

The bailiffs were all members of the guild appointed to this office by the guild itself, without any contribution from non-members, and it is highly unlikely that anyone outside that exclusive membership was consulted about Benedict's admission. What was in it for Benedict, apart from the status? It seems that being a guildsman brought many additional benefits. The charter, conferring the liberty and right to Winchester to run its own affairs through a ruling council of guildsmen under a mayor, absolved that group from having to pay tolls and customs. His elevation to the guild also made him a citizen, which gave him the ability he had lacked as a Jew to own tenements and houses. (Jews were not allowed to own property outright other than the houses they occupied or rented to other Jews.) He immediately acquired many houses and shops in Winchester, some bought at probably advantageous prices from his fellow guildsmen, and several from Simon Draper, within five days of his elevation. He also bought from other associates such as Adam Gurdon, who was often a witness for some of Benedict's transactions. This was the same Adam Gurdon who, having fought on the losing side during the Barons' Wars, followed a career leading the outlaws of Alton woods, waylaying travellers on the London road, before managing to return to respectability by fighting a duel with Prince Edward, which he (probably strategically) lost.[12] He was knighted later in life. In addition Benedict acquired property elsewhere in the country, such as a house in Coney Street, York for his daughter Rose, which could have been a marriage gift, and a house in Winch Street, Bristol.[13]

If it is true that the king encouraged Simon Draper to elevate Benedict to the guild, then clearly he was hoping that, if this was accomplished without too much dissension, it would not only increase his potential income from Benedict and other Jews, but bring into his grasp more property whenever he wanted it. His tacit approval, at least, could indicate that this may have been yet another attempt by the king to try and dodge his own laws. Unfortunately for him, the reaction in Winchester was one of outraged uproar and rioting. The election of a Jew to this powerful group was described as, 'a manifest scandal to all Christian men'.[14] The king backtracked at this point and ordered an explanation, to which Simon Draper replied that Benedict had not been made a full member, only an associate, but this clearly contradicts the text of the Patent Roll.

The furore resulting from Benedict's admission to the guild in Winchester erupted with lawsuits, riots and ferocious attacks on individual Jews, as well as conflict between the ordinary people or the 'commune' and the ruling guild and their supporters. In 1270 the king had to appoint another set of guardians for the Jewish community in Winchester, although several of them had been among the 1264 guardians, such as Henry the Cordwaner, Adam de Northampton and John Cobbe who, with Simon Draper, had been or were currently Christian chirographers, while others had held office as bailiffs or coroners.[15] The wording of the order to the named guardians is illuminating:

> because of a matter of contention between some of the king's citizens of Winchester and Benedict fil Abraham, Jew of that city, the king has taken the Jews of that city into his special protection appointing them to be their guardians and protectors; and commanding them to cause proclamation to be made throughout the city that none do them harm on pain of life and limbs, and to protect the said Jews, their households, lands, houses, things, rents and possessions, and if harm be done to them to have it amended at once.[16]

Despite this, there were many attacks on individual Jews, among them Benedict and Belassez, and Deudonne, the other Jewish chirographer. Unspecified physical injury to Benedict and Belassez was caused by Prior Valentine and his supporters during the assault on the Jews. In an enquiry in 1269 Benedict was awarded the considerable sum of £100 against Valentine and the Priory.[17] Whilst this figure may never have actually been paid over, the size of this award indicates the severity of the attack; Belassez may even have died as a consequence of the assault. She was still alive in 1267 but died some time afterwards, for Benedict subsequently remarried around 1274. Life for the rest of the community must have become even more difficult, and probably was never again as peaceful and relatively safe as it had been, but this tense situation was not confined to Winchester alone.

Eventually, early in 1274, and following more violence, this time with one of the sides in the dispute attempting to take over the Priory, the city administration had to admit that it could no longer govern Winchester, and the king had to take the city into his own hands. By September 1274 King Edward had eventually returned to England from the Crusades to take up the vacant throne after his father's death in 1272, and the whole situation changed again. Another hearing at the king's court was set up and all twenty-four members of the merchants guild, only three of whom had not been 1270 guardians, were accused by twelve of 'the more discreet' members of the community chosen as prosecutors. In October the city administration of Winchester was placed in the hands of the clerk to the king, Adam of Winchester, and was not restored until January 1276, when Roger Dunstable became mayor. He had been one of the 1270 guardians as a member of the guild, but had changed sides by 1273 and subsequently led rioters who assaulted Deudonne the chirographer and stormed his house.[18]

BENEDICT THE BUSINESSMAN

From 1268 Benedict's various deals multiplied both in volume and complexity.[19] Although he had suffered by the destruction of the *archa* with the rest of the Winchester money-dealers, many of his transactions before the war had been in the neighbouring counties and even further afield where the *archae* had not been attacked, and he was able to bounce back after Evesham and continue his business activities at once.

In 1274 Benedict supported the nomination of Richard of Stockbridge as Christian chirographer, in succession to Henry Crabbe, another guildsman. Richard subsequently became embroiled with Benedict's son Abraham over a parcel of gold and precious stones in 1280. Besides his business contacts, there were also those who had sold Benedict houses when he became a guildsman, and those who benefited from the windfall of the bargain sale of all his houses after his death in 1279/80. They included John Mouraunt the gold merchant, a guardian and guildsman who bought Benedict's house in Calpe Street, perhaps the building called Moraunt's Hall in later years.

What is clear is that Benedict was very closely involved with his fellow guildsmen both as chirographers and business partners, and in particular he was very close to the mayor, Simon Draper, for many years, to their mutual financial advantage. The mayor and the guildsmen met frequently at the Guild Hall where, as well as discussing and deciding matters and making business arrangements, a lot of drinking went on. Generally, heavy drinking, particularly with Christians, was discouraged among the Jewish community, although Joseph Jacobs quotes a ruling that social drinking while pursuing business with Christians might be permitted.[20] The other Winchester Jewish chirographer, Deudonne fil Isaac, was a moderately successful moneylender but he was never as close to the guardians and the Christian chirographers as Benedict, and he was either more unpopular or less closely linked to the influential citizens, for he was assaulted more often during anti-Jewish riots and with more serious results. Perhaps Deudonne was reluctant to break the general religious ban on drinking, or maybe he was just less affable or obliging than Benedict. The guildsmen and other leading citizens had good reason to be protective of the Jewish moneylenders. Their business affairs were closely linked and any raid on the Jewry that deprived the town of a source of money could be contrary to their own interests.

One particular business transaction continued over many years, with many changes and unlooked-for implications that illustrate some of the many twists and turns of financial dealings in this period. Benedict had loaned fifty marks to Alexander, whose surname is variously given as Hulse, Ace or Huse. Alexander had served the king very well during the Barons' Wars, and in 1266 Henry pardoned him his debt to Benedict, either to reward him, or possibly provide him with a salary.[21] Prince Edmund intervened at this point to remind his father that he had promised Benedict not to interfere with any of his debts for five years, as compensation for his losses at the hands of the followers of Simon de Montfort. The king first rescinded his gift to Alexander and then, at the urging of his other son, Prince Edward, reinstated it.

The following then appeared in the Exchequer Rolls: 'We are minded to show Benedict special favour', which could have been a reference to the pardoned debt of Alexander Huse.[22] The Exchequer officials were instructed to produce and deliver to Benedict two ancient debts, both of which link his story to that of Chera's family. The first was for £30 and six quarters of corn owed by William de Baloyne of Easton to Abraham Pinche, Chera's son. Pinche had, as we know, been hanged in 1234,[23] as a result of which all of his property and chattels had been confiscated by the Crown, and this debt with others had then sat in the Exchequer files, apparently uncollected, and generating no interest.[24] Whoever was the descendent of the original debtor could then be called upon to pay the thirty-four-year-old debt, plus any interest that might accrue after its emergence back into circulation.

The second debt given to Benedict was one owed to Elias, Abraham Pinche's brother, and Elias's son Abraham, for twelve marks and eight shillings. It was a debt which John de Froyle, as tenant of Michael de Columbar, keeper of Chute Forest, had been responsible for repaying at least a part. It may well have been a debt that was incurred long before by the first husband of one Alicia of Grunestede. He had died in 1232 and his widow had taken Elias and Abraham to court to claim that, under the Magna Carta, her young son was immune from having to pay this debt or perhaps just the interest as he was entitled to support from her late husband's estate. In 1232 she was keeper of some woods near Durley in Hampshire. She seems to have taken as a second husband Michael de Columbar, who was obviously managing her estates.

Both of these debts were valued together at a total of fifty-seven marks, which was seven marks over the Alexander Huse debt. Benedict was ordered to pay the surplus back to the Treasury. The Froyle debt, in particular, turned out to be a complex transaction.

It seems that the unlucky heir of the Froyle debt was Rosamund Ernham of Froyle or Holebury, John of Froyle's daughter, or perhaps his daughter-in-law.[25] She still lived in Froyle near her mother, Margery, and she may have been the tenant, sister or close relative of one Richard of Ernham, who had fought for the barons during the recent civil war. He was identified as having taken part in the fighting in Southampton. As such he may have lost his estate but been allowed to ransom it for several times its annual income under the settlement of the Dictum of Kenilworth, which allowed the defeated to repossess their lands. When Rosamund begins appearing in the long story of her dealings with Benedict, she seems to be struggling to repay a considerably larger amount than John's original debt. It may have been that she was involved in repaying Richard of Ernham's ransom for his forfeit property, or she may have been consolidating her debts by agreeing with her debtors to pay them all as one sum. Rosamund had made an agreement with Benedict in 1266 to pay over a fee-rent of £14 per annum to stay on her lands, which were security for the debt, but was plainly running into difficulties in finding this sum. The fee-rent a means by which a debtor in difficulties could convert their debt to an annual fixed payment to the lender on their property; even this, however, seems not to have helped Rosamund. By 1270 she was desperate enough to break into her own house that had been seized by Benedict. She stole back some of her own belongings, among them two carpets, and two linen cloths valued at six shillings, as well as twenty shillings sterling. Hugh Scot, who had been installed by Benedict as agent at the house, raised a hue and cry and she was captured and forced to make another agreement with Benedict and his new partner, William Somerfield, Queen Eleanor of Castile's tailor.[26] William was told he could collect five marks a year for two years, which would go towards the ransom that Richard had to pay, but if he chose to keep the land he would be entitled to take no ransom. It would seem he chose the latter, more profitable course.

Following this incident, Rosamund came to a new agreement which cancelled all her previous debts and arrears, in return for which she granted to William Somerfield all her tenements and attached properties in Froyle, North Froyle, Ernham, Holybourne and elsewhere, together with the dowers held by her mother for which she gave William a charter of enfeoffment. Benedict is absent from this agreement; he had sold his interest to William in 1269, probably because he could not be involved in dealing with the land pledge.[27] Subsequent records refer to the quitclaims of her debt issued by Benedict and Elias's widow Floria.[28]

In 1271 Benedict came up against an allegation from Peter, the son of Robert of Mapledurham, that Benedict had not only trespassed on his estate but had falsified a charter, purporting to come from Robert, concerning a debt of £64 to Elias the son of Chera whom we have met before. Benedict seems to have acquired several of Elias's debts at various times, which might indicate some sort of relationship to him via his mother, or his widow, Floria. Abraham, Elias's son, must have died by that time, as his widowed mother is the only one mentioned in connection with his surviving business interests. This particular bond had been placed in the *archa* in 1272 when Sir William de Watford was justice to the king's treasury. This shady character had since been dismissed for corrupt practices. Peter then accused Benedict of causing him £100 worth of damage while in seisin of the land, taking chattels, goods, horses, cattle and crops. Benedict said that William of Watford should answer the charge of falsifying a document but, with the support of Robert of Mapledurham, the plaintiff's father, he was able to prove that the debt was given to him by the king, but he returned it for Peter's use as a result of the enquiry. Thomas de Tychesye also had his cattle carried off. Both men subsequently came to an agreement of some kind with Benedict.[29]

While Benedict was probably closer to his Christian neighbours than any of his co-religionists except those who actually did convert, his was a high-wire act, a delicate balance between his close relationship with those in power, and the resulting envy and hatred from some of his Christian – and Jewish – neighbours. That the powerful support he so carefully cultivated sometimes melted away, precipitating him into highly exposed and dangerous situations, did not seem to concern him. Repeated crises only seemed to teach him that he always would emerge relatively unscathed, and his actions became more arrogant and over-confident.[30] He was surrounded by Christian dealers, who were equally ruthless in their business practices.[31] He was accused of asset-stripping pledged land and properties that were legally his only for one year and one day in order to use the income for gaining back some of the debt. This was a frequent practice of Christian moneylenders and debtors too, and Benedict was no different from them.

In the same Patent Roll recording Benedict's elevation to guildsman is a letter from the papal legate, Ottobuoni, who asked that Benedict be excused aids, loans, pledges, demands and tallages for three years, adding considerably that the resulting tallage burden should not fall on the poorer members of the Winchester Jewry.[32] Even though the two letters appear side by side in the Patent Rolls, it may well have been that he had no knowledge of Benedict's elevation. In any case this request included another moneylender, M. Elias fil Mosse of London, so it seems more likely that this was a favour purchased or otherwise owed to the two men rather than evidence that the legate was a client of the moneylenders or involved in Benedict's promotion. The legate was after all a very wealthy man who could access more acceptable sources of credit. Ottobuoni Fieschi later became Pope Adrian V for just thirty-five days in 1276, and for that time perhaps Benedict could enjoy the thought that he had known the pope.

NOTES

1. *Pat. R. Henry III, 1247–1258*, p.442.
2. In 1266 he was permitted to seize pledges in compensation for 'damages and grievances by the king's enemies in the time of the disturbance of the realm': *Pat. R. Henry III, 1258–1266*, p.585.
3. Michael Adler, 'The Jews of Bristol in Pre-Expulsion Days', *TJHSE*, 12 (1928–31), pp.117–86, at 173 and 183. See also *PREJ*, II, p.61, where Benedict stands surety for the new chirographer of Bristol.

4. *PREJ*, I, p.143.
5. See below, p.132.
6. *PREJ*, V, p.37, entry 248.
7. *PREJ*, I, pp.292–3; *PREJ*, II, pp.1–2.
8. *Rokeah*, p.73, entry 305.
9. *Cl. R. Edward I, 1272–1279*, p.128 documents the order for Simon and others to answer to the community of Winchester for their 'enormous trespasses'; the order to arrest Simon is ibid., p.163.
10. Benedict's elevation was first discussed by Michael Adler, 'Benedict the Gildsman of Winchester', *MJHSE*, 4 (1942), pp.1–9, but Adler was sure that Benedict son of Licoricia and Benedict the guildsman were two different people, an error followed by Carpenter Turner in her work on Winchester. See above, Chapter 5, note 1.
11. *Pat. R. Henry III, 1266–1272*, p.223, dated 5 May 1268.
12. Alexander McCall, *The Medieval Underworld* (London: Sutton, 2004) pp.97–9.
13. For example, *Pat. R. Henry III, 1266–1272*, p.226, listing properties he acquired in Winchester and York. *Ch. R. 1253–1300*, p.222, records the York house in 'Kuningestrete' late of Benedict of Winchester in 1279. Bristol: see above, note 3.
14. Derek Keene, *Survey of Medieval Winchester*, Winchester Studies 2, 2 vols (Oxford: Clarendon Press, 1985), I, p.78, citing *Cl. R. Edward I, 1278–1288*, pp.128 and 163 and PRO KB 27/14 m.10. See also *Pat. R. Edward I, 1272–1281*, p.60.
15. The 1264 list is at *Pat. R. Henry III, 1258–1266*, p.323. The 1270 guardians are listed in *Pat. R. Henry III, 1266–1272*, p.417.
16. *Pat. R. Henry III, 1266–1272*, p.417.
17. Adler, 'Benedict the Gildsman', p.5.
18. *PREJ*, II, pp.196 and 227.
19. For example, *Rokeah*, p.80, entry 318.
20. Joseph Jacobs, *The Jews of Angevin England* (London: David Nutt, 1893), p.269.
21. Original pardon: *Cl. R. Henry III, 1264–1268*, pp.214–15, followed by compensation to Benedict, ibid., pp.411–12.
22. *PREJ*, I, p.196.
23. See above, p.42.
24. While debts were in the custody of the Crown it was forbidden to collect any interest, although this was sometimes ignored.
25. *PREJ*, II, p.152. See also *Rokeah*, p.160, entry 620.
26. *Rokeah*, p.60, note 25 identifies William *le Taillur* with William Somerfield on the basis of a reference in John Carmi Parsons, *The Court and Household of Eleanor of Castile in 1290* (Toronto: Pontifical Institute of Medieval Studies, 1977), pp.65–6.
27. *Pat. R. Henry III, 1266–1272*, p.360.
28. In 1272 Rosamund is recorded trying to pay off some of her debt to William, but he was 'unwilling to receive the money himself or by agent', so she deposited it with Richard Russel until William would collect it: *Rokeah*, p.92, entry 375. See also *PREJ*, I, pp.307–9.
29. *Rokeah*, p. 94, entry 381, where Manser son of Aaron and Aaron Crespin of London were mainperned to produce Benedict to answer the charge; p.96, entry 383 for the detail and p.186, entry 703 for the settlement.
30. The Rolls record a settlement after Benedict's death of a rental 'unjustly' sold by Reginald le Parmenter to Benedict, suggesting that Benedict would participate in questionable deals: *Rokeah*, p.311, entry 1037.
31. For example, Alexander Le Parmenter, one of the Jewish guardians of 1270, had no hesitation in exercising unlawful distraint against Benedict in 1275: *PREJ*, II, p.287.
32. *Pat. R. Henry III, 1266–1272*, p.223 (1268).

CHAPTER EIGHT

After the Wars

The Barons' Wars form something of a hiatus in the histories of Licoricia, Belia and their family members, and were, for some of the individuals we have met, a defining moment in their fortunes. In this chapter we pick up some of their stories again, and see the variety of experiences and outcomes that this period of upheaval brought to them.

ASSER/SWEETMAN'S STORY

Licoricia's son Asser Sweetman was too young to be seriously involved in moneylending until the mid-1260s, a time of upheaval and violence when we know increasingly less about the family's commercial activities due to the destruction of so many of the records. Nevertheless, he benefited from a rich inheritance from his father, David of Oxford. We know he was born about 1242, and he is mentioned in 1253 when his father's first wife, Muriel, left the house that had been assigned to her in Oxford and it reverted to Asser, who could then have been only around 11 years old, and Licoricia his mother.

Asser moved back to Winchester with Licoricia after his father's death, but by the 1260s he had based himself in Marlborough in Wiltshire.[1] This might have been an extension of the family business, although there is no evidence of such cooperation. He certainly represented his mother in some of her more far-flung transactions, and appeared jointly with his half-brother Benedict in others, but he had many enterprises of his own. While he should have been extremely wealthy with the inheritance from his father, and was a fairly successful dealer in later life, he appears never to have been as prosperous as his parents or Benedict, but he was working in far less secure circumstances. His clientele were mostly minor gentry and he was not as well connected or influential as his parents had been. Mundill identifies him as 'a plutocratic financier . . . dominating the business of the [Devizes] archa' before 1275, but as Devizes was not among the richest Jewries in the country, this is not saying much.[2]

Sweetman is among those named individuals given permission to search for evidence of dealings in other chests across the country, the Winchester *archa* having been destroyed, or otherwise disappeared. Some of his bonds may have been his father's or Licoricia's, which he had managed for them. One of these, dating from 1267, had been that of Ralph, son and heir of Ralph de Secherval, whose tenant now responsible for the payments was the unfortunate Henry de Chambernon, and who was continuing to appear at the courts some eight years later when the original loan of ten marks stood at ten shillings and £15 interest.[3]

Asser married another moneylender, Muriel fil Samuel, who appeared with her husband in 1272 in a case against Thomas of Chilwarton,[4] but they do not appear to have had any children: perhaps Asser inherited his father's low fertility. What Licoricia made of a daughter-in-law of the same name as David's first wife is a matter of conjecture, particularly taking into account the fact that Sweetman lived mainly in Wiltshire, away from Winchester and his powerful mother. He still held houses in Oxford that had been inherited from his father, David, and in 1268 he paid a fine of five marks for permission to sell one of them to Walter of Witney, who was also fined the same amount for permission to buy it. Some fifteen years later the sheriff of Oxford was instructed to impound chattels to this value from Walter, who had plainly not paid the fine.[5]

In the 1270s, Asser figured in a series of court cases, which were nominally Licoricia's, involving William Sharpe of Upavon, in Devon. He was also engaged in a dispute with the sheriff of Wiltshire, Stephen de Eddesworth, and in 1275 the barons of the Exchequer were ordered to investigate it. The dispute concerned whether the debt of £40 that Stephen owed Sweetman on the security of the lands that he rented from Gilbert Conon, and previously from Adam Gurdon who had ejected Stephen from his lands, was the responsibility of either of these landlords.[6] Gilbert was called as a witness that the obligation to repay the debt can only have been Stephen's and not Adam's. The argument was still raging in 1277 when Benedict represented his brother, although it later appears that the debt of £40, with £90 interest, was one of their few joint enterprises.[7] Sweetman subsequently dismissed his brother from any involvement in the disputed estate before discharging the debt entirely. Was there a disagreement between Benedict and Sweetman? They did not have many cases in common, and rarely acted for each other.[8] Perhaps Benedict had been reluctant to settle the debt for a smaller amount, or that the pressure was heavier on Sweetman to find money for his tallage, or it may have been vice versa, but it was Sweetman who immediately acquitted Gilbert Conon of the debt.

An examination of some of the various persons involved in this case demonstrates the tangled relationships that developed in the local business world. Some three years earlier, Gilbert Conon had been part of the sheriff of Hampshire's entourage, including the sheriff himself, Henry of Schotesbrok, which escorted Benedict's fellow chirographer, Deudonne of Winchester, to Southampton so that he could collect the debts owed to him there. The Jews had been expelled from Southampton in 1236, but in 1274 Benedict, Deudonne and the moneylenders Josce of Germany and Solomon fil Solomon of Winchester all paid a fine to be allowed to have houses in Southampton to carry on their business activities.[9] They could stay there while pursuing their debts, which were mostly loans to the town's merchant oligarchy who controlled business in Southampton and commerce through the port.

On this occasion in 1274, as Deudonne and the sheriff entered the city, a blacksmith noticed them and rang the tocsin, summoning his fellow citizens to the defence of the liberty of Southampton. This liberty had been granted under a charter in 1256, which declared that the citizens were free from arrest or loss of goods for unpaid debts unless the burgesses had gone surety for the debt. This, combined with civic pride, gave a sense of inviolability and independence, leading them to assume they were exempt from the demands of law officers attached to the county sheriff or the courts. On this occasion, the townspeople fell upon the intruders, attacking them with arrows, axes, swords and stones. One of Deudonne's debtors dragged him from his horse, stabbed him in the arm and tore some of his rich clothing from his back. Plainly, theft was another motive of the attack for some of the crowd, as the sheriff also lost his rich clothes and money as well as seeing his horse, no doubt an expensive animal, stabbed. The sheriff's men, who included the future sheriff, John of Havering, fared worse. One, Adam, was shot through the shoulder by an arrow which could not be removed. Gilbert Conon suffered worse than anyone, having his left cheek slashed open by an axe, and being taken prisoner and held for several days. In the subsequent court cases he was described as being 'like to die', which could have been an exaggeration for the benefit of the prosecution, or perhaps he was much stronger than first appeared, because he certainly survived the attack.

The court cases arising from this episode involved the sheriff and Deudonne in trying to gain compensation from a bewildering miscellany of Southampton men, who came at some times but not at others, and which trailed on for two years.[10] One of the individuals found guilty of the attack on John of Havering was named as James Isambard, a rich merchant of Southampton who forfeited his land and houses, which included 'Bulehuse' in Bull Street, and West Hall. Both Benedict and Sweetman had individually lent money to Bartholomew de Bulehuse, a prominent citizen of Southampton, and Sweetman paid a fine to be allowed to sell his debt on to a yeoman of Queen Eleanor of Castile called Monterelli. Bartholomew's surname referred to the house of that name in Bull Street, which he had sold to James Isambard, and James lost it to the king when he was found guilty of being involved in the attack. Significantly, all those who were individually penalized for the ensuing riot were punished, not for attacking Deudonne, but for their injuries to the sheriff and his men.

In the end, King Edward took Southampton 'into his own hands', which meant it lost its liberties, in 1275. The following year the burgesses paid the large sum of £20 to buy them back but the king ordered that this amount be added to the annual *ferm*, or community tax which the city paid to the treasury, and they continued paying it until the reign of Henry VIII. By 1278 the justices of the Jewish Exchequer were told that the innocent townspeople should not be molested any more for Deudonne's injuries.[11]

The Marlborough Jewish community was one that fell foul of Queen Eleanor in 1275, when they were expelled. Asser appears to have moved to Wilton, but may have lost property as a result of the expulsion, as the queen sold off a messuage in Marlborough, 'late of Sweteman', to her usher in 1281.[12] Asser seems to have got on well with his half-brothers, and he worked with all of them over the years, as well as occasionally acting as Licoricia's agent in some of her more distant enterprises, such as one in Devon.[13] This may have been one of the debts he inherited from his father; it could have been that all their shared business had originally been David's, but Licoricia had not handed it over entirely to him. Perhaps he only fully acquired what was left of his patrimony on his mother's death in 1277, by which time it was worth a lot less. Sweetman continued to hold property in Winchester, acquiring Samarian's house in Jewry Street, and by 1285 he held several houses in Jewry Street, some of which may have been his mother's.[14]

LICORICIA'S FINAL YEARS AND DEATH

The upheavals of the Barons' Wars appear to have had a significant effect on Licoricia's fortunes, and she seems to have retreated from business activities in the 1260s and 1270s. She is only rarely found in the records, and her business does not seem to have been as well protected against the depredations of the mid-1260s as Benedict's. In 1266, at the urging of Prince Edmund, she had been permitted by the king to seek evidence of her debts in other *archae*.[15] When Licoricia's bonds were being assessed for tallage in 1275, authority was given to the treasury officials to search in the chests of Wiltshire, Surrey, Warwickshire, Norfolk, Bedfordshire and Oxford, as well as Hampshire for evidence of her transactions. Some of these may have been debts she had inherited from David, which would illustrate the extent of his business activities as much as hers, but there is little confirmation that anything was found at these centres.

On a spring day early in 1277, the bodies of Licoricia and her Christian maid, Alice of Bicton, were found by a woman described as Belia, Licoricia's daughter, at her mother's house in Jewry Street, lying on the floor, having died of stab wounds.[16] This is the only reference to Belia, daughter of Licoricia, anywhere in the records. While it could have been Belia of Bedford, it seems much more likely that Licoricia had a daughter named after her earliest colleague in Winchester. They had been close friends and colleagues before their second marriages parted them and several of their children shared the same names.

Alice of Bicton (or Bighton as it is now known, a village near Alresford in Hampshire), should not have been employed by Licoricia as a maid, as Christians were forbidden to work for Jews by the Third Lateran Council in 1179, an edict reinforced by the Fourth Lateran Council in 1216 and by several church directives thereafter. It would be nice to think that it was a sense of loyalty, rather than economic pressure, that kept Alice working there, but whatever the reason, Alice paid for it with her life. In all the subsequent confused investigations and enquiries, no further hard facts emerged as to the perpetrator or the motive, although there was an assumption of robbery. Certainly, there were sporadic outbreaks of violence at that time in Winchester; another Jewish woman, Pucelle the widow of Bonavye of Newbury, was also found murdered in Winchester in the same year.[17]

Because Licoricia was such a prominent member of the Jewry, her murder attracted a lot of attention, and news of it even spread as far as Germany, where it was referred to in a Jewish chronicle of the time. An inquest was requested and paid for by her sons, Cokerel and Sweetman, and a jury of eighteen men from Winchester and the Bighton area was ordered to assemble. At the first inquest no jurors appeared, but the sheriff subsequently ensured that fourteen attended. These included at least three of the guildsmen who had also been appointed guardians of the Jews in 1270, and who would have known Licoricia and her family extremely well. One of them, Henry of Durngate, was a close colleague of Benedict.

Licoricia's house was sealed to prevent any of her goods from being spirited away by members of the family or stolen before they could be assessed for the king's share. Excited local speculation put the possible total of Licoricia's wealth at the over-inflated amount of £10,000. This should be compared with the value of the chattels and bonds kept at the house by Cokerel and his son, who requested access to them.[18] It seems extremely unlikely that Licoricia was worth anything like the rumoured amount because, as we have seen, she was in less affluent circumstances than before the Barons' Wars.[19] We shall never know how much was actually there, because the house was subsequently broken into and much was lost in the burglary.

The three men who were initially named as chief suspects, Robert le Scerre and Adam le Seeler with John le Sclatiere as an accomplice, were acquitted, and the enquiry concluded that the culprit was a poor saddler called Ralph, who was of the same profession as Adam.[20] Ralph, who had opportunely left or perhaps fled the area, had abandoned his personal belongings, which amounted to the value of two shillings. The enquiries were at best cursory, and it is likely that Ralph provided the townsmen with an easy target for this accusation, relieving them of the burden of accusing neighbours, who may have had much more influence, or relatives who could have taken revenge on the prosecutors. It is also entirely possible that poor men actually accepted payment to flee a town and take the blame for a crime or misdemeanor, thus relieving the pressure on the jurors from royal officials to find the culprit. Although in theory an individual banished or outlawed could be arrested or even killed anywhere in the kingdom, there were no nationwide law officers who could enforce the arrest of a wanted man beyond their area of jurisdiction. The Winchester enquiry into Licoricia's murder declared Ralph guilty and outlawed him, and nothing more was heard of him. Because the murders had occured in daylight, the city was found to be derelict in its duty, condemned for failing to call a hue and cry the minute the bodies were found, and heavily fined.

BENEDICT'S FAMILY TRIALS

Benedict had at least seven surviving children by Belassez: four sons – Lumbard, Cokerel, Abraham and Aaron – and three daughters including Avegaye (see Figure 8).[21] Lumbard worked most closely with his father and may have been named after Benedict's maternal grandfather or his brother. When in 1273 Benedict became assessor and moved to London, Lumbard became a Winchester chirographer in his place.[22] Although closely involved with his father in his business, Lumbard seemed to be less ruthless in his dealings. Abraham, who could have been the eldest, was possibly named after Benedict's father, but his career was a highly chequered one that ruled out any close business partnership within the family. Both became entangled in the fallout from their grandmother's death when judicial concern moved from the murders to the theft from Licoricia's house.

Initially accused of breaking the seals on the Jewry Street house and stealing the murdered woman's property were the sheriff of Hampshire himself, John of Havering, and two of his men, William of Chichester and Thomas de la Mare. Also accused, however, were Benedict's two sons Abraham and Lumbard, although it is not clear if they were supposed to be working with the sheriff's men or on their own. If they were involved, it would have been to try and keep some of their grandmother's business interests from falling into the hands of the king, who initially would have taken all of it while it was being assessed. The sons would then be allowed to buy back two-thirds of the business, although they would not necessarily have had the right to select the most valuable assets. The practice of hiding large amounts of a deceased dealer's chattels to prevent them falling into the hands of the Exchequer was common practice among wealthy Jews' families. It was a form of tax evasion, and was precisely the sort of situation that Benedict had been appointed assessor to investigate and prevent.

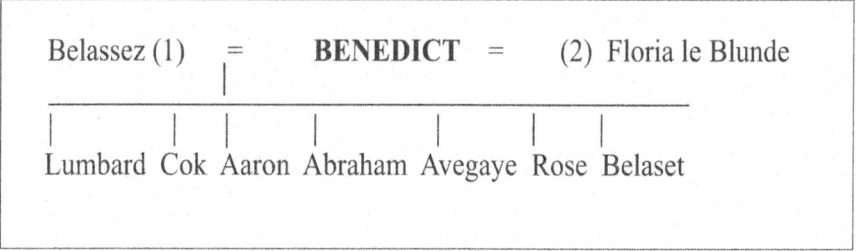

Figure 8. The Family of Benedict

By the second inquisition into the burglary, Lumbard was no longer accused, but the accusation against Abraham still stood. He was the family black sheep: one historian says of him, 'No category of crime would be complete without Abraham fil Benedict'.[23] He is rarely seen operating with other family members, and then only with his father. Following the burglary, enquiries found him to be in London, without any property in Winchester by which he could be secured or forced to return to undergo trial. He may have been recovering from an assault on him in 1277 by Edward de Sutton that left him with wounds to his head, right shin and suffering from 'other outrages'. This was the outcome of a row between Abraham and Edward Sutton's father-in-law, Hugh of Fulfloode, which seems to have come to blows.[24] He may also have got himself committed to prison on a lesser charge to escape the more serious accusation in Winchester. Over the years, he was accused of theft with and without violence, causing death, and very questionable business practices. Ironically, he seems to have escaped most of these charges and survived into the 1280s at least. In 1281 he is recorded as being imprisoned in the Tower, accused of killing a man in Winchester.[25]

The sheriff, John of Havering, was able to prove he was in London on the day of the burglary and therefore the accusation against him was dropped. He was, however, a very shady character who would subsequently be found to have withheld money collected for the Crown and silver accrued at the time of the coin-clipping accusations of 1278/79, and by 1279 wound up in the Tower of London for these offences and various other instances of contempt of court. His two servants had fled Winchester and, like the poor saddler found guilty of Licoricia's murder, afforded an easy solution to the case. Together with Abraham, they were found guilty and outlawed.

The question arises as to why the influential Benedict took no part in the enquiry into his mother's murder, leaving it to his brothers to apply for the inquest. He seems to have distanced himself from the whole proceedings, probably because as escheator he had to remain uninvolved. He was under considerable pressure in London to pay off his outstanding taxes, and he was also facing an accusation in the courts of wrongdoing. Overshadowing all of this was the new threat that was growing for the Jews, and which culminated in complete disaster for Benedict and most of English Jewry later in the year. This was the pogrom unleashed by the accusation of coin-clipping that raged from the autumn of 1278 through to May 1279. This will be discussed presently.

Benedict's third son, Aaron, was encouraged by King Edward to move to Canterbury and was then made a chirographer. It is claimed that this followed Aaron transferring a £5 debt to the prince.[26] However shortly afterwards Aaron and two of the other chirographers, one of them Christian, were accused of wrongfully removing two charters from the Exchequer chest. One was for ten shillings, which they agreed was removed in error, and they were ordered to compensate for its loss. They insisted that the other one, valued at two marks, was dealt with correctly, but they were sent for trial. The final verdict is unrecorded but Aaron was still living in Canterbury at the Expulsion, suggesting that he was acquitted.[27] With him were his brother Cokerel and their sister, Belaset. Another sister, Avegaye, moved to Oxford, possibly on her marriage, although we do not know the identity of her husband.[28] There may have been yet another sister named Rose living in York, in a house in Coney Street that belonged to Benedict, and it too could have been part of a marriage settlement. Although most of Benedict and Belassez's children appear to have survived until close to 1290, there seems to be little mention of them and no grandchildren are named.

Benedict took advantage of his permission to occupy a Southampton house to carry on other business activities such as exporting goods, probably wool, and he was also involved in the wine trade. The house was called Ronceval, and was positioned near the West gate with a stone undercroft, which could be used as a warehouse to store his goods, and access to the quay below. It was obviously a large house, as he paid an annual rent of forty shillings, and from there he and his son Lumbard operated their import-export business, despite the fact that Jews were not allowed to trade overseas. Benedict acquired one of the first of the scarce licences to deal in wool at this time, as did Simon Draper, for which no doubt they had to pay a tidy sum. However there is evidence that, like his fellow guildsmen, he was also dealing in wine as well as salt and wheat.

The house itself belonged to the prior of St Denys, who had leased it for life to Claremunda, the daughter of William of Gloucester and the sister of Richard of Gloucester who was her heir. She was a Christian moneylender and dealt in a considerable amount of local property. When she died in 1260 Richard claimed the house as his inheritance, but Petronilla, the widow of Nicholas, another of the Gloucester family, took it over. She subsequently leased it to Benedict, but the following year Richard and his brother threw Benedict and Lumbard out of Ronceval and took some twenty shillings' worth of their goods that had been stored there. Benedict got reinstated but there seems to be no word of compensation for his lost goods. Eventually he handed back the lease of Ronceval to Petronilla the widow in exchange for a tun of kosher wine or sixty shillings.[29]

BENEDICT'S NEW WIFE AND CHANGING ROLE

Benedict's fortunes appeared to flourish during the early 1270s. He did not emerge entirely unscathed from all the upheavals caused by his becoming a guildsman and the civic scandals of the Oysun case in Winchester, for he seems to have been attacked again. His wife Belassez disappears from the records at this time and must have died, perhaps as a result of the earlier assaults, which may account for the size of the compensation awarded to him. Some time around 1273/74 he married again. His new wife was Floria Le Blunde, daughter of Aaron Le Blunde II, and the widow of Benedict's friend and colleague Solomon L'Eveske, with whom he had shared many business interests.

Solomon was one of the L'Eveske dynasty,[30] whose surname implied 'bishop', but more probably was a misunderstanding or misuse of the name Cohen, which was taken by the hereditary religious leaders among Jews. Solomon had been dealing since 1234 and in some of his business transactions had been in partnership or working with some of the leading Jews of his day, including Benedict of Winchester. Other members of his family had worked with David of Oxford and all the leading Jewish dealers earlier in the century, including members of the Le Blunde consortium. The marriage of Solomon and Floria would therefore have been an alliance between two of the most successful Jewish families, and she was involved jointly with her husband in some of the loans, as early as 1247. There do not seem to have been any children by this marriage, although the editor of a collection of starrs and charters thinks it possible that Solomon had a son named Benedict after his paternal grandfather, who married a Sarah.[31]

Solomon had become an expert in collecting gold for the king whenever he needed it, although his relationship with the monarch had its ups and downs. In 1241 he was in the Tower of London over some misdemeanor involving a debt. He was released when Aaron le Blunde, his father-in-law, paid his fine of ten marks. Later, Solomon's usefulness to the Crown was such that in 1252 he was granted immunity from paying tallage of more than £20 per year for four years.[32] One donation by Solomon into the King's Wardrobe lists eighty-five gold marks, gold bezants worth twenty-six marks, thirty-one marks' worth of obols of Muscat, and gold leaf, money and ingots, demonstrating the assortment of coins and bullion in use, particularly needed for travel abroad.[33] Gold coins were not minted in England until Henry tried, unsuccessfully, to issue a gold mark coin for the first time when Richard of Cornwall was overseeing the production of a new coinage to replace the devalued, lightweight money. In 1255 Solomon and his two brothers were nominated as guarantors for the London tallage, which meant that they would have to produce any missing amount from the expected tallage target.[34]

In 1259 Solomon was in trouble again, accused of forgery, and his lands and property vulnerable to being confiscated.[35] He and Floria fled the kingdom early in the following year. Just how important he was to the king was demonstrated in 1261, when a royal pardon was issued to him, guaranteeing safe conduct and explaining that 'the king has necessity that he return to the realm, for business specially affecting him'.[36] As well as having all bonds and securities returned to him, he was also offered the inducement of two years' freedom from tallage at the urging of Queen Eleanor.[37] He and Floria returned, and Solomon worked for the king and queen until he died at some time in 1268.[38] The king's third of his estate might have been part of the 1271 'gift' of 6,000 marks levied from the Jewry to fund Prince Edward's journey to the Crusades. Solomon's loans ranged in value from six to 300 marks, with additional amounts of interest which the king himself could not benefit from directly once they came into his custody because that would be regarded as usury; he could, however, raise revenue when he sold them on to other Jews. Those debts listed include locations in ten counties, although many of them would have been negotiated in London. The unfortunate tenants on land that was security for the loan must have felt that the sky had fallen on them when their share of the debt was demanded.

Floria, therefore, would have been an extremely wealthy woman when she married Benedict, and given her relatively advanced age, it is tempting to view this as a marriage of assets. Her share in the two-thirds remainder of Solomon's estate – some of which were her own debts – would have been a powerful attraction to someone like Benedict. By 1275 Floria was apparently dead: an order dated 15 November that year by Queen Eleanor granted Benedict all of the possessions of Floria 'late his wife', as well as all the goods she had the day he married her, and the debts of Solomon L'Eveske 'sometime her husband'. Floria had granted the goods to the queen, 'whereby the latter had her action against Benedict', but Benedict had now satisfied her and took possession of the goods.[39] The same year, Benedict was called upon to pay 350 marks owing from the tallage of Solomon and Floria, of which he paid fifty marks to Walter of Kent, Keeper of Queen Eleanor's gold, a post he himself subsequently occupied. Benedict paid the outstanding 300 marks with a bond of £300, the debt of Sir William of Dartford to Queen Eleanor, and who may well have demanded this bargain herself, but it paid to stay on the right side of the rapacious Queen.

Benedict proved his undoubted talent for wheeling and dealing amidst adverse circumstances in the confused and dangerous world of Winchester and London in the 1270s. England had suffered much unrest following Evesham and the end of the civil war, with many disaffected supporters on the losing side, having lost their estates and status, reacting with violence to any cause for disagreement with the authorities or their previous enemies. In such a volatile atmosphere, it was the Jewish community that became the focus of attacks from both sides. The records are full of former rebels being accused of murder during the wars and, astonishingly, they all seemed to be discharged, probably on payment of a heavy fine. None of the victorious side, of course, were prosecuted for the same offence. This spirit of forgiveness pervaded the Edict of Kenilworth, where estates were returned to their previous owners on payment of a sum worth seven times the annual income. This forced many to turn to the Jewish moneylenders to fund the reclamation of their own property, which went some way to restore the battered Jewries to financial health. Scenting a source of future profit, many Christians entered into partnerships with Jews, whereby the Jews lent money and could obtain the usury, while being able to realize the security of the land in the event of the debtor's failing to repay the agreed instalments. The Christian partners could and did sell the land that was pledged, and for them this was a cheap source of considerable profit. Many well-connected Englishmen climbed on the bandwagon, including court officials, churchmen, members of the aristocracy and Queen Eleanor herself.

While Benedict was taking part in this bonanza, he was also suffering from attacks fuelled by the lingering resentment of the still-smouldering dispute between the merchant guildsmen of Winchester and the commonalty. Eventually he was removed from the Winchester scene to become an Exchequer official, the Jewish Escheator, or evaluator of Jewish tallage based in London in 1273. This appointment was made on the instruction of the new king, Edward I, who was abroad on a crusade followed by some touring and junketing at the French court until 1274. When he made this appointment, it is clear that Edward had no idea what the duties of an escheator might be, and the wording of the appointment said something to the effect that Benedict 'should do whatever it was that the escheator did'. The post had been vacant for four years, and seemed to involve the investigation of the chattels and wealth of Jews who died in order to assess the amount due to the Exchequer, but other duties could be added as needed. Whatever he was supposed to do, Benedict's new role exposed him to further risk, as pressure increased on the Jewish communities in the late 1270s, culminating in the coin-clipping disasters at the end of the decade.

NOTES

1. He is recorded in Marlborough in 1270: *PREJ*, I, p.220. A note of a debt sold by Sweetman fil Davy was lodged in the chest at Devizes, reinforcing Asser's Wiltshire interests: *PREJ*, V, p.50, entry 313 (1278 – the purchaser from Asser sells the debt on).
2. Robin R. Mundill, *England's Jewish Solution: Experiment and Expulsion, 1262–1290* (Cambridge: Cambridge University Press, 1998), p.206.
3. *PREJ*, I, pp.279 and 290; ibid., II, pp.2, 72 and 90; ibid., III, p.281; ibid., IV, p.103.
4. *PREJ*, I, p.294.
5. Sale: Robin R. Mundill, 'The Jewish Entries from the Patent Rolls, 1271–1292', *JHS*, 32 (1990–92), pp.25–88, at 75. Walter's debt: *Rokeah*, pp.278, entry 944 and 292, entry 978.
6. The initial order appears in the Memoranda Rolls: *Rokeah*, p.165, entry 635. See also *PREJ*, II, pp.134 and 290–1 (1275) and ibid., III, pp.152–3 (1276).
7. *Cl. R. Edward I, 1272–1279*, pp.386–7. The document suggests that Benedict was planning to buy out Sweetman's part of the debt but that Stephen defaulted.
8. Indeed, in 1274 Benedict had been mainperned to produce Asser to answer for a debt to the queen, or face settling it himself, which can hardly have helped relations between them: *Rokeah*, p.137, entry 539.
9. Deudonne's right to a house in Southampton was upheld in 1275: *Cl. R. Edward I, 1272–1279*, p.259.
10. Initial pleas: *PREJ*, II, pp.130–1, 132, 200, 220; the defence begins, ibid., pp.216–17; the defendants fail to appear, ibid., p.219; a date set for the hearing, ibid., p.286; an order to round up the suspects, ibid., p.302. *Cl. R. Edward I, 1272–1279*, p.439 (1278) records an order to the justices of the Jews not to molest the citizens of Southampton because of the actions of some against Deudonne, indicating the lingering tension after the case.
11. Patricia Allin, 'Medieval Southampton and Its Jews', *TJHSE*, 23 (1970), pp.87–95, at p.87. Deudonne's story ends with his being hanged in 1280: Mundill, 'Jewish Entries', p.34.
12. Mundill, 'Jewish Entries', p.71 for the grant to Eleanor of the property.
13. *PREJ*, III, p.273 (1277) records him as 'Asser fil David, Jew of Exeter'.
14. Derek Keene, *Survey of Medieval Winchester*, Winchester Studies 2, 2 vols (Oxford: Clarendon Press, 1985), II, p.647, entry 260; Michael Adler, 'An Unpublished Pipe Roll of 1285: Inventory of the Property of Condemned Jews', *MJHSE*, 2 (1935), pp.56–71, at p.61 and p.71, includes the sale of an item from the chattels of 'Sweteman of Winchester/Wilton', suggesting that he did not survive beyond this date.
15. *Pat. R. Henry III, 1258–1266*, p.585.
16. *PREJ*, III, pp.292–3, and Zefira Entin Rokeah, 'Crime and the Jews in Late 13th-Century England: Some Cases and Comments', *HUCA*, 55 (1984), pp.95–197, at pp.126–7 and 156–7.

17. *PREJ*, V, p.185, entry 955.
18. Cokerel had £10 6s 3d, Abraham his son 54s 4d: *PREJ*, III, p.258.
19. A debt to her of £72 (and presumably sold or passed on) is recorded among the debts owed to Lumbard of Cricklade in 1278: *PREJ*, V, p.165, entry 888.
20. Accusation of the three men: *PREJ*, III, p.248. Acquittal of the trio and condemnation of Ralph: ibid., pp.292–3.
21. Avegaye's property in Oxford is recorded after the Expulsion: *Ch. R. II, 1253–1300* (London: HMSO, 1906), p.415.
22. *PREJ*, II, p.108.
23. Rokeah, 'Crime and the Jews', p.134.
24. *Pat. R. Edward I, 1272–1281*, pp.244–5 orders a hearing 'concerning persons who lately assaulted Abraham fil Benedict so that his life was despaired of'.
25. *PREJ*, VI, p.294, entry 1223.
26. M. Adler, 'The Jews of Canterbury', *TJHSE*, 7 (1911–14), pp.19–96.
27. Ibid., pp.80, 85 and 86 records debts owed to Aaron and also to a Cok of Winchester, both now termed 'Jews of Canterbury'.
28. See above, note 21 for Avegaye.
29. Allin, 'Medieval Southampton and Its Jews', p.87.
30. See Joe Hillaby, 'London: The 13th-Century Jewry Revisited', *JHS*, 32 (1990–92), pp.89–158 for recent work on this family.
31. *Starrs and Jewish Charters* II, p.341, note 1520.
32. *Pat. R. Henry III, 1247–1258*, p.130.
33. *Pat. R. Henry III, 1258–1266*, p.48 (1259).
34. *Pat. R. Henry III, 1247–1258*, p.439.
35. H.P. Stokes, *Studies in Anglo-Jewish History* (Edinburgh: JHSE, 1913), p.16.
36. *Pat. R. Henry III, 1258–1266*, p.149.
37. Ibid., p.177.
38. Some of his property is recorded as escheated to the king in that year: *Pat. R. Henry III, 1266–1272*, pp.235 and 430.
39. *Pat. R. Henry III, 1272–1281*, p.113. See also *PREJ*, II, p.52 (1273), recording Benedict as already a widower, and ibid., III, p.57 (1275), where he is still liable for a tallage payment of Floria and Solomon.

CHAPTER NINE

The Coin-Clipping Pogrom

King Henry III died in 1272, and many of the benefits that a royal connection brought to Licoricia and her family seem to have disappeared with his death. In Henry the Jews lost a king who had offered them some protection, but only in order to use them for his own purposes. He had been an erratic protector who was mostly open to bribery and who had formed relationships with individual Jews such as David of Oxford and Licoricia. But even though they knew that they could not rely on him, they must at times have used this royal connection for the benefit of themselves and the wider community. His brother, Richard of Cornwall, who had sometimes interceded for Jews facing Henry's wrath, died in the same year.

Henry had never hesitated to employ individual Jews to try and circumvent feudal law when it was to his personal advantage. We have seen how he would have benefited from allowing Jews to become citizens, thus enabling them to own property. The case of Licoricia and Thomas of Charlecote was another example of Henry trying to circumvent the laws which limited the time a Jewish moneylender could hold pledged estates.

With King Edward, however, the Jewish community found themselves dealing with a totally different ruler. Edward was a crusader, perhaps more zealous than his father, perhaps more consistent in his religious beliefs, but he also brought back with him from the Crusades an increased intolerance that amounted to profound hostility towards non-Christians. In his dealings with Jews as reflected in the records, he was plainly out of sympathy and indifferent to the sufferings his actions caused them, opportunistic about using Jewry for his own financial benefit, yet without any recognition that he should husband the moneylenders in order to be able to employ them in the future. Edward appeared to believe that the Jewish community could produce limitless resources for him whenever they were called for. Given the custody of the Jews in order to be able to farm them for the money he needed for his crusades, Edward's response was to build a prison for those whom he considered too slow in their payments.

The first two years of Edward's reign saw him still abroad, taking part in a crusade where he did little to further his reputation, although he gained valuable experience which would serve him well in future campaigns against the Welsh and Scots. He had also noted how some of the other Christian rulers dealt with their Jewish subjects. Despite knowing of his father's death he took his time to return, touring through France and Italy, secure in the knowledge that the kingdom was well run in his absence. He returned, however, to numerous complaints against his judiciary, and one of his first actions was to discharge the most corrupt among them.

Edward was very much preoccupied with the question of money-dealers and the usury they levied on loans, which was anathema to the church. Despite this, he returned from abroad owing some £3,000 to the Riccardi family of Italian bankers from Lucca. They continued to fund his Wardrobe in return for the entire management and receipts of the customs and a portion of taxes. When he eventually dismissed the Riccardi in 1294 they were bankrupt, and he was forced to rely on the more conventional forms of royal income.[1] While this source of finance was in operation, Edward probably felt himself to be less reliant on Jewish funds. On his leisurely progress homeward he sent ahead to his treasurer, the Hospitaller Joseph de Chauncy, to find 'any merchant-usurers in the city of London or elsewhere and cause them and all their chattels to be arrested and kept safely'. This was aimed at the Christian moneylenders, but it does not seem to have been a curb on the activities of the provincial guildsmen, as was the case in Winchester.

THE STATUTE OF THE JEWRY, 1275

Once back in England, Edward turned his attention to his Jewish subjects. In April 1275 a parliament was summoned where the Statuta de Judaismo or Statute of the Jewry was unveiled.[2] This was a mountain of restrictions heaped on the Jewish community, some of them old ones that had been allowed to lapse, but the majority were new. Jews were forbidden to practise unrestrained moneylending, and were forbidden to extend credit on the security of land or rents. Usury on old debts was restricted, and had to be acquitted by Easter – this was announced on 25 April – but creditors could keep enough of their income to live on. Debts could not be collected from heirs or tenants, and only on part of the land, not including the main house. Jews could no longer acquit Christian debts without a royal licence. Pawnbroking, both a minor source of credit for the poorest, and a necessary sideline when selling off surrendered pledges, was outlawed.[3]

The Statute then addressed the question of how Jews were going to make an alternative living. They could become merchants like everyone else, and those who did would be allowed to own their own house; if they became farmers, they would be allowed to buy land on a ten-year lease. But as the new restrictions also restated the law that all Jews live in the *archa* towns[4] (which had consistently been breached by individuals choosing new areas in which to operate, with and without permission from the Crown), farming was practically impossible, and living in the countryside would in any case expose the Jewry to attacks.

The Jewish community protested against the implications of these restrictions in a letter begging for mercy to the Councillors in 1276. It was unjust, they said, that they could only claim from part of the land, and what if the debtor only had one house on his land? If repayment could not be claimed from heirs or tenants when the original debtor had died, then where was it to come from? They asked that existing debts should be allowed to be paid. The poorer Jews could not become merchants and were reduced to trying to sell their houses to the richer members, and where they could not, they demolished them for the price of the building materials. For the poorer Jews who had been earning their living in the various spin-offs from moneylending, such as pawnbroking and the selling of the lower grade pledges such as clothing and household goods, this ban deprived them of any chance of earning a legitimate livelihood, and many turned to criminal activities.

Those who might have been willing to try and become a merchant knew they could not compete with Christian merchants in the extension of credit, and in any case could be undercut by them. They could not join any of the guilds, assuming that they were even admitted, because of the requirement for Christian oaths. If they were restricted to the *archa* towns, they could not move to sell goods in the rest of the country. The ways in which Benedict altered his business practices and continued his dealings are instructive as to how some of the wealthiest Jews were able to survive. As we have seen, he forged closer partnerships with Christians, which enabled a certain amount of evasion of these rules, and he was also granted exceptional licence to trade.[5] The involvement of powerful 'protectors' such as Edmund, the king's brother, and Queen Eleanor, was to their mutual benefit; and other partnerships with the lesser nobility and men 'on the make' blossomed. Yet the failure to take up alternative employment and give up moneylending became the justification for the Expulsion fifteen years later.

The social restrictions enforced by the Statute on the whole community had a profound effect. The wearing of the badge was re-imposed, and a new tax, a *chevage* or poll tax on all Jews, male and female, of three pence per head per annum was declared, the proceeds to go to the maintainence of the converts in the Domus Conversorum. Provocatively, converts were sometimes used to collect this, and were attacked on more than one occasion.[6] The tax yielded an income of £11 3s 9d, excluding London and Canterbury, for which the records are missing. The king also ordered a series of compulsory services where the Jews were forced to listen to preachers urging conversion.

Despite imposing restrictions on the ability of Jews to conduct their business, the king seemed to believe, unrealistically, that he could still expect a huge income from the Jews. Despite his legislation, there may still have been some Jewish moneylending going on, but in the late 1270s Edward instigated the tragedy of the coin-clipping pogrom which, along with his unrealistic demands, totally impoverished and ruined the community beyond recovery.

COIN-CLIPPING

Money in the form of coinage had circulated in England for centuries, evidenced by the sophistication of Anglo-Saxon recalls and reissues of coinage. The use of money was similarly sophisticated, with a face value which usually exceeded the actual weight of the metal used in its production, but which was nevertheless affected by the practice of filing or clipping metal from around the edge. While King Henry III had a few gold crowns struck, they were not a success, being of too high a value in such insecure times and it was not until the fourteenth century that gold nobles were minted again.

Coins were increasingly minted locally in Saxon England and mints were located in several towns, initially serving local kings but eventually becoming centralized under one monarch. Under the Normans lower denomination coins were created by physically cutting them into halves and quarters, although a certain amount of bartering in goods continued. Goods recorded as interest on the repayment of loans included clothes, horses, wine, grain and wool. Benedict rented out one of his houses in Micheldever for one pound of peppercorns per year, which was then no trifling sum. This method of payment was a gamble, for the value of spices fluctuated wildly, depending on the security of the supply routes during wars and crusades. Philip, Benedict's Micheldever tenant, fell into arrears and by 1276 was owing sixteen pounds of peppercorns, which establishes that Benedict owned the house as early as 1260.[7]

Coins did not necessarily contain metals of a worth equal to the coin's nominal value, but there was profit to be made by paring off tiny quantities of the metal. The clippings were then melted down into silver plates or ingots and sold to silversmiths, for whom they were a cheap source of precious metal. Sometimes they were swindled into buying ingots that enclosed a certain amount of lead, making a heavier weight. There were also exchangers who charged for changing bad coins for good. All these activities were criminal, and incurred the severest penalties. Those Jews involved in moneylending were well situated to employ these underhand methods, as were the jewellers, but Christians were also engaged in shady monetary dealing. The sheriff of Hampshire, John of Havering, who had been implicated in the theft from Licoricia's house in 1277, was said to have been such a trader, but there were other government officials who were not averse to dealing in silver clippings.

This repeated debasing of the coinage constituted a damaging drain on the country's resources. As early as 1206 it was ordered that anyone found with clipped money should be imprisoned and his goods confiscated. Light coins were to be perforated and so continue to be used, presumably at less than face value, by Jews, foreigners and jewellers. Matthew Paris, commenting on the state of the coinage in 1238, said, 'No foreigner let alone Englishmen could look on an English coin with a dry eye and an unbroken heart'.[8] Indeed the Jewish business community at that time was so concerned that they paid for a countrywide investigation. David of Oxford, Benedict's future stepfather, then led a mixed group of Jews and Exchequer officials round the country enquiring into coin-clipping, larceny and receiving stolen goods among the various Jewish communities. They requested that the punishment for these offences be made more severe, with exile as the penalty, instead of fines and confiscation of property. David's involvement in this appeal for a more severe penalty lends a rather sad resonance to what happened to his stepson some forty years later. By the 1270s coin-clipping had become a capital offence, although some of the accused escaped abroad while others merely had all of their possessions forfeit.[9]

The only way of dealing with corrupted money was to recall and exchange it for a new coinage, which happened several times during the thirteenth century. In order to prevent clipping, the design of the coins changed, and the invention of the long penny, with the legs of the cross on its reverse side almost reaching the edge, might have seemed the answer, but it soon proved just as vulnerable to trimming, and light coin was once more in circulation. From 1274 the tide of accusations of coin-clipping steadily rose. The record of fines against the London Jewry, and those Christians visiting it for questionable dealings in coin-exchange, show a steady increase. During those years the penalties for illegal exchange of money, the sale of silver plates probably made from coin-clippings, dealing in lightweight pennies and actual coin-clippings incurred fines some of which were for sums as considerable as £10. By 1278 the king was faced by another crisis over the money in circulation, which this time coincided with a rising tide of general unrest and growing intolerance of the Jews.

This increased debasement of the coinage called for a much harsher strategy. Those found guilty would incur the death sentence and the confiscation of all their property, while others found guilty of lesser currency offences either lost everything or had to pay huge fines that consumed most of their wealth. If they or their families could not pay, they too were executed. By 1278 there was a mounting crescendo of accusations against both Jews and Christians.[10] That an estimated ten times as many Christians were arrested during the coin-clipping episode indicates that they were just as deeply involved as the Jews. There can be no doubt that a lot of the accusers were settling old scores and made false claims, and there are references to evidence such as the instruments for clipping being planted. As whole families were arrested and imprisoned, their houses were ransacked and in some cases destroyed. It has also been suggested that some agent provocateurs were planted, among them a convert, Henry of Winchester, who had been regularly used by King Henry for various ploys and investigations concerning the Jewish community since the 1250s. He was able to act unobtrusively, gathering information about coin-clipping by both Jews and Christians, and collecting samples of bars made of clippings. He was even arrested and imprisoned in Bristol Castle for a while, himself accused of illegally dealing in plate. He was well rewarded for his services to the Crown.[11]

IMPRISONMENT

Jews were liable to experience imprisonment at many points in their lives.[12] They would go voluntarily to gaol in search of protection at times of danger and attack, although it must be said that only the wealthiest seemed to avail themselves of this opportunity. It may have been that the poorer members could not have afforded to pay for their keep while there, or the fine that had to be paid for their release. Jewish servants were left in the houses to safeguard property, and as a result were the first to be slaughtered whenever there were massacres. The wealthiest were likely to be imprisoned in advance of any projected Jewish tallage, to enforce payment from their families. King John went so far as to torture individual Jews to try and enforce the early settlement of their taxes. As in the case of Licoricia, wives could be imprisoned at the death of their husbands to prevent interference with his estate before it could be assessed for the king's share. More obviously, those accused of crimes were put in prison to await trial, and at the time of accusations of child-murder this could mean whole communities, or at least the entire leadership. The numbers who were imprisoned in advance of the coin-clipping trials were, however, far greater than anything known before.

It is estimated that some 680 Jews were confined in London alone, and prisons across the country must have been filled to overflowing with the many more Christians who were at first accused, as well as some local Jews. A particular problem presented itself at the Tower of London, where extensive rebuilding was in progress; ironically, this had been partly paid for by the income from Jewish taxation.[13] The clearest picture of conditions in the prisons emerges from London in a series of lists of the fines and penalties paid by the prisoners in the Tower for various liberties and supplies, as well as for misdemeanors.[14] There could not have been adequate accommodation for 600 in any case, but people were crammed into every available space. Whole communities were accommodated elsewhere, some in the Fleet and Newgate prisons. Named communities housed in the Tower included those from Norwich, York, Lincoln, Oxford, Stamford, Bedford and Hereford. Some of the communities fined for the favour of being jailed together; the Londoners paid to be housed together in the Guildhall, and the Stamford community also paid to be kept together. In the Tower itself, all available space was occupied; one woman paid a fine of eight shillings to be accommodated in the elephant house. This was built in 1255 to house a gift from the King of France to Henry, a second-hand elephant which had probably been an unwanted gift in the first place. King Henry was known to have an extensive menagerie kept in the grounds of the Tower; he ordered his sheriffs to build the elephant house at their own expense, and in a rare burst of economic foresight, required them to make sure it was suitable for other uses. The poor beast died two years later, but the resulting house, which measured twenty by forty feet, proved a very useful addition to the accommodation available for the flood of prisoners in 1278.[15] The White Tower, the tiled stables, Brother John's Tower and its cellar, and another tower in addition were all pressed into use.

It should be remembered that those in prison were not just the accused individuals, but their families too. There is a surviving instruction from 1277 that those accused Jews of York who were unable to pay for their transport should be funded by the rest of the community.[16] Another instruction states that wives and families were to pay to be transported to jail with their husbands. Where sheriffs submitted costs for this requirement, it is unclear whether these were receipts for money already received from the Jews themselves or if they were bills for the Exchequer to remunerate. In 1280 the sheriff of Oxford and Berkshire, Alan son of Roald, charged the Crown not only for carrying Jews to Newgate, but also for baptizing some of their children en route.[17] The families could not be left to fend for themselves on their own, and wives would probably have wanted to accompany their husbands. Some of them were business partners of their husbands and would have been valuable as witnesses if not accused themselves, such as Floria of Kingston, who was a known dealer in silver clippings, sought out by silversmiths in search of cheaper sources for their raw materials.

Initially, those arriving at the prisons would have been fettered to each other and chained to the floor or walls, but there was a menu of freedoms that could be bought for a sliding scale of fines, depending on the wealth of individuals. Some could not afford any of these freedoms and remained chained for their entire imprisonment, others had some of the privileges bought for their whole community, such as being free of chains, or from being attached to others.[18] The ability to move around the Tower outside their cells, and the liberty to leave the Tower and travel around the city, could also be bought. This last was essential if the prisoners were to earn the money to pay for their food and for such basics as blankets and fuel, a requirement for all prisoners. The consequences of not being able to do so are revealed in an earlier reference to seven Christians unable to fund their keep and who had died of starvation while in prison. This was in addition to the Jews' existing impoverishment, commented upon by Matthew Paris as early as 1250.[19] In some cases, the husbands left their families behind in prison, while in others, whole families could afford to pay the fines to go out raising money where they could. Those who could afford the fine carried on their money-dealing or exchanging, returning to the prison at night. Two husbands paid forty shillings for their pregnant wives to be allowed to go and stay in the London Jewry, which seems to prove that not all the Jews were in prison and there was still a community existing outside.

While it was the usual practice to confiscate the property of all prisoners, even those awaiting trial, it raises the question as to what business remained available to them, and it seems clear that they were able to go on collecting on their debts and even to continue money-dealing, until found guilty. Clues for this can be found in the list of fines, particularly of those Christians caught trying to enter the Tower to contact their creditors. They were apparently eager to redeem their pledges and paid a hefty fine to do so, for even if their debts fell into the control of the Treasury and they might not have to pay interest in future, the king might give their bonds to more ruthless Christians, eager to get their hands on the land or other valued objects given as a pledge, and who would be less restricted in their practices than the original Jewish creditors. Other Christians were caught attempting to exchange their money despite the difficult circumstances in which their exchangers found themselves. Alice of Hackney was caught bringing in silver plate, while John of Woodstock, a merchant, came to reclaim his pledged jewels. Emma of Cornhill, a Christian exchanger, was also found visiting the Tower, while an unknown Christian woman suspected of coming to the Jewry to exchange, fled dropping 100s in the process.

The lists of the fines collected by the Sergeant of the Tower responsible for the Jews give a clear impression of life for those prisoners. The food they paid to import and eat in the Tower included 'a custom of herrings' costing 32s, two calves and the services of a kosher butcher or *shochet*, and the Rosh Hashana New Year meal for four Jews, who also paid to be allowed to keep Yom Kippur. Some poor Jews fined for permission to be allowed to be servants to the others. The 'Jewish vice' of gambling still carried on, as witnessed by the many fines for dicing, and also the fighting that sometimes followed a heated game. There were other outbursts of violence, such as a man attacking someone else's wife, and various scuffles with individual Christians. The servants of Nicholas, a wealthy convert, appear to have come into the Tower and either attempted to repossess some silver cups and spoons or perhaps sell them, and got embroiled in fighting in the process. This could have been a manifestation of the bad feelings against converts that most Jews felt, exacerbated by being under the threat of the trials and their outcome. Spitting as an expression of contempt and insult appeared to be a common feature of medieval life, but one that incurred fines for those in prison. There is some evidence of a little defiance where one man was fined for gainsaying the Sergeant, while a woman dealer paid for a hue and cry when she was robbed. Manser Despenser was accused of pretending to be a bailiff, presumably to illegally collect fines.

BENEDICT ACCUSED AND EXECUTED

Among the individuals to be found imprisoned at the Tower was Licoricia's son, Benedict of Winchester. Ironically, some three years earlier he had been a guarantor for the appearance of two of the Tower's sub-constables who were charged with some offences. In the last reference to him alive, he is described as being in 'his' tower and paying thirteen shillings and four pence, presumably for being free of shackles. Prior to this, he appeared to be riding high, appointed by the king himself as assessor with access to the king and his court. He had become a Keeper of the Queen's Gold in 1275, safeguarding her interests in her rights to the fines paid by Jews.[20] His business interests continued to prosper and his position must have seemed inviolate. As late as June 1277 he was granted the right to trade anywhere in the kingdom, a licence which had to be obtained following the Statute of the Jews.

There were, however, hints of his overstepping the mark on various occasions. Benedict's removal to London as an assessor might have been part of the strategy to defuse the continuing animosity against his elevation in Winchester. Several court cases against him were still on-going at the time of his imprisonment. One was over land, he claimed, as a forfeit pledge from Thomas Peynell and his tenant Geoffrey of Worldham. He had taken over the property from Thomas and Geoffrey, who had then forcibly ejected him, causing considerable damage. In October 1277 Thomas Peynell had been in the king's service and as such possessed the king's writ to 'have such terms for repayment that will cause him not much trouble by payment'. Benedict had been reinstated to the land but the court case continued after his death, being finally resolved in 1281.[21]

Another case concerned Hugh of Fulfloode, whose son-in-law, Edmund de Sutton, had been found guilty of attacking and wounding Benedict's son Abraham, perhaps as a consequence of the bad feelings between the two families that had arisen out of a disagreement over a tally for an alleged loan made on 14 September 1277. The loan had been witnessed by Simon Draper, another indicator of the extent to which Simon was increasingly involved in Benedict's affairs. The enquiry into this wounding was conducted by the justices, Hamo de Hautun and William de Braybeouf, on 18 October 1277. Benedict appeared on behalf of his son and agreed compensation of forty marks and a cask of wine worth four and a half marks. It should be remembered that Benedict was also a wine merchant at this time, as was Simon Draper. Some four and a half years after his father's death, Abraham tried to claim compensation of a hundred marks from Edward de Sutton, only to hear that it had been settled with his father for forty marks and the price of the wine, except for ten marks that had been paid to the King as part of Benedict's chattels. This may have been news to Abraham or he may have known it very well but decided to try his luck. From what we know of both of them, either explanation seems likely. The sum involved in Hugh of Fulfloode's debt was for £60, and Benedict had demanded £40, which he said was outstanding.[22]

As well as occasionally sailing close to the wind while pursuing his business interests with some vigour, Benedict was not slow to protect his own rights. The king specifically referred to his nagging over some bonds that the Exchequer had been slow in returning to him. On another occasion he reactivated a promise that Henry, the king's father, had made to him to give him £60, and which had still not been paid to him when the king died. King Edward was reluctant to fulfil his father's promise unless Benedict could prove its existence, which he did, and the king paid over the sum in bonds.

These importunities would not have endeared him to Edward, particularly as he had also been dragging his feet over paying his taxes dating from 1272, when he had been assessed at £300. He had paid £100 in land to augment Winchester Castle, and another £100 in rent and land near Winchester, but £100 was still outstanding three years later, and the chirographers were ordered to withdraw £50 worth of his 'better bonds' towards it. This may have been a way of putting pressure on him to pay up, and it seems to have worked, for the bonds were returned to him soon afterwards.[23]

Although he was among the most influential and wealthy Jews of his time, Benedict's success seems to have led to him overstepping the line of what was acceptable once too often. The animosity which he attracted culminated in an accusation of coin-clipping, and he was imprisoned in what had probably been his official accommodation, as a servant of the Exchequer, in his rooms in the Tower. He might have suspected that nemesis was approaching, for he was in a position to hear and sense the rumours at court and to have realized that attitudes towards the Jews were worsening; he had lived through similar times before. He may have been arrogant enough to expect that his elevated position might save him. Some of his fellow dealers, who had friends or supporters among the leading nobility or perhaps who bribed them enough, were able to escape the worst punishments. For example, Aaron fil Vives, who was assigned to Prince Edmund, the king's brother, had his protector intercede for him and he was excused from even appearing in court to answer any accusation. He sold his London house soon afterwards, which might have been in order to pay off Prince Edmund.

Benedict, surprisingly, seems to have been unable to command that sort of influence, despite working for Queen Eleanor, and having had Prince Edmund intervene for him before. Perhaps he could not collect a sufficient bribe in time, or he may have been one of the first to be accused, condemned and executed before he even considered that a possible outcome. Maybe, like Abraham Pinche earlier in the century, he was just too unpopular. At some time between 1278 and 1279, Benedict was hanged in London.[24] In all further references to him over the following years, his name is always followed by the words 'who was hanged'.[25]

ASSESSING BENEDICT'S WEALTH

It was the practice of the Treasury to seize the goods of executed felons, and the fate of Benedict's property was no different. The list of Benedict's goods that were confiscated gives a vivid impression both of his personal wealth, and the variety of the goods he took as pledges for loans.[26] There was much 'broken' gold and silver, which was not only used in the manufacture of jewellery but was urgently required whenever a new coinage was being minted. (It must be remembered that Solomon L'Eveske had been recalled from exile specifically because of his ability to gather large amounts of the precious metals.) Benedict left twenty-three gold brooches, ninety-nine gold rings and two golden seals as well as broken gold which brought the estimated value of this collection of bullion alone to £15 15s 9d. Another £20 10s 11d was the total from the silver collection that included six cups with feet and eight without, one silver goblet, two basins, 165 spoons, three large spoons, a penner and inkhorn (a writing set), a key, a girdle of silver thread, a brooch, thirteen rings, a lidded salt cellar and forty-one French silver coins. The broken silver was worth £23 20d, and this could have been cited in the accusation of coin-clipping. Other goods included twenty-three silk girdles and seven of leather barred with silver, old chests and an inkhorn made from wild-ox horn. Other goods acknowledged as being pledges were two gold brooches, five gold rings and a silver cup.

In a subsequent report of the sale of these goods, a somewhat different and more extended list appears, some of which might have come to light after the first list. There are thirty gold brooches, 124 gold rings, and two gold seals that are worth 79s 6d on their own. Most of the combined list was sold, but there remained eight brooches and twenty-five rings valued at £28 11s 2d. The list of silver also varied in that the number of cups had risen to thirteen footed cups, and nine without, and 196 spoons. Left unsold at that time were eight cups and twenty-eight spoons. An additional list of goods, previously unlisted, included precious stones that were found among Benedict's chattels and which included 105 garnets and twenty-four peridots. This seems to indicate that Benedict, or some of his associates, were jewellers in addition to their moneylending activities, but they could have been a collection made as an investment, or again pledges for loans to members of the clergy, or to Jewish jewellers, among others. There were also two cups of jasper, five more silk and eight leather girdles, and as an indication of the worth of his possessions, the five girdles that had not yet been sold were valued at sixty shillings.[27]

The later list included forty-nine books of Jewish law, which Benedict may have inherited from the magnificent library of his stepfather, David of Oxford. He also left fifty-four Latin books, which had probably been placed with him as securities for debts, a 'certain book' valued at nine shillings and eight Jewish books belonging to other Jews, possibly held by Benedict for their debts, or just for safekeeping. This was an outstanding collection to be owned by one individual. The Jewish books that the Exchequer gathered from executed Jews at this time were sold largely abroad, some of them finding their way on to the markets in Germany.

Benedict's houses and some plots of land that he owned in Winchester were sold for £207 7s 8d, and these included two houses in Alwarene Street, and others sited in Wonger Street, Parchment Street, and Calpe Street. Another house in Shorten Street might have been Licoricia's, but was liable for only 5s per annum in landgable, which was a much lower assessment than some of the other properties and seems to indicate something much smaller. Licoricia's house might have gone to the Exchequer in payment of her inheritance fine, or Cokerel may have bought it back from the Crown. Benedict's Shorten Street house went to William de Seleburn, who continued to owe money for it many years later, which implies that some of those who took part in the land-grab of forfeit Jewish houses overstretched their resources. Benedict's houses in Winch Street, Bristol and his daughter Rose's house in Coney Street, York, which Benedict had bought from Aaron of York's widow, were eventually sold too. His Drayton estate in 1281 became the property of Walter of Kent who, as Keeper of the Queen's Gold, may have received it from her, or was holding it for her; a dispute over its boundaries continued for a while. The manor of Chilwarton, formerly Benedict's, was given to Hugh son of Otto,[28] and the house Benedict owned in Romsey Road, which may have afforded access to the Jewish cemetery, seems to have been left for the use of the Jewish community, although the rent for the cemetery remained unpaid for many years by the time of the Expulsion in 1290.

Benedict seems to have taken some steps to safeguard his property in Winchester before his death. He may have made an arrangement with his fellow guildsman and friend, Henry Durngate, who had been involved in many of his business activities in the past, to safeguard some of his valuables. Certainly, Henry was found to be in possession of much of Benedict's property and was accused of buying the goods of hanged Jews including clothes, furs and copper lamps, all of which are absent from the list of the property that was confiscated and sold after Benedict's execution. Henry was fined the massive sum of £1,000, and sent to prison until he could pay it.[29] He remained there for over ten years, before he was allowed to leave on condition that he could find twelve people willing to guarantee that he would pay the balance. It might have been that he was given exemplary punishment because of his close links to Benedict, or that he used that friendship and his knowledge of what Benedict possessed in order to gather as much as he could to sell on.

SURVIVORS AND VICTIMS OF THE POGROM

And what of those whose stories we have related so far? Also mentioned as being in the Tower was Floria of Winchester. Although Floria was a fairly common name, this could have been Benedict's wife. She incurred a minor penalty of six pence, although her offence is not stated. She also paid two shillings to be allowed out of the Tower, which again, if she was Benedict's wife, might have required a bigger payment under the sliding scales that operated.

Of Benedict's brothers, Sweetman escaped with a heavy fine, having to pay over part of a costly golden canopy, and Lumbard was also fined for an Exchange offence in April 1278, when Hildebrand of London, the sheriff of Wiltshire, was instructed to take forty marks from Lumbard's chattels.[30] Cokerel seems to have escaped the accusation. An Abraham son of Benedict also paid some kind of fine in the record, but seems to have committed no other misdemeanour. If this is Benedict's son, he must have been unusually well behaved, although he might have been recovering from his wounds after having been attacked in Winchester the previous year. We know that he survived the trials of 1278/79, unlike so many others. Lumbard, Benedict's closest son, who became chirographer in Winchester when his father went to London, was imprisoned and hanged, probably in Winchester, although his place of execution is never mentioned. Deulebene, the other Jewish chirographer who worked there with Benedict and with Lumbard after his father had gone to London, was also executed in Winchester.

Among the Bedford Jews executed was Benedict, Belia's son, accused of passing light halfpennies in the fish market, and her other son Jacob, who was hanged.[31] Their property was granted to Newnham Priory.[32] A Bella de Bedford is mentioned as being imprisoned in the Tower. If this was our Belia, then it is the last time that we hear of her too. Three members of the Crespin family are also recorded in prison; presumably they would have been in the Guildhall, together with the rest of their community.

NOTES

1. D.A. Carpenter, *The Struggle for Mastery: Penguin History of Britain, 1066–1284* (London: Penguin, 2004), p.479.
2. *Rokeah*, p.185, entry 701, has the king ordering copies to be made for the justices of the Jews. The text is translated in Robin R. Mundill, *England's Jewish Solution: Experiment and Expulsion, 1262–1290* (Cambridge: Cambridge University Press, 1998), pp.291–2.
3. Mundill, *Solution*, p.119 ff. has a discussion of the economic implications of the Statute.
4. *Rokeah*, p.134, entries 530 and 531, show that orders to this effect had already been issued

in 1273.
5. Robin R. Mundill, 'The Jewish Entries from the Patent Rolls, 1271–1292', *JHS*, 32 (1990–2002), pp.25–88, at p.33.
6. For example, *Select Pleas, Starrs and Other Records from the Rolls of the Exchequer of the Jews, AD 1220–1284*, J.M. Rigg (ed.) (London: Selden Society Publications 15, Bernard Quaritch, 1902), p.113.
7. *PREJ*, III, pp.151–2.
8. *Matthaei Parisiensis Chronica Majora*, ed. H.R. Luard, 7 vols (London: Rolls Series, 1872–83), V, p.15.
9. Mundill, 'Jewish Entries', p.63, shows how Winchester Christians benefited from this windfall by buying the goods of hanged Jews and selling them on.
10. Ibid., p.62.
11. Robert C. Stacey, 'Conversion of the Jews to Christianity in Thirteenth-Century England', *Speculum*, 67 (1992), pp.263–83, at pp.276–8.But see now Paul Brand, 'Jews and the Law in England, 1275-1290', *HER*, 115 (2000), 1138–58.
12. A good survey of imprisonment in this period is R.B. Pugh, *Imprisonment in Medieval England* (Oxford: Oxford University Press, 1968).
13. London had been the power base for the Montfortian rebels, and the Tower, where the Treasury had been stored, had been vulnerable. Edward spent more on the rebuilding of the Tower than any other of his extensive castle-construction projects, except Caernarvon. The improvements included strengthening the walls, moat and the Watergate, took ten years to complete and cost some £21,000: Carpenter, *Struggle for Mastery*, p.468.
14. *PREJ*, IV, pp.148–94 has an edition and translation of the lists.
15. James Parkes, *The Jew in the Medieval Community* (London: Soncino Press, 1938; 2nd edn, New York: Herman Press, 1976), p.264.
16. *PREJ*, III, p.277.
17. *Rokeah*, p.258, entry 904.
18. The so-called 'bona' or 'libera' imprisonment: Pugh, *Imprisonment*, p.168.
19. *Matthaei Parisiensis Chronica Majora*, V, p.114.
20. *Rokeah*, p.191, entry 716.
21. *PREJ*, IV, p.104; Lumbard son of Benedict pursued the case later: *PREJ*, VI, p.92, entry 91.
22. An inquisition into the dispute between Benedict and Hugh in 1278 involved ten Christian jurors and six Jews, who included Benedict's brother Cokerel, his half-brother Sweetman, Abraham son of Cokerel and three others. Despite the strong representation of Benedict's family on the jury, Hugh was let off: *PREJ*, V, p.94, entry 543.
23. *Rokeah*, p.99, entry 387 (original assessment), p.106, entry 425 (removal of all Benedict's charters from the Winchester *archa*), p.111, entry 440 (Benedict's terms for payment agreed), p.111, entry 443 (the charters returned), p.169, entry 647 (removal of the 'better and clearer debts') and p.173, entry 656 (Benedict's acknowledgement that he still owes £100).
24. Carpenter Turner says he was hanged in Winchester but it is unlikely that all the condemned Jews were returned to places of origin, particularly as he had been living in London for two years by this time.
25. *Rokeah*, p.262, entry 911 (1281): 'Benedict de Winton, the recently hanged Jew'.
26. Michael Adler, 'Inventory of the Property of the Condemned Jews (1285): Part of a Pipe Roll in the Public Record Office', *MJHSE*, 2 (1935) pp.56–71; Benedict's goods are listed at pp.59–60. The same document shows Deudonne of Winchester's goods were also sold, to Master Ralph the king's *salsarius*.
27. Ibid., pp.66–7.
28. Mundill, 'Jewish Entries', pp.27 and 66.
29. *Fin. R. Edward I, 1272–1307*, p.144. See also *Rokeah*, p.355, entry 1162.
30. *Rokeah*, p.220, entry 812.
31. B. Lionel Abrahams, 'Condition of the Jews in England at the Time of the Expulsion', *TJHSE*, 2 (1894–95), pp.76–105, at p.86, says that Benedict was forcibly baptized and that Jacob then held their joint property until he was hanged. Jacob: *Pat. R. Edward I, 1281–1292*, p.183 and *Rokeah*, pp.339–40, entry 1110.
32. *The Cartulary of Newnham Priory*, I, Joyce Godber (ed.) (Bedford: Bedfordshire Historical Record Society Publications 43, 1963), pp.34 and 35.

CHAPTER TEN

The Final Decade and Expulsion of the Jews

THE AFTERMATH OF THE COIN-CLIPPING POGROM

With the decimation of their numbers by execution, English Jewry across the country had been severely impoverished by the loss of their leading and wealthiest members, and was never able to regain their previous prominent position. Benedict of Winchester was one of some 269 Jews who were executed, including some of the women dealers, the most famous of whom was Belaset of Lincoln, whose stone house stands there to this day. If Christians were ten times more likely to be accused of offences against the currency than Jews, the reverse proportion was true for the numbers executed. During the orgy of executions that swept the country in the winter of 1278/79, orders had to be given to try and halt the looting of empty Jewish houses, and the planting of false evidence. The confiscated property of the victims poured into the Treasury, which benefited by an estimated £10,000.

Those spared capital punishment, such as Asser Sweetman, still incurred heavy fines. Specially appointed officials were put in charge of collecting, evaluating and selling confiscated goods. John le Falconer was appointed to supervise the collection in south-west England but he died before he could take up his duties. His place was taken by William de Braybeouf, a senior justice, local landowner and sheriff of Hampshire from 1278 until his death in 1280. Those in charge kept records of what they found, most of which have long vanished, but among those surviving are some for Winchester, Bristol and Devizes, compiled by William and issued by his widow as executor of his will. It includes the list and estimated value of Benedict's chattels, some of which had been put in the care of the abbot of Waverley, probably by order of the authorities for safekeeping at the time of his arrest, but it is not clear what, if any of the property listed, had come from that subsequently found in the keeping of Henry of Durngate.

The Jewish chattels confiscated or held in safekeeping provided a bonanza for many others besides the king. Some were illegally sold to

Italian merchants and to many others. Apparently well-meaning neighbours and friends who had undertaken to look after belongings for those Jews threatened with imprisonment at the least, kept them after the owners had been executed. Others broke into the Jewish houses when the occupiers were in prison awaiting trial, taking not only the contents but also, in some cases, the fabric of the buildings. The king had ordered that they be repaired: this had less to do with pity for the returning survivors than with concern for the value of the property that became the king's to sell after a finding of guilt. Six years later, an investigation was ordered in an attempt to evaluate how much had been looted and how much lost to the monarch.

While the king seemed satiated by the flood of wealth that had poured into the Exchequer, he was well aware that others had benefited and were still creaming off some of the treasures that should have been his. In March 1278 he postponed for two years another intended tallage on the Jews and this delay, perhaps acknowledging the devastation he had caused, or merely that his clerks had enough to collect in for the time being, makes clear his belief that the Jews could still make up their losses, and that their new riches would be at his disposal. For the surviving Jewish population, the pogrom had been disastrous. Nearly every family had lost at least one member, and in some cases entire families had died. Those who had been found guilty and survived were crippled by the confiscation of most of their property. Others who were allowed to pay a fine for their freedom now had to find the money required, at a time when they were mourning their lost relatives, and attempting to come to grips with a greatly changed financial position. In some cases, they faced complete poverty, and their homes were wrecked or impounded. Those families who had lost none of their immediate members were nevertheless caught up in helping the less fortunate, and even the poorest, who had largely escaped from the accusations, found that they had lost the employment and the income they had previously enjoyed from the wealthier Jews.

By Easter 1279, the Exchequer clerks were struggling to cope with the torrent of riches, and the king piously declared a halt to the executions over Easter. By 1 May, an edict was issued by the king to stop further accusations and trials, if those still in prison paid a fine for their release. Among those allowed to go home were 'Jewesses who were the wives of those condemned or forfeit', but unless they could prove the house had been part of their *ketuba*, they would have no homes to which to return; they would have had to rely on their extended family or the surviving local Jewish community for the payment of their release fine and for their support. On 7 May, a further statement from the king ordered that, 'all those charged and convicted have been punished by death. Because some Christians have attempted to accuse certain Jews and threaten them, those Jews not yet charged must not be charged. They may fine for their release'.

As the Jews struggled to adjust to their utterly changed circumstances, life around them appeared to be much as before. They were still required to attend court hearings into previous debts which had vanished into the Treasury, sometimes on behalf of the their dead relatives. The case of Hugh of Fulfloode against Benedict was first postponed as all the Jews involved were in prison and Benedict had been hanged. Finally, it came back into court, where Benedict's surviving brothers, Sweetman and Cokerel, Cokerel's son Abraham and Cresse, Belia's son, declared that the debt had been settled.

By 1283 King Edward had to face up to the failure of his attempts to stamp out moneylending for interest. Jewish and Christian money-dealers had found various stratagems to circumvent the restrictions of the Statute of Jewry. Fee-rents had developed as a means of dealing with bad debtors and to raise at least some income. Many had for a number of years been dealing in 'futures', that is, investing in goods against the worth they might accrue later; after the Expulsion, many deals involving cereals and wool were recorded. Yet the increasingly hostile legislation from the throne, demands for more restrictions and the enforcement of the Fourth Lateran Council strictures from the pope and other churchmen demonstrated the worsening situation for Jewry. In 1279 a mandate was issued that all the Jews were to 'hear the word of God' preached by the friars.[1] Increasingly during the 1280s, those who could afford to leave the country did so, and by 1289 Edward found that most of the richest Jews had left.

Not all their Christian neighbours were alienated. Among others, some of the senior churchmen sympathized with the ruined Jews and deplored what had happened. For many others, the new situation offered opportunities to benefit from the collapse of the Jewish moneylenders and there was a steep rise in the amount of Christian moneylending carried on at all levels of society. This was despite the disapproval of the church and the threat of damnation, because there always had been Christian competitors offering loans. Some were foreigners, Lombards, Cahorsins and Italians, but Englishmen at all levels of society were involved in monetary dealing, which increased dramatically to take advantage of the collapse and restrictions on Jewish dealers.

QUEEN ELEANOR AND THE JEWS

A supreme example of a Christian who took advantage of the opportunities to make a financial killing from the vacuum in the credit market, following the elimination of so many Jewish dealers in the coin-clipping disaster, is that of the king's wife, Queen Eleanor of Castile.[2] Until she came to the throne, queens had little income of their own, depending on their husband's financial support and whatever they had brought with them from their parents. The institution of the Queen's Gold had been created as a way of supplying them with an income of their own, and they were entitled to 10 per cent of all the fines that the Jews paid. From 1268, Eleanor began to ruthlessly pursue her rights to the Queen's Gold, and she was able to have the fund extended to include the entire belongings of those who were executed or had been allotted to her. This had been operational in earlier times, but was never so ruthlessly pursued by previous queens. The establishment of the Jewish Exchequer and the accounting and documentation it instituted meant that this fund became more accessible. Eleanor saw it as her personal income, a fund to safeguard her position and that of her family, and on acquiring Jewish debts, she foreclosed on selected debts where she wanted the pledged lands to extend her estates. She dealt in the debts themselves, giving them to her servants as payment or as gifts, and she employed her own Jews, accountable to herself, to farm the debts for the usury they brought in.

There was a sequence of Queen's Jews over the years, most notably Hagin fil Cresse, who was granted to her with all his debts in 1275 when he had been excommunicated from Jewry by the Beth Din. Three years later, Eleanor had got hold of his debts, worth a total of £5,262 6s 8d. In acquiring them, she let him continue to manage some on her behalf, presumably the ones where the property pledges were of lesser interest to her, and at her request he was made archpresbyter of the Jews in 1281, hardly a diplomatic appointment in view of his earlier excommunication. This was an appointment made by the king, and he was meant to be a spokesman with some jurisdiction over his co-religionists. Needless to say, this appointment was most unpopular with the Jewish community who requested that in future they name their own leading spokesman. Hagin was still serving the queen in 1290 and she obtained a licence for him to sell his houses in London, so that he could carry his remaining wealth into exile.

Eleanor also appointed Keepers of the Queen's Gold at the Jewish Exchequer, to look after her interests and monitor the Jewish fines for her share. Richard de Bures, her household controller, was one of these, as were Walter of Kent and Walter de Albini, but she also appointed Jews to safeguard her interests, with their inside knowledge of Jewish wealth. Jacob of Oxford was one of these. She had had dealings with him since 1268, and while he was not her exclusive possession like Hagin, he worked for her until 1276, when he went mad and died, whereupon she claimed that he had been 'her' Jew and confiscated his entire estate, leaving his widow, Hannah, destitute. To replace him, she chose Benedict of Winchester, who as we have seen had recently been appointed an assessor at the Exchequer, estimating the levels of tallage to be paid by the Jewish community. She had been involved with him since 1268 when her father-in-law, King Henry, had allowed her the management of two estates, one of which was the Ernham debt in which Benedict had been so closely involved. The following year she had specifically requested that he should have the freedom to hunt through the chirograph chests across the country in search of evidence for his charters that had disappeared during the upheaval of the Barons' Wars.

The queen herself was generous to her servants, advancing their interests where she could. Her tailor, William Somerfield, whom we have already met as the ultimate beneficiary in the Ernham case,[3] was not merely her outfitter, but the collector of her precious metals and jewellery. With her help, he had begun to take advantage of the new licences to buy bonds from Jews.[4] He became very wealthy, and after her death made a donation in her memory at St Paul's, an appreciation perhaps of how much he owed his status and wealth to her.

This was also a time when there were many instances of Christians forming alliances with Jewish moneylenders, to their mutual advantage. The Jews could lend money against securities of land which they could not sell, but in a joint deal their Christian partners would buy from them. This was of course profiting from the forbidden usury, and the archbishop of Canterbury, John Pecham, repeatedly warned the queen that her soul was in jeopardy.[5] Yet, devoted Christian as she undoubtedly was, she ignored his warnings and admonishments to give up dealing in Jewish debt and the land she acquired through foreclosing on them which, he said, was tantamount to usury and generated scandal throughout the kingdom.

Eleanor of Castile was secure in the love and admiration of her husband the king, who supported his queen in her pursuit of wealth. After her death in 1290, the grieving husband had the Eleanor Crosses set up wherever her coffin rested on its way back to London. He knew that what she had been doing was very questionable, both morally and legally, as revealed by the £1,000 he donated towards compensation to be allocated by an enquiry that he commissioned into the complaints against her after her death. This was carried out by Ralph of Ivinghoe in three centres, Westminster, Bury St Edmunds and Salisbury, so that it could be reasonably near to her greatest estates. For the poor people from Hampshire, the Isle of Wight and distant Devon, it was still a considerable distance to travel, and once there, they would have to spend a long time waiting around to be called. One hundred and ten cases were heard from individuals coming from nineteen different counties, including twenty-nine from Norfolk, twenty-one from Kent, fourteen from Exeter and eleven from Hampshire.[6] The testimony of those who appeared before the enquiry told of events that were barbarous even by the standards of the day, involving beatings, a baby abandoned by the roadside, torture, imprisonment for long periods, unlawful dispossession and death. Eleanor's victims, the debtors and tenants who lost their land and livelihood, bitterly resented the queen's activities. A verse dating from that time reflects the general view: 'The king would like to get our gold / The queen our manors fair to hold'.[7]

While the worst of these atrocities were carried out by the queen's agents, particularly Walter of Kent, the queen was named as the source of their injustices. Mundill terms her 'particularly anti-Jewish'.[8] Even when the courts had ruled that some of the dispossessed should be reinstated and that certain illegal payments be repaid, her officials had simply ignored the courts. Sixty to seventy wrongful land seizures were recorded, the majority of them in the south-western and southern counties. The £1,000 pounds allocated as compensation was not fully paid out; the poorest could not travel to the courts, and some must have suspected that they were unlikely to benefit. Although when on her deathbed, the queen had requested that if anyone had suffered they should be compensated, she did not refer specifically to her business deals. That Edward had called for such a hearing at all is quite extraordinary, and the fact that he caused the Eleanor Crosses and the inquiry to be set up shows a recognition of both contradictory aspects of his wife's character. Parsons calls her 'hard-nosed and downright heartless' and refers to the 'unpleasant contradictions' in her personality. But Edward was devoted to her, and they had some fifteen or sixteen children, of whom only one son and five daughters were surviving when she died. Edward had helped her in her financial acquisitions, turning a blind eye to some of her excesses, and indulging her demands for still more rights to Jewish wealth, which not only reduced the need for him to pay for her extravagances out of his own pocket, but would in the long run benefit himself and their many children. Parsons declares that, 'Edward so tangled her finances with Jews only expulsion (of them) could untangle her'. Indeed, it has been suggested that by letting Eleanor preoccupy herself with the acquisition of land and wealth, the king was able to keep her from meddling in affairs of state and out of his own political concerns. Queen Eleanor of Castile died on 28 November 1290, just three weeks after the date set for Jews to be finally expelled.

EXPULSION

By 1290 Edward had long decided to expel the Jews from England. The pressures on him to do so were financial and political, as well as his personal wish to rid his realm of non-Christians. The Jews themselves, although slowly recovering from the impoverishment following the limitations of the Statute for Jews of 1275 and the coin-clipping pogrom, were still demoralized and unable to produce the level of finance that the king required and expected from them.

By 1286 Pope Honorius IV had demanded increasing restrictions to emphasize the separation of Christians and Jews, and Edward was inclined to follow this path more enthusiastically than any other monarch. He had re-imposed the 'badge', and had since June 1280 been pursuing a rigorous campaign of conversion, which involved enforced attendance of the Jewish community at special meetings run by Franciscan monks. Simultaneously, he opened more houses for the converted in London and reviewed the provisions for them. As an inducement, he waived his claim to converts' property for the first seven years following conversion, and then promised they could keep half, but all of this failed to produce the mass conversions he hoped for. The houses for converts were funded by a special poll tax called a *chevage* on all Jewish males above the age of eleven, and females of twelve.

David Carpenter believes that, during a bout of severe illness while in Gascony, Edward made a pledge to God to expel the Jews if he recovered.[9] He went on to expel his Jews from the region and had confiscated property and chattels, as well as acquiring all the registered bonds, which had yielded a nice little windfall for the king. Edward found it increasingly difficult to secure a steady and adequate income for his extensive castle-building programme and his wars in France, Wales and Scotland. He relied on Italian bankers, such as the Riccardi family of Lucca for his everday maintenance, and he was able to placate them for a while by allowing them to collect his taxes. Another money-raiser was the customs duty collected from the export of wool, but he was anxious to establish his income on a more reliable footing. The Jews had failed to recover enough to meet his tallage demands, and although parliament had previously denied him a financial lifeline, he was made aware that this would be granted if he evicted the Jews.

It has also been suggested that his mother, Eleanor, had been urging him to do this. She had, with his permission, expelled the Jews from all her dower towns in England in 1275, among them Asser Sweetman from Marlborough, whence he had gone to Devizes. Over the years Jews had been evicted from many towns across the country, and generally they either were made to go to named towns or they moved where they had family or friends. This increased the congestion in the favoured towns and caused some tensions. Because some of them still had business in the towns they had left, they fined for permission to visit them and in some cases were allowed to retain houses to stay in while pursuing their debts.

By the 1280s there is plenty of evidence of Jews operating in unapproved localities elsewhere in the country. The instruction that they should move to those towns where *archae* were supervised by chirographers had been repeated many times, and sheriffs were specifically ordered to bring in those reported to be living outside these centres. By 1290, the Jews were confined to living in just twenty towns, thirteen of which, including Winchester, had contained a Jewish population residing there continuously for some 150 years.

By the summer of 1290 the king had summoned a parliament to discuss the possibility of a tax being granted, although he had probably been sounding out this possibility for some time. Before the parliament could actually meet, he had apparently decided instead to expel the Jewish community. He ordered his sheriffs to make certain that the Jews were not molested and enabled to leave in safety. They were to be allowed to take with them whatever money and valuables they could carry, and their bonds, although a time limit was placed on the settlement of loans and the return of pledges. It is not in any case clear what they could do with these bonds once they were abroad, and certainly most were left behind and continued to be dealt with over very many years after the Expulsion.[10]

During the seventeenth century, an historian called Patrick Junius examined the ruins of Winchester where he found an inscription carved on a wall in what he called 'an old vault in the South Tower', which was probably the remains of the Jews' Tower, where the Jews were imprisoned or offered sanctuary. The inscription was in Hebrew: 'On Friday, eve of the Sabbath in which the pericope Emor is read, all the Jews of the land of the isle were imprisoned. I, Asher, inscribed this . . . "

This must refer to the imprisonment of Jews on 2 May 1287 in advance of a tallage for 20,000 marks. Junius reported his discovery to John Selden, the renowned historian and map maker.[11] Here, according to Roth,[12] we have the voice of Licoricia and David's son echoing across some five centuries after he was expelled. There is no evidence for such an identification, other than the comparative rarity of the name. The inscription does not survive, but it is a fitting end to our story of the family, and one which demonstrates the spirit of the medieval Anglo-Jewish community even in extreme adversity.

NOTES

1. Robin R. Mundill, 'The Jewish Entries from the Patent Rolls, 1271–1292', *JHS*, 32 (1990–92), pp.25–88, at pp.39 and 61.
2. The following discussion is largely based on John Carmi Parsons, *Eleanor of Castile: Queen and Society in 13th-Century England* (London: Macmillan, 1995) and John Carmi Parsons, *The Court and Household of Eleanor of Castile* (Toronto: Pontifical Institute of Medieval Studies, 1977).
3. See above, p.102.
4. *Pat. R. Henry III, 1266–1272* (Hereford, 1913), p.360.
5. He is quoted in Parsons, *Eleanor of Castile*, p.120.
6. Muriel Fenwick, 'The Inquiry into Complaints against the Ministers of Eleanor of Castille, 1291-2: Its Administrative and Legal Significance'. MA thesis, University of London, 1931.
7. Walter of Guiseborough, quoted in Robert C. Stacey, 'Parliamentary Negotiation and the Expulsion of the Jews from England', in M. Prestwich, R.H. Britnell and R.R. Frame (eds), *Thirteenth-Century England, VI: Proceedings of the Durham Conference, 1995* (Woodbridge: Boydell, 1995), pp.77–101, at p.81.
8. Mundill, 'Jewish Entries', p.28.
9. D.A. Carpenter, *The Struggle for Mastery: Penguin History of Britain 1066–1284* (London: Penguin, 2004), p.489.
10. Lionel B. Abrahams, 'Condition of the Jews in England at the Time of the Expulsion', *TJHS*, 2 (1894–95), pp.76–105, at p.86 onwards, lists the goods of Jews granted in 1291 to eighty-five recipients. The property includes corn owned by Cok and Aaron, sons of Benedict of Winchester, at Canterbury, Belia widow of Jacob, Avegaye's house in Oxford, Sweetman's house and tenement in Winchester, plus twenty-four quarters of corn, £140 of Sweetman son of David of Oxford, and a house and *scola* (school) of Jacob son of Cokerel at Winchester owing rent to the abbey of Hyde.
11. John Selden, *Treatise on the Jews in England* (1617).
12. Cecil Roth, *A History of the Jews in England* (Oxford: Clarendon Press, 3rd edn 1965), p.273.

Epilogue: Looking for Licoricia

Sue Bartlet spent over a decade looking for Licoricia, and wrote several pieces about her research.[1] Just as Licoricia had died in suspicious circumstances, so the rediscovery of what was believed to be Winchester's Jewish cemetery, where she was almost certainly buried, attracted a similar level of attention and comment. No sooner had human remains been found than a deputation from the Chief Rabbi visited Winchester and demanded to take them away for reburial.[2] They now lie in a cordoned-off part of the Jewish cemetery in Manchester. The excavation, which was in advance of redevelopment, did not reveal the full extent of the cemetery, but the section which was excavated contained mainly the remains of children and women. It seems unlikely that we shall ever have the opportunity to investigate the make-up of Winchester's Jewish population from its physical remains, as was done so successfully in York. Nor is it easy to reconstruct Jewish social life in medieval England from the largely fiscal documents. But Sue's painstaking enquiry into Licoricia and her friends and family will surely stimulate other scholars to look again at the Winchester Jewry, and give this community the attention it surely deserves.

NOTES

1. See above, Editor's Preface, p.x, note 1.
2. *The Observer*, 16 June 1996, carries the story.

Bibliography

UNPUBLISHED SOURCES

Winchester Museums Service, papers on the defences of Winchester, held at Hyde Historic Resources Centre, Winchester.

PRIMARY SOURCES IN PRINT

Abrahams, I., 'The Northampton *Donum* of 1194', *MJHSE*, 1 (1925), pp.59–87.

Adler, Michael, 'Inventory of the Property of the Condemned Jews (1285): Part of a Pipe Roll in the Public Record Office', *MJHSE*, 2 (1935), pp.56–71.

Annales Monastici, ed. H.R. Luard, 5 vols, II: Winchester and Waverley; IV: Oseney (London: Rolls Series, Longman and Green, 1864–69).

Building Accounts of King Henry III, H.M. Colvin (ed.) (Oxford: Oxford University Press, 1971).

Calendar of the Charter Rolls of the Reign of Henry III: 1226–1257 (London: HMSO, 1903).

Calendar of the Fine Rolls of the Reign of Henry III, I, 1–8 Henry III (1216–1224), Paul Drybergh and Beth Hartland (eds) (London/Woodbridge: National Archives/Boydell, 2007).

Calendar of the Fine Rolls: Edward I 1272–1307 (London: HMSO, 1911).

Calendar of Inquisitions Post Mortem in the Public Records Office: I: Henry III (London: Public Records Office, 1904).

Calendar of Inquisitions Post Mortem in the Public Records Office: II: Edward I (London: Public Records Office, 1906).

Calendar of the Liberate Rolls: Henry III 1226–1240 (London: HMSO, 1916).

Calendar of the Liberate Rolls: Henry III 1240–1245 (London: HMSO, 1930).

Calendar of the Liberate Rolls: Henry III 1245–1251 (London: HMSO, 1937).

Calendar of Patent Rolls of the Reign of Edward I: 1272–1281 (London: HMSO, 1901).
Calendar of Patent Rolls of the Reign of Edward I: 1281–1292 (London: HMSO, 1893).
Calendar of the Patent Rolls of the Reign of Henry III: 1216–1225 (London: HMSO, 1891).
Calendar of the Patent Rolls of the Reign of Henry III: 1225–1232 (London: HMSO, 1903).
Calendar of the Patent Rolls of the Reign of Henry III: 1232–1247 (London: HMSO, 1906).
Calendar of the Patent Rolls of the Reign of Henry III: 1266–1272 (London: HMSO, 1913).
Calendar of the Plea Rolls of the Exchequer of the Jews, I, J.M. Rigg (ed.) (London: Macmillan for the Jewish Historical Society of England, 1905); II, J.M. Rigg (ed.) (Edinburgh: Ballantyne for JHSE, 1910); III, Hilary Jenkinson (ed.) (London: Spottiswoode for JHSE, 1929); IV, H.G. Richardson (ed.) (London: JHSE, 1972); V, Sarah Cohen (ed.) (London: JHSE, 1992); VI, Paul Brand (ed.) (London: JHSE, 2005).
The Cartulary of Newnham Priory, I, Joyce Godber (ed.), 2 vols (Bedford: Bedfordshire Historical Record Society Publications no. 43, 1963–64).
Cartulary of Oseney Abbey, ed. H.E. Salter, 6 vols (Oxford: Clarendon Press, 1929–36).
Charter Rolls 1194–1216 (see *Rotuli*).
Charter Rolls II: 1253–1300 (London: HMSO, 1906).
The Chronicle of Richard of Devizes, John T. Appleby (ed.) (London: Nelson, 1963).
Chronicles of the Reigns of Stephen, Henry II and Richard I, Richard Howlett (ed.), 4 vols (London: Longman, 1884–89).
Close Rolls 1204–1227 (see *Rotuli*).
Close Rolls of the Reign of Henry III: 1227–1231 (London: HMSO, 1902).
Close Rolls of the Reign of Henry III: 1231–1234 (London: HMSO, 1905).
Close Rolls of the Reign of Henry III: 1234–1237 (London: HMSO, 1908).
Close Rolls of the Reign of Henry III: 1237–1242 (London: HMSO, 1911).
Close Rolls of the Reign of Henry III: 1242–1247 (London: HMSO, 1916).

Close Rolls of the Reign of Henry III: 1247–1251 (London: HMSO, 1922).
Close Rolls of the Reign of Henry III: 1251–1253 (London: HMSO, 1927).
Close Rolls of the Reign of Henry III: 1253–1254 (London: HMSO, 1929).
Close Rolls of the Reign of Henry III: 1254–1256 (London: HMSO, 1931).
Close Rolls of the Reign of Henry III: 1256–1259 (London: HMSO, 1932).
Close Rolls of the Reign of Henry III: 1259–1261 (London: HMSO, 1934).
Close Rolls of the Reign of Henry III: 1261–1264 (London: HMSO, 1936).
Close Rolls of the Reign of Henry III: 1264–1268 (London: HMSO, 1937).
Close Rolls of the Reign of Henry III: 1268–1272 (London: HMSO, 1938).
Corcos, Ada, 'Extracts from the Close Rolls, 1279–1288', *TJHSE*, 4 (1899–1901), pp.202-19.
Curia Regis Rolls of the Reigns of Richard I and John, VII: 1213–1215 (London: HMSO, 1935).
Documents Illustrative of English History in the 13th and 14th Centuries: Selected from the Records of the Department of the Queen's Remembrancer of Exchequer, Henry Cole (ed.) (London: Eyre and Spottiswoode, 1844).
English Episcopal Acta 9: Winchester, 1205–1238, N. Vincent (ed.) (Oxford: Oxford University Press, 1994).
English Historical Documents, III: 1189–1327, Harry Rothwell and D.C. Douglas (eds) (London: Methuen, 1975).
Excerpta è Rotulis Finium in Turri Londiniensis Asservatis, II (1246–1272), C. Roberts (ed.) (London: Public Records, 1836).
Great Roll of the Pipe for the 8th Year of King John, D.M. Stenton (ed.) (London: Pipe Roll Society, 1942).
Jacobs, Joseph, (ed.), *The Jews of Angevin England: Documents and Records from Latin and Hebrew Sources* (London: David Nutt, 1893).
Matthaei Parisiensis Chronica Majora, H.R. Luard (ed.), 7 vols (London: Rolls Series 57, 1872–83).
Medieval English Jews and Royal Officials: Entries of Jewish Interest in

the English Memoranda Rolls, 1266–1293, Zefira Entin Rokeah (ed. and trans.) (Jerusalem: The Hebrew University Magnes Press, 2000).
Medieval Jewish Documents in Westminster Abbey, Ann Causton (ed.) (London: JHSE, 2007).
Prynne, William, *The Second Part of a Short Demurrer to the Jews* (London, 1652).
Receipt and Issue Rolls in the 26th year of the Reign of King Henry III, 1241–2, R.C. Stacey (ed.) (London: Rolls Series, NS 49, 1992).
Records of the Wardrobe and Household, B.F. and C.R. Byerly (eds), 2 vols (London: HMSO, 1977 and 1986).
Rotuli Chartarum, 1194–1216 (London: Record Commission, 1837).
Rotuli Litterarum Clausarum in Turri Londinensi Asservati, T.D. Hardy (ed.), 2 vols (London: Records Commission, 1833–44).
Royal and Other Historical Letters Illustrative of the Reign of King Henry III, W.W. Shirley (ed.), 2 vols (London: Longman, 1862–66).
Select Pleas, Starrs and Other Records from the Rolls of the Exchequer of the Jews, AD 1220–1284, J.M. Rigg (ed.) (London: Selden Society Publications 15, Bernard Quaritch, 1902).
Shetaroth: Hebrew Deeds of English Jews before 1290, M.D. Davis (ed.) (London: Jewish Chronicle, 1888).
Starrs and Jewish Charters Preserved in the British Museum, Israel Abrahams and H.P. Stokes (eds) with additions by Herbert Loewe, 3 vols, I (Cambridge: Cambridge University Press for the Jewish Historical Society of England, 1930); II and III (London: Spottiswoode for the Jewish Historical Society of England, 1932).
Winchester College Muniments, vol. 3: Estates, Sheila Himsworth, Peter Gwyn and John Hooper Harvey (eds) (Chichester: Phillimore, 1976).

SECONDARY WORKS

Abrahams, B. Lionel, 'Condition of the Jews in England at the Time of their Expulsion in 1290', *TJHSE*, 2 (1894–95), pp.76–105.
—— *Expulsion of the Jews from England in 1290* (Oxford: Oxford University Press, 1895).
Abrahams, Israel, *Jewish Life in the Middle Ages* (Philadelphia, PA: Jewish Publication Society of America, 1896).
Abulafia, Anna Sapir, 'An Attempt by Gilbert Crispin, Abbot of Westminster, at Rational Argument in the Jewish-Christian Debate', *Studia Monastica*, 26 (1984), pp.55–74.

────── 'From Northern Europe to Southern Europe and from the General to the Particular: Recent Research on Jewish-Christian Co-existence in Medieval Europe', *JMH*, 23 (1997), pp.179–89.

Adler, Michael, 'The Jews of Canterbury', *TJHSE*, 7 (1911–14), pp.19–96.

────── 'The Jews of Bristol in Pre-Expulsion Days', *TJHSE*, 12 (1928–31), pp.117–86.

────── 'Jewish Tallies of the 13th Century', *MJHSE*, 2 (1935), pp.8–24.

────── 'An Unpublished Pipe Roll of 1285: Inventory of the Property of Condemned Jews', *MJHSE*, 2 (1935), pp.56–71.

────── 'The Testimony of the London Jewry against the Ministers of King Henry III', *TJHSE*, 14 (1935–39), pp.141–85.

────── *Jews of Medieval England* (London: JHSE, 1939).

────── 'Benedict the Gildsman of Winchester', *MJHSE*, 4 (1942), pp.1–9.

Allin, Patricia, 'Medieval Southampton and Its Jews', *TJHSE*, 23 (1970), pp.87–95.

────── 'Richard of Devizes and the Alleged Martyrdom of a Boy at Winchester', *TJHSE*, 27 (1978–80), pp.32–9.

Amt, Emily, *Women's Lives in Medieval Europe: A Sourcebook* (London: Routledge, 1993).

Ashe, Lincoln F., *The Legal Background to the Starrs* (London: Edward Goldston, 1932).

Bailey, Jo, 'City Walls Project, 1984–5', *Find*, 36 (1984).

Bale, Anthony P., 'Richard of Devizes and Fictions of Judaism', *JCH*, 3 (2001), pp.55–72.

────── 'Fictions of Judaism in England before 1290', in Patricia Skinner (ed.), *Jews in Medieval Britain*, (Woodbridge: Boydell, 2003), pp.129–44.

Bartlet, Suzanne, 'Three Jewish Businesswomen in Thirteenth-Century Winchester', *Jewish Culture and History*, 3 (2000), pp.31–54.

────── 'Women in the Medieval Anglo-Jewish Community', in Patricia Skinner (ed.), *Jews in Medieval Britain*, (Woodbridge: Boydell, 2003), pp.113–27.

────── 'Discovering Licoricia', *The New Light*, 46, 2 (Winter, 2003), pp.35–6.

Bartlett, Robert, *England under the Norman and Angevin Kings, 1075–1225* (Oxford: Clarendon Press, 2000).

Baskin, Judith R., 'Jewish Women in the Middle Ages', in Judith R.

Baskin (ed.) *Jewish Women in Historical Perspective*, (Detroit, MI: Wayne State University Press, 1991), pp.94–114.

Biddle, Martin, 'Excavations in Winchester', *Antiquaries Journal*, 45 (1965), pp.258–60.

—— *Wolvesey* (London: English Heritage, 1986).

—— *King Arthur's Round Table: An Archaeological Investigation* (Woodbridge: Boydell, 2000).

—— and Clayre, Beatrice, *Winchester Castle and the Great Hall* (Winchester: Hampshire County Council, 1983).

Blair, I., J. Hillaby, I. Howell, R. Sermon and B. Watson, 'The Discovery of Two Medieval *Mikva'ot* in London and a Reinterpretation of the Bristol *Mikveh*', *JHS*, 27 (2002), pp.32–4.

Bowers, R.H., 'From Rolls to Riches: King's Clerks and Moneylending in 13th-Century England', *Speculum*, 58 (1983), pp.60–71.

Boyle, David, *Blondel's Song: The Capture, Imprisonment and Ransom of Richard the Lionheart* (London: Viking, 2005).

Brown, R. Allen, 'Royal Castle-Building in England, 1154–1216', *English Historical Review*, 70 (1955), pp.353–98.

—— and Colvin, H.M., 'The Royal Castles, 1066–1485', in H.M. Colvin, *History of the King's Works*, 6 vols (London: HMSO, 1963–82), vol. II, pp.706–29.

Carmi Parsons, J., *The Court and Household of Eleanor of Castile in 1290* (Toronto: Pontifical Institute of Medieval Studies, 1977).

—— 'The Patronage of Queens: Margaret and Isabella', in M. Prestwich, R.H. Britnell and R.R. Frame (eds), *Thirteenth-Century England, VI: Proceedings of the Durham Conference, 1995*, (Woodbridge: Boydell, 1995), pp.145–56.

—— *Eleanor of Castile: Queen and Society in 13th-Century England* (London: Macmillan, 1995).

Carpenter, D.A., *The Struggle for Mastery: Penguin History of Britain 1066–1284* (London: Penguin, 2004).

—— 'An Unknown Obituary of King Henry III in 1263', in D. A. Carpenter, *The Reign of Henry III* (London: Hambledon and London, 2003).

Carpenter Turner, Barbara, 'The Winchester Jewry', *Hampshire Review* (1954), pp.17–21.

—— 'The Winchester Jewry', *Anglo-Jewish Association Quarterly*, 1, no. 4 (March 1956), pp.120–5.

—— 'Benedict the Guildsman', *Hampshire Chronicle*, 27 January 1962.

—— *A History of Winchester* (Chichester: Phillimore, 1992).

Chazan, Robert, *In the Year 1096: The First Crusade and the Jews* (New York: Jewish Publication Society, 1997).
Chew, Helena, 'A Jewish Aid to Marry, 1221', *TJHSE*, 11 (1924–27), pp.92–111.
Cheney, C.R. (ed.) *A Handbook of Dates for Students of British History*, (Cambridge: Cambridge University Press, 2nd edn, 2000).
Cohen, Sarah, 'Oxford Jewry in the 13th Century', *TJHSE*, 13 (1932–35), pp.293–322.
Coulton, G.G., *A Medieval Panorama*, (Cambridge: Cambridge University Press, 1938).
Cramer, A.C., 'Origins and Functions of the Jewish Exchequer', *Speculum*, 16 (1941), pp.226–9.
Cunliffe, Barry, 'The Winchester City Wall', *Hampshire Field Club Papers*, 22 (1961), pp.51–81.
——— *Winchester Excavations, 1949–1960*, I (Winchester: City of Winchester Research and Libraries Committee, 1964).
Davies, J.S., *History of Southampton* (Southampton: no pub., 1883).
Davies, R., 'The Medieval Jews of York', *Yorkshire Archaeological Journal*, 3 (1875), pp.148–97.
Davis, M.D., 'Early Winchester Jews', *Jewish Chronicle*, 16 September 1892.
——— 'An Anglo-Jewish Divorce', *JQR*, 5 (1893), pp.158–65.
Dobson, R.B., *Jews of Medieval York and the Massacre of March 1190* (York: Borthwick Papers 45, 1974).
——— 'The Decline and Expulsion of the Medieval Jews at York', *TJHSE*, 26 (1974–78), pp.34–52.
——— 'The Jews of Medieval Cambridge', *JHS*, 32 (1990–92), pp.1–24.
——— 'The Role of Jewish Women in Medieval England', in D. Wood (ed.), *Christianity and Judaism: Studies in Church History* 29 (Oxford: Blackwell for the Ecclesiastical History Society, 1992), pp.145–69.
——— 'The Medieval York Jewry Reconsidered', in Patricia Skinner (ed.), *Jews in Medieval Britiain*, (Woodbridge: Boydell, 2003), pp.145–56.
Dubrowolski, P., 'Women and their Dower in the Long 13th Century, 1265–1329', in M. Prestwich, R.H. Britnell and R.R. Frame (eds), *Thirteenth-Century England, VI: Proceedings of the Durham Conference, 1995*, (Woodbridge: Boydell, 1995), pp.157–64.
Epstein, I., 'Pre-Expulsion England in the *Responsa*', *TJHSE*, 14 (1935–39), pp.187–205.
Fenwick, Muriel, 'The Inquiry into Complaints against the Ministers of

Eleanor of Castile, 1291–2: Its Administrative and Legal Significance'. MA thesis, University of London, 1931.

Fletcher, Richard, *Bloodfeud: Murder and Revenge in Anglo-Saxon England*, (London: Penguin, 2003).

Fletcher Jones, Pamela, *The Jews of Britain: A Thousand Years of History* (London: Windrush, 1990).

Frassetto, Michael (ed.) *Christian Attitudes toward the Jews in the Middle Ages*, (New York: Routledge, 2007).

Gilbert, Martin, (ed.), *The Jewish Historical Atlas* (London: Weidenfeld, 3rd edn, 1985).

Gomersall, Malcolm, 'The Jewish Population of Medieval Winchester', *Winchester Museum Service Newsletter*, 15 (July 1992), pp.3–6.

Gross, C. 'The Exchequer of the Jews of England in the Middle Ages', *Anglo-Jewish Historical Exhibition Papers* (London: Anglo-Jewish History Society, 1888), pp.170–210.

Grossman, Avraham, 'Medieval Rabbinic Views on Wife-Beating', *Jewish History*, 5 (1991), pp.53–62.

Hampshire Treasures Survey (Winchester: Hampshire County Council, 1953).

Harding, A., *England in the 13th Century* (Cambridge: Cambridge University Press, 1993).

Hillaby, Joe, 'Hereford Gold, Irish, Welsh and English Land: The Jewish Community at Hereford and its Clients, 1179–1253', Parts 1, 2 and 3, *Transactions of the Woolhope Naturalists Field Club*, 44 (1984), pp.358–419; ibid., 45 (1985), pp.193–270; ibid., 46 (1990), pp.432–87.

―――― 'A Magnate among the Marchers: Hamo of Hereford, His Family and Clients,1218–1253', *JHS*, 31 (1988–90), pp.23–82.

―――― 'The Worcester Jewry, 1158–1290: Portrait of a Lost Community', *Transactions of the Worcestershire Archaeological Society*, 3rd ser. 12 (1990), pp.73–122.

―――― 'Beth Miqdash Me'at: The Synagogues of Medieval England', *Journal of Ecclesiastical History*, 44 (1993), pp.182–98.

―――― 'London: The 13th-Century Jewry Revisited', *JHS*, 32 (1990–92), pp.89–158.

―――― 'The London Jewry: William I to John', *JHS*, 33 (1992–94), pp.1–44.

―――― 'Testimony from the Margin: The Gloucester Jewry and Its Neighbours', *JHS*, 37 (2002), pp.41–112.

―――― 'Jewish Colonisation in the Twelfth Century', in Patricia Skinner (ed.), *Jews in Medieval Britain* (Woodbridge: Boydell, 2003), pp.15–40.

Honeybourne, M.J., 'The Pre-Expulsion Cemetery of the Jews in London', *TJHSE*, 20 (1964), p.146.

Hurnard, N.D., *The King's Pardon for Homicide before AD 1307* (Oxford: Clarendon Press, 1969).

Hyams, Paul, 'The Jewish Minority in Medieval England, 1066–1290', *Journal of Jewish Studies*, 25 (1974), pp.271–93.

Jacob, W.H., *The History .... and Survey of the Antiquities of Winchester*, 2 vols (Winchester, 1809).

——— 'The West Gate of Winchester', *Hampshire Field Club Papers*, 4 (1893–1903), pp.51–8.

Jacobs, Joseph, 'London Jews in 1290', *Anglo-Jewish Historical Exhibition Papers* (London, 1888), pp.20–53.

——— *The Jews of Angevin England* (London: David Nutt, 1893).

James, T., *The Book of Winchester* (London: Batsford for English Heritage, 1997).

Jenkinson, Hilary, 'The Records of the Exchequer Receipts from the English Jewry', *TJHSE*, 8 (1918), pp.19–54.

——— 'Jewish Entries in the Curia Regis Rolls and Elsewhere', *MJHSE*, 5 (1948), pp.128–35.

——— 'Medieval Sources for Anglo-Jewish History: The Problem of Publication', *TJHSE*, 18 (1955), pp.285–93.

Jolles, Michael, *A Short History of the Jews of Northampton, 1159–1196* (London: Jolles Publications, 1996).

Jordan, W.C., *The French Monarchy and the Jews: From Philip Augustus to the Last Capetians* (Philadephia, PA: University of Pennsylvania Press, 1989).

Katz, D., 'The Marginalisation of Early Modern Anglo-Jewish History', in T. Kushner (ed.), *The Jewish Heritage in British History: Englishness and Jewishness* (London: Frank Cass, 1992).

Keene, Derek, *Survey of Medieval Winchester*, Winchester Studies 2, 2 vols (Oxford: Clarendon Press, 1985).

Kisch, G., 'The Yellow Badge in History', *Historica Judaica*, 4.2 (1942).

Kitchen, G.W., *Winchester* (London: Historic Towns Series, 1890).

Kushner, Tony, *Anglo-Jewry since 1066: Place, Memory, Locality* (Manchester: Manchester University Press, 2009).

Labarge, Margaret Wade, *Simon de Montfort* (New York: Norton, 1963; repr. London: Eyre and Spottiswoode, 1975).

——— *Mistresses, Maids and Men* (London: Phoenix Press, 2003).

Langmuir, G., 'Jews and the Archives of Angevin England: Reflections of Medieval Antisemitism', *Traditio*, 19 (1963), pp.183–244.

—— 'The Faith of Christians and Hostility to Jews', in D. Wood (ed.), *Christianity and Judaism: Studies in Church History 29*, (Oxford: Blackwell for the Ecclesiastical History Society, 1992), pp.77–93.

Levi, Naphthali, 'Letter on Jewish Divorce in 1242', *Jewish Chronicle*, 30 December 1892.

Lincoln, F.A., *The Legal Background to the Starrs* (London: E. Goldston, 1932).

Lipman, V.D., 'The Anatomy of Medieval Anglo-Jewry', *TJHSE*, 21 (1968), pp.65–77.

—— *The Jews of Medieval Norwich* (London: JHSE, 1967).

—— 'Jews and Castles in Medieval England', *TJHSE*, 28 (1981–82), pp.1–19.

Lloyd, S., 'Crusader Knights and the Land Market in the 13th Century', in P.R. Coss and S.D. Lloyd (eds), *Thirteenth Century England II: Papers from the Newcastle-upon-Tyne Conference* (Woodbridge: Boydell, 1988), pp.119–37.

Maccoby, Hyam, *Judaism on Trial: Jewish-Christian Disputations in the Middle Ages* (Rutherford, NJ: Fairleigh Dickinson University Press, 1982).

Maddicott, J.R., 'The Crusader Taxation of 1268–70 and the Development of Parliament', in P.R. Coss and S.D. Lloyd (eds), *Thirteenth Century England II: Papers from the Newcastle-upon-Tyne Conference* (Woodbridge: Boydell, 1988).

Martin, C. Trice, 'Documents Relating to Jews in the 13th Century', *TJHSE*, 3 (1899), pp.187–213.

McCall, Alexander, *The Medieval Underworld* (London: Sutton, 2004).

McCulloch, Paul, 'Archaeological Evaluation at Winchester Barracks', *Winchester Museum Service Newsletter*, 25 (August 1996).

Meekings, C.A.F., 'Justices of the Jews, 1218–1268: A Provisional List', *BIHR*, 28 (1955), pp.173–88.

Menache, Sophia, 'Matthew Paris's Attitudes towards Anglo-Jewry', *Journal of Medieval History*, 23 (1997).

Moore, Ellen Wedemeyer, *Fairs of Medieval England* (Toronto: Pontifical Institute of Medieval Studies, 1985).

Mundill, Robin R., 'Anglo-Jewry under Edward I: Credit Agents and Their Clients', *TJHSE*, 31 (1988–90), pp.1–21.

—— 'Lumbard and Son: The Businesses and Debtors of Two Jewish

Moneylenders in Late 13th-Century England', *JQR*, 82 (1991), pp.137–70.

——— 'The Jewish Entries from the Patent Rolls, 1271–1292', *JHS*, 32 (1990–92), pp.25–88.

——— 'Rabbi Elias Menachem: A Late 13th-Century English Entrepreneur', *TJHSE*, 34 (1994–96), pp.161–89.

——— *England's Jewish Solution: Experiment and Expulsion, 1262–1290* (Cambridge: Cambridge University Press, 1998).

Nisbett, N.C.H., *Winchester: Its History, Buildings and People* (Wells: Winchester College Archaeological Society, 1933).

Norgate, K., *The Minority of King Henry III* (London: Macmillan, 1912).

Page, W., 'A History of Winchester and the Isle of Wight', in *Victoria History of the Counties of England and Wales*, vol. 5 (London: Institute of Historical Research, 1973).

Parkes, James, *The Jew in the Medieval Community* (London: Soncino Press, 1938; 2nd edn, New York: Herman Press, 1976).

——— 'The Jewish Moneylender and the Charters of English Jewry in Their Historical Setting', *MJHSE*, 3 (1940), pp.34–41.

——— *A History of the Jewish People* (London: Pelican, 1964).

Pevsner, N., and D. Lloyd, *The Buildings of England: Hampshire and the Isle of Wight* (London: Penguin, 1967).

Platt, Colin, *Medieval Southampton: The Port and Trading Community* (London: Routledge and Kegan Paul, 1973).

Pollock, F., and F.W. Maitland, *History of English Law before the Time of Edward the First*, I (Cambridge: Cambridge University Press, 2nd edn, 1968).

Poole, A.L., *Domesday Book to Magna Carta, 1087–1216* (Oxford: Oxford University Press, 1951).

Portal, W., *The Great Hall and Winchester Castle* (London: Warren, 1899).

Pugh, R.B., *Imprisonment in Medieval England* (Oxford: Oxford University Press, 1968).

Reader, Rebecca, 'Sweet Charity and Sour Grapes: The Historical Imagination of Matthew Paris', *Medieval History*, 4 (1994), pp.102–19.

Richardson, H.G., *The English Jewry under Angevin Kings* (London: JHSE/Methuen, 1960).

Richmond, Colin, 'English and Medieval Anglo-Jewry', in T. Kushner (ed.), *The Jewish Heritage in British History: Englishness and Jewishness* (London: Frank Cass, 1992), pp.42–59.

Rokeah, Zefira Entin, 'Some Accounts of Condemned Jews' Property in the Pipe and Chancellor's Rolls', *BIJS*, 1 (1973), pp.19–42; ibid., 2 (1974), pp.59–82; ibid., 3 (1975), pp.41–66.

—— 'Crime and the Jews in Late 13th-Century England: Some Cases and Comments', *HUCA*, 55 (1984), pp.95–197.

—— 'Money and the Hangman in Late Thirteenth-Century England, parts 1 and 2', *TJHSE*, 31 and 32 (1988–90 and 1990–92), pp.83–109 and pp.159–218.

—— 'A Hospitaller and the Jews: Brother Joseph de Chauncey and English Jewry in the 1270s', *TJHSE*, 34 (1994–96), pp.189–209.

Roth, Cecil, *Medieval Lincoln Jewry and its Synagogue* (London: JHSE, 1934).

—— *The Jews of Medieval Oxford* (Oxford: Oxford Historical Society NS 9, 1945–46).

—— *A History of the Jews in England* (Oxford: Clarendon Press, 1941; 2nd edn, 1942; 3rd edn, Oxford, 1964).

—— *Essays and Portraits in Anglo-Jewish History* (Philadelphia, PA: Jewish Publication Society of America, 1962).

—— *The Intellectual Activities of Medieval English Jews* (London: British Academy/Oxford University Press, n.d.).

Rye, Walter, 'Persecutions of the Jews', *Anglo-Jewish Historical Exhibition Papers, 1887* (London: Anglo-Jewish History Society, 1888).

Salter, H.E., 'Was There a *Domus Conversorum* in Oxford?', *MJHSE*, 2 (1935), pp.29–32.

Saltman, Avram, *The Jewish Question in 1655: Studies in Prynne's 'Demurrer'* (Ramat Gan, Israel: Bar-Ilan University Press, 1995).

Samuel, Edgar, 'New Light on the Selection of Jewish Children's Names', *TJHSE*, 23 (1970), pp.64–86.

Saunders, Frances Stonor, *Hawkwood: Diabolical Englishman*, (London: Faber and Faber, 2004).

Schechter, F.I., 'The Rightlessness of Medieval English Jewry', *JQR*, 4 (1913–14), pp.121–51.

Seror, Simon, 'Les nommes des femmes juives en Angleterre au moyen age', *REJ*, 154 (1995), pp.295–325.

Shahar, Shulamith, *The Fourth Estate: A History of Women in the Middle Ages* (London: Routledge, 1983).

Skinner, Patricia (ed.), *Jews in Medieval Britain: Historical, Literary and Archaeological Perspectives* (Woodbridge: Boydell, 2003).

Stacey, Robert C., 'Royal Taxation and the Social Structure of Medieval

Anglo-Jewry: The Tallages of 1239–42', *HUCA*, 56 (1986), pp.175–249.

——— *Politics, Policy and Finance under Henry III, 1216–1245* (Oxford: Oxford University Press, 1987).

——— 'Conversion of the Jews to Christianity in Thirteenth-Century England', *Speculum*, 67 (1992), pp.263–83.

——— 'Parliamentary Negotiation and the Expulsion of the Jews from England', in M. Prestwich, R.H. Britnell and R.R. Frame (eds), *Thirteenth-Century England, VI: Proceedings of the Durham Conference, 1995* (Woodbridge: Boydell, 1995), pp.77–101.

——— 'Jewish Lending and the Medieval English Economy', in R. Britnell and B.M.S. Campbell (eds), *A Commercialising Economy: England 1086 to c.1300* (Manchester: Manchester University Press, 1995), pp.78–101.

Stephenson, D., 'Colchester: A Smaller Medieval English Jewry', *Essex Archaeology and History*, 16 (1985), pp.48–52.

Stokes, H.P., *Studies in Anglo-Jewish History* (Edinburgh: JHSE, 1913).

——— 'The Relationship between the Jews and the Royal Family of England in the 13th Century', *TJHSE*, 8 (1918), pp.163–5.

——— *A Short History of the Jews in England* (London: SPCK, 1921).

——— 'A Jewish Family in Oxford in the 13th Century', *TJHSE*, 10 (1921–23), pp.193–206.

——— 'Extracts from the Close Rolls, 1289–1368', *MJHSE*, 1 (1925), pp.6–18.

Tallan, Cheryl, 'The Medieval Jewish Widow: Powerful, Productive and Passionate'. MA thesis, University of York, 1989.

——— 'Opportunities for Medieval Northern Jewish Widows in the Public and Domestic Spheres', in Louise Mirrer (ed.), *Upon my Husband's Death* (Ann Arbor, MI: University of Michigan Press, 1992), pp.115–31.

——— 'Structures of Power Available to Two Jewish Women in Thirteenth-Century England', in Mordechai Altschuler (ed.), *Proceedings of the Twelfth World Congress of Jewish Studies, Jerusalem 29 July–5 August 1997, Div. B: History of the Jewish People*, (Jerusalem: Magnes Press, 2000), pp.77–84.

Tovey, D'Blossiers, *Anglia Judaica (1738)*, Elizabeth Pearl (ed.) (London: Weidenfeld and Nicolson, 1990).

Turner, H., *Town Defences in England and Wales* (London: Archon Books, 1971).

Turner, Ralph V., *King John* (London: Longman, 1994).

Urry, Willam, *Canterbury under the Angevin Kings* (London: Athlone Press, 1967).

Valente, C., 'The Cult of Simon de Montfort', *JMH*, 21 (1995), pp.27–49.

Victoria History of the Counties of England: Hampshire and the Isle of Wight, V. W. Page (ed.) (London: Constable, 1912).

Vincent, Nicholas, 'Jews, Poitevins, and the Bishop of Winchester, 1231–1234', in D. Wood (ed.), *Christianity and Judaism: Studies in Church History 29* (Oxford: Blackwell for the Ecclesiastical History Society, 1992), pp.119–32.

────── 'Two Papal Letters on the Wearing of the Jewish Badge, 1221 and 1229', *JHS*, 34 (1994–96), pp.209–24.

────── *Peter des Roches: An Alien in English Politics, 1205–1238* (Cambridge: Cambridge University Press, 1996).

Watt, J.A., 'The English Episcopate, the State and the Jews', in P.R. Coss and S.D. Lloyd (eds), *Thirteenth Century England 2: Papers from the Newcastle-upon-Tyne Conference* (Woodbridge: Boydell, 1988), pp.137–49.

Williams, Daniel, 'Simon de Montfort and His Adherents', in Mark W. Ormrod (ed.), *England in the Thirteenth Century: Proceedings of the 1984 Harlaxton Symposium* (Woodbridge: Boydell, 1985), pp.166–77.

Wolf, Lucian, 'The Middle Age of Anglo-Jewish History, 1290–1656', *Publication of the Anglo-Jewish History Exhibition of 1887 at the Albert Hall* (London, Anglo-Jewish History Society, 1888), pp.53–80.

Index

Aaron, son of Benedict, 111, 113
Abraham, son of Benedict, 95, 99, 111, 112, 129, 133
Abraham, son of Isaac/Cokerel, 79, 137
Abraham of Kent, 22, 25, 26, 28, 38, 78
Archae, 4, 6, 57, 88, 89, 90, 91, 94, 95, 99, 102, 106, 109, 121, 139, 142
Asser, son of Licoricia, 24, 57, 60, 78, 79, 84, 105–8, 109, 133, 135, 137, 142, 143
Avegaye, daughter of Benedict, 111, 113

Barons' Wars, 10, 75, 85–92, 94, 96, 97, 100, 105, 109, 110, 139
Basingstoke, 40, 83
Bedford, 41, 48, 90–2, 96, 125
Belaset, daughter of Benedict, 113
Belassez, wife of Benedict, 93, 94, 98, 111, 113
Belia of Bedford, 42, 44–5, 48, 54, 71, 74, 76, 81, 90–2, 105, 109, 133
 Sons of, *see* Benedict, Cresse, Jacob, Lumbard, Moses
Belia, daughter of Licoricia, 109
Benedict, son of Belia, 44, 48, 91, 133
Benedict, son of Licoricia, 1, 15, 24, 25, 37, 39, 67, 70, 71, 78, 82–3, 88, 90, 93–103, 105, 106, 107, 108, 109, 112, 114–17, 121, 122, 128–32, 135, 137, 139
 children of, *see* Aaron, Abraham, Avegaye, Belaset, Cokerel, Lumbard, Rose
Beth Din, 55, 56, 138
Bristol, 3, 30, 93, 124, 132, 135

Cambridge, 3, 4, 91
Canterbury, 3, 22, 91, 113, 122
Castles, 12, 16, 29, 37, 65
Cemeteries, Jewish, 37, 43, 132, 144
Charlecote family, 72–5, 80
Chera, 27–30, 33, 40–4, 48, 50, 67, 78, 100
 Sons of, *see*, Abraham Pinche, Deulebene, Elias
Chichester, 16
Child murder, accusations of, 25–6, 38, 42, 125
Chirographers, 6, 28, 39, 40, 41, 88, 93, 94, 98, 99, 100, 111, 113, 129, 133, 142
 See also Deudonne, Isaac
Coinage
 clipping, 6, 13, 14, 29, 53, 83, 112, 122–33, 138
 exchange of, 14, 53, 81, 83, 123, 124, 127, 133
 minting, 13, 115, 122, 130
Cokerel, son of Benedict, 111, 113
Cokerel, son of Licoricia, *see* Isaac
Conversion, converts, 40, 58, 81, 122, 124, 126, 128, 141
Crespin, Abraham, 28, 41
Crespin, Benedict, 27, 41, 42, 43, 52, 53, 54, 59, 69
Cresse, son of Belia, 48, 137

David of Oxford, 23, 24, 50, 51–60, 67, 72, 76, 78, 80, 96, 105, 106, 108, 109, 114, 119, 123, 131
De Montfort, Simon, the elder, 4, 7, 39, 52, 67, 75, 87, 96
Des Roches, Peter, 16, 34, 42–3, 51, 65, 86
Deudonne, 39, 98, 107–8
Deulebene, son of Chera, 28, 41, 44
Devizes, 84, 105, 135, 142
Devon, 41, 106, 108, 140

Edward I, King, 15, 35, 70, 81, 89, 97, 99, 108, 113, 115, 117, 119–20, 129, 136, 137, 140–1
Eleanor of Castile, Queen, 15, 35, 92, 102, 108, 116, 121, 128, 130, 138–41
Eleanor of Provence, Queen, 4, 65, 84, 90, 108, 115, 142
Elias, son of Chera, 25, 28, 42, 44, 45, 54, 101, 102
Execution, 42, 100, 124, 130, 133, 135
Expulsion, 12, 17, 37, 82, 84, 113, 132, 141–3

Floria, wife of Benedict, 114–16, 133
France, 2, 3, 29, 34, 56, 66, 87

Gershom, Rabbi, 17, 55

Henry III, King, 8, 9, 13, 30, 33, 35, 63–7, 73, 80, 86, 90, 91, 119, 122, 124, 126, 129, 139
Henry of Durngate, 94, 110, 132, 135
Hyde Abbey, *see* Winchester

Imprisonment, 37, 58, 81, 112, 120, 125–8, 132, 143
Isaac the Chirographer, 28, 40, 41
Isaac/Cokerel, son of Licoricia, 24, 67, 70, 73, 74, 78, 79–82, 109, 110, 132, 133, 137

Jacob, son of Belia, 44, 48, 91, 133
Jewish Badge, 72, 122, 141
Jewish Exchequer, 4, 6, 68, 91, 108, 138
John, King, 12, 29, 34, 86, 125

Ketuba, 41, 49, 50, 55, 57, 136

Landholding, 15, 69, 73, 103, 121
Lateran Councils, 13, 14, 72, 109, 137
Law, 27, 49, 73, 74, 98, 119
Licoricia, 1, 10, 15, 21, 26, 29, 33, 42, 44, 45, 48, 50, 55–60, 63–76, 78–84, 88, 89, 90, 96, 105, 106, 108, 109–12, 119, 125, 131
    Children of, *see* Asser, Belia, Benedict, Isaac/Cokerel, Lumbard
Lincoln, 16, 24, 51, 125
London, 3, 29, 57, 69, 89, 92, 111, 112, 115, 116, 120, 122, 124, 125, 127, 139
    Sheriff of, 10
    Tower of, 5, 41, 45, 54, 58, 68, 75, 76, 80, 81, 92, 93, 112, 114, 125–8, 133
    See also Westminster Abbey
Lumbard, son of Belia, 44, 48
Lumbard, son of Benedict, 39, 111, 112, 113, 133
Lumbard, son of Licoricia, 24, 25, 67, 78, 80, 83–4, 133

Maimonides, 17, 58
Marlborough, 4, 84, 105, 108, 142
Moses, son of Belia, 44, 48
Muriel, wife of David of Oxford, 55–7, 105

Naming, 21, 22–3, 24, 25, 48, 51, 78, 82
Northampton, 4, 24, 57
Norwich, 3, 38, 125

Oxford, 3, 11, 22, 51, 57, 58, 63, 105, 106, 109, 113, 125, 126
    See also David of Oxford

Paris, Matthew, 53, 63, 123, 127
Pictavin, husband of Belia, 48, 90, 92
Pinche, Abraham, 25, 28, 40, 42, 43, 67, 69, 100, 130

Richard I, King, 6, 16, 64
Romsey, 4, 30, 39
Rose, daughter of Benedict, 97, 111, 113, 132

Simon Draper, 88, 94, 95, 97, 98, 100, 113, 129
Southampton, 4, 39, 101, 107–8, 113
Statute of the Jews, 11, 120–2, 128, 137, 141
Sweetman, *see* Asser
Synagogues, 44, 51, 68, 69, 70, 93

Tallage, 6, 16, 29, 37, 45, 51, 53, 54, 57, 59–60, 76, 80, 91, 106, 115, 122, 125, 129, 136, 142, 143

Westminster Abbey, 10, 59, 65
Wilton, 23, 108
Winchester, 22, 26, 29, 32, 40, 45, 48, 51, 55, 57, 63, 69, 76, 85–90, 92, 93, 95, 99, 105, 108, 109, 110, 112, 116, 120, 131, 135, 142
    Bishop of, 36, 41, 86-88, 89
    Castle, 32–5, 65, 88, 129
    Great Hall, 33, 65
    Guild of, 97–9, 100
    Hyde Abbey, 28, 34, 41, 85, 89
    Walls, 32, 88
    Wolvesey, bishop's palace at, 32, 34, 35, 65, 87
    See also Des Roches, Peter
Worcester, 4, 51, 54

York, 3, 29, 97, 113, 125, 126, 132